THE CHILD, THE STATE,
AND THE VICTORIAN NOVEL

VICTORIAN LITERATURE AND CULTURE SERIES

Karen Chase, Jerome J. McGann, *and* Herbert Tucker, *Editors*

THE CHILD,
THE STATE,
AND THE
VICTORIAN NOVEL

———··◦❈◦··———

Laura C. Berry

UNIVERSITY PRESS OF VIRGINIA
Charlottesville and London

The University Press of Virginia
© 1999 by the Rector and Visitors of the University of Virginia
All rights reserved
Printed in the United States of America

First published 1999

∞ The paper used in this publication meets the minimum requirements of the
American National Standard for Information Sciences—Permanence of Paper
for Printed Library Materials, ANSI Z39.48-1984.

Library of Congress Cataloging-in-Publication Data
Berry, Laura C., 1957–
    The child, the state, and the Victorian novel / Laura C. Berry.
        p.   cm. — (Victorian literature and culture series)
    Includes bibliographical references and index.
        ISBN 0-8139-1909-6 (alk. paper)
            1. English fiction—19th century—History and criticism.
    2. Children in literature.   3. Literature and society—Great
    Britain—History—19th century.   4. Dickens, Charles, 1812–1870—
    Characters—Children.   5. Children—Great Britain—Social
    conditions.   6. Social problems in literature.   7. State, The, in
    literature.   I. Title.   II. Series.
    PR878.C5B47—1999
    823'.809352054—dc21   99-35304
                                                                       CIP

for Elliot and Alice

"How long," they say, "how long, O cruel nation,
    Will you stand, to move the world, on a
    child's heart,—
Stifle down with a mailed heel its palpitation,
    And tread onward to your throne amid the mart?
Our blood splashes upward, O gold-heaper,
    And your purple shows your path!
But the child's sob in the silence curses deeper
    Than the strong man in his wrath."

Elizabeth Barrett Browning, "The Cry of the Children"

Contents

Acknowledgments

A PROJECT THAT unfolds over such a long period of time has at least the advantage, when it is done, of allowing one to remember and to thank the many people who were a part of its evolution at one time, and in one way, or another. I recall with pleasure and gratitude the insights of the teachers and friends I associate with Berkeley: Janet Adelman, Kate E. Brown, Evelyn Carr, Carol Christ, William Cohen, Simone Davis, David Karp, Laura Green, and Catherine Robson were all tough and generous critics who helped me to imagine and define what I was doing. Thomas Laqueur made it possible for me to think about my work in an entirely new way, and Catherine Gallagher urged me to articulate that newness with greater complexity. Her influence is present in the best of what I have written here.

I have been extraordinarily lucky, in more recent times, to have found smart and skeptical friends and colleagues whose confidence in my own and the book's development was very often enough. Susan Brown, Christina Crosby, Jehanne Gheith, Janet Jakobsen, Ina Milloff, Katherine Morrissey, and Maja-Lisa Von Sneidern have provided intellectual insight as well as encouragement. Dianne Sadoff is a teacher and friend who first sparked my interest in the Victorian novel—should I say it?—almost twenty years ago, and is still a constant model and inspiration for my work. My colleagues at the University of Arizona have made the English Department a happy and productive place in which to work and think; particular thanks to Susan Hardy Aiken, Joan Dayan, Ed Dryden, Larry Evers, Jerrold Hogle, and Rudy Troike, all of whom have a share in making the book possible. I am tremendously grateful for the meticulous attentions Peggy Flyntz paid to the manuscript. Two readers for the University Press of Virginia—Audrey Jaffe and John Kucich—offered smart criticism, as well as encouragement that made the last revisions bearable.

If Scott Treimel had not been in my life over the last twenty-one years—advising, analyzing, enduring, and, mostly, being my friend—I might have written the book, but I would not have learned nearly so much from doing it. My thinking about childhood in the nineteenth century, and every aspect of the process of writing the book itself, was enriched, challenged, and complicated by my own children, whose very real presence meant (among other things) that I was always reflecting on the relationship between writing and real life. To Elliot, whose birth coincided with the beginnings of the idea of this book, and to Alice, whose arrival in its later stages brought more joy and more chaos, I am grateful for the dailiness, the love, and the sense of urgency that entwine my working life. I am also thankful for the patience and efforts of David Berry, whose contributions to this and to all the parts of my life cannot be tallied.

I am grateful to the Department of English and the College of Humanities at the University of Arizona for leaves of absence and financial support that made research for parts of the book possible. I have also been supported by grant of admission by the Greater London Record Office and the Family Welfare Agency (England). Archivists and librarians at the Greater London Record Office, the University of San Francisco Medical Library, and the Law Library at the University of California at Berkeley were of tremendous assistance in locating papers that have been central to the writing of the book.

A version of chapter 3 appeared under the title "In the Bosom of the Family: The Wet-Nurse, the Railroad, and *Dombey and Son*" in *Dickens Studies Annual* 25 (1996). A version of chapter 4 was published as "Acts of Custody and Incarceration in *Wuthering Heights* and *The Tenant of Wildfell Hall*" in *Novel: A Forum on Fiction* 30.1 (fall 1996). I am grateful to the editors of both publications for permission to reprint the essays here, in somewhat different form.

THE CHILD, THE STATE,
AND THE VICTORIAN NOVEL

Introduction: The Rise of the Child Victim and the State of the Novel

As the family comes before the State in order of time—as the bringing up of children is possible before the State exists, or when it has ceased to be, whereas the State is rendered possible only by the bringing up of children; it follows that the duties of the parent demand closer attention than those of the citizen. Or, to use a further argument—since the goodness of a society ultimately depends on the nature of its citizens; and since the nature of its citizens is more modifiable by early training than by anything else; we must conclude that the welfare of the family underlies the welfare of society. And hence knowledge directly conducing to the first, must take precedence of knowledge directly conducing to the last.

Herbert Spencer, "What Knowledge Is of Most Worth?"

THIS IS A BOOK about the familiar figure of the child victim in nineteenth-century English writing: its dominance, its various forms, and, above all, its importance to Victorians' ideas of self and state. At an uncertain point in the nineteenth century, the welfare of the family, especially the state of the child, was intertwined with debates about the welfare of the state in England. Earlier figurations of the relationship between the family and the state correlated the power of the monarch with the authority of a father. But this patriarchal model had begun to erode by 1859 when Herbert Spencer, with an almost casual familiarity, linked the welfare of the individual family with that of all society. In Spencer's sweeping and even startling statement, child welfare—and, presumably,

the institutions that the guardianship of England's children would require—was to be given pride of place over the more traditional projects
and institutions of the state. The private and privately governed domain
of the home was now permeable territory, increasingly subject to such
diverse and evolving authority as the educational and legal systems, the
medical establishment, and the apparatus of social welfare. Even before
some of these institutions had any formal existence, their development
was supported by the fact that *childhood* and *the child* had become unquestioned and unquestionably public categories. Publicly and politically
imagined, the child was frequently and often sensationally represented as
an innocent imperiled by cruelties as likely to be administered at the hand
of a relative as by an administrative arm of the state. Although endangered
children are a dominant presence in Victorian novels—not just in the
infant mobs of Dickens's fiction, but in the work of George Eliot, the
Brontës, Lewis Carroll, and Charles Kingsley, to name only a few examples—stories of victimized innocence are by no means restricted to
fiction. Outside the novel, especially in discourses of social reform, children were routinely said to be the victims of an uncaring society bent on
progress.

A public discourse concerning the need to protect children had
been at work in England at least since Jonas Hanway's efforts on behalf
of the chimney sweeps, or in Lord Shaftesbury's speeches, as well as in
the legislative attempts to regulate apprenticeships in the early part of the
century. These early protective efforts represent a fledgling version of
the complex social apparatus that would eventually function in the name
of the child's "best interests," contributing to the development of social
welfare by the end of the century. What is especially notable in the early
Victorian period, however, is that the child's "interests" were as likely to
be articulated in poetry as in a pamphlet. Virtually from the start, social
reform writings on child protection were linked with and supported by
the efforts of *literary* writers. This linkage is explicitly materialized in
James Montgomery's 1824 anthology, *The Chimney-Sweeper's Friend, and
Climbing-Boy's Album,* which combines tracts decrying the apprenticing
of boys as sweeps with poetry and short fiction espousing a similar aim.
The Climbing-Boy's Album literally enacts a pairing of literature and reform writing that continued, if less obviously, throughout much of the
nineteenth century.

This pairing sets early and mid-Victorian writing about child victimization apart from similar narratives at other historical moments: Victorian representations of the endangered child, and pleas for social action, cross generic boundaries with relative ease. A nineteenth-century reader was as likely to find an impassioned argument against child labor in Elizabeth Barrett Browning's poetry ("The Cry of the Children") as in a parliamentary blue book. Similarly, Anne Brontë was as ardent a speaker for a mother's right to custody of her child (in *The Tenant of Wildfell Hall*) as was Caroline Norton in her pseudonymous pamphlets and letters distributed to Parliament. Although not always anthologized in a single volume, the story of the victimized child is told in the Victorian period with increasing frequency and, often, with greater sensation, both in and out of fiction. Even as George Eliot's novel *Silas Marner* (1861) chronicled the politics of paternal abandonment and rescue, the usually sober London *Times* linked childhood to an originating story of destructive patriarchal control, noting that "Infancy in London has to creep into life in the midst of foes," for "The age is the same as in the massacre which Christendom annually remembers, but the size of this great metropolis causes it to out-Herod Herod" (29 April 1862). Meanwhile the *Times,* in the passage just quoted, itself seeks to out-Dickens Dickens in its description of a world fiercely hostile to children.

In examining the predominance of the narrative of child victim, I want to ask new questions about the place of that narrative in nineteenth-century culture. Why is the story of the victimized child told in specific and culturally unique ways in England in the early and middle periods of the nineteenth century? How does that story find its way into such different generic categories at this particular historical moment? What might be understood differently if we read the rise and dominance of the child victim in the Victorian period as something more than a literary gesture, and as something less than a record of historical truth? What can be learned by interpreting the importance of the child as a widespread social phenomenon in Victorian England, recognizable in literary as well as social discourse?

This book examines the intense nineteenth-century fascination with victimized children to show how novels and reform writings authoritatively reorganize ideas of self and society as narratives of childhood distress. I examine the links among subjectivity as represented through the victimized child, Victorian projects of social reform, and the articulation of the state. Representing childhood as endangered is instrumental to nineteenth-century debates about stratifications among individuals, and also negotiations between the private self and the broader demands of social life and institutions in England. The child victim's omnipresence, as well as the details of the discrete narratives in which he or she appears, allows a critical way of understanding the self to seem natural and at times inevitable. Portraying the Victorian child as a victim enables the imagining of a version of selfhood in which a subject may be taken as self-determining and individualized, but inextricably (and simultaneously) dependent upon social formations, especially institutions, outside the self. Children in distress can be seen, in this context, as *little citizens*—persons whose sovereignty as selves is secured by their unformed and innocent status as children, but whose relation to the social realm is made necessary by the fact of their endangerment.

The endangered child-subject is a focal and unique position that intersects with foundational epistemological categories of this period, specifically social welfare. Although it constitutes a recognizable and familiar social category, as does "gender" or "race" or "class," "childhood" is unique because the child occupies a position that homogenizes rather than fragments the social community. Simply put, everyone can lay claim to membership, at least for a time, in the community of children, because everyone must have been a child. The necessary fact of childhood changes the way that this particular subject position functions socially.

Nineteenth-century children are often represented in the way that Blake saw them: as repositories for a culturally powerful and undeniable innocence, at the same time that they are subject to the experience, and restrictions, of the social world. To put it another way, the endangered child in the nineteenth century can be imagined as a liberal subject, a free and self-determined individual; and he or she can at the same time be understood as subject to the realm of the social. Thus, personal sovereignty and social indebtedness can coexist in the child victim, who is not fully confined or defined by either representation. The victimized child is never fully constituted as Foucauldian subject, who must always be constructed by social forms outside the self; but neither is the victimized child represented or imagined as free of those social forms. Rather, the self is represented as a child victim so that individual and social claims are, for a time at least, simultaneously endorsed. In the world of fiction, indeed in writing of all kinds, children need never grow to maturity. Even as discourses of child endangerment overtly urge social action, they covertly and simultaneously maintain the child *as* a child, thereby preserving the idea of individual selves in perpetual relation to the social world.

To endorse the self and the social, and to do so at the same time, is important in the nineteenth century because—especially in the early part of the century—social mobility is imagined as both more possible and more likely than ever before, an anxiety expressed in many of the writings discussed in this book. Reasserting the claims of the self is obviously crucial at moments of social flux: simultaneously affirming the need for a social sphere allows for the legislative construction of a (social welfare) realm that purports to accommodate the needs, and remedy the failures, of those whose status is subject to change.

Early and mid-Victorian concerns about changes in social rank are articulated in many ways, one of the most important of which is hunger. Exploring the uneven development of the narrative of the child victim is also, in part, to trace the coincident and related relationship between social mobility and anxieties about hunger in literary as well as social-reform texts concerned with the lives of children. In many of these writings, children are crucial to mediating anxieties about hungry others because the representation of endangered children allows the transformation of powerful adult appetites into the pitiable needs of an innocent (and therefore socially pure) victim. In other instances, the representation of hunger brings social anxieties to the foreground without imaginatively resolving them. By the end of the mid-Victorian period, in the works examined here, references to hunger and to voracious appetites subside. But the animalistic self, to which writings about hunger often refer, remains present. This animalistic self can at times be prized as an instinctual, evolutionary being; this is the case, for example, in George Eliot's novel *Adam Bede*. These themes of hunger and of beastliness are often found in narratives of child victimization, and their importance is discussed throughout the book.

Two defining discursive and social practices are the subject of this book. The first of these is the dominant literary form in the period, the novel. In particular, the focus is on novels that are not explicitly connected to social reform and political debates, although they may comment upon issues relevant to those debates. More specifically, with the possible exception of Dickens's *Oliver Twist,* this book considers novels other than those conventionally associated with particular social problems, especially the so-called industrial novels. I am thus concerned to reveal the ways in which fictions that purport to deal with private life, particularly the private domain of the family, nevertheless intervene in public and social debates, an assumed relationship almost a commonplace since Nancy Armstrong elaborated the idea in *Desire and Domestic Fiction.*[1]

Alongside the novel I read the inchoate discourses of social welfare, drawn from medical, legal, charitable, and poor relief documents. These "social" writings include parliamentary debates and committee reports, pediatric manuals and essays in medical journals, legal documents and trial transcripts, and pamphlets on the appropriate distribution of charity, as well as newspaper and magazine accounts. Together these writings describe the role of governmental, professional, and private entities in the lives of Victorian families with children. They further provide crucial sources in the history of social welfare and modern modes of representing the family decades before the existence of what we now call the "welfare state." Many of the practices examined here, particularly medicine and law, find a formal place in the administration of relief to the poor, and in interventions into private life by the twentieth century. But although these documents trace a kind of prehistory of welfare, they do not locate the origins of welfare in nineteenth-century reform efforts. Measured against nineteenth-century fiction, these nonliterary texts instead chart epistemological changes endemic to this period, showing a genealogy of "self" and "family" that supports the predominance of the child victim over a Foucauldian account of the self, or a humanistic account of the liberal individual.[2]

In much Victorian discourse, children are seen as mutable subjects who can transgress the social boundaries that adults cannot. Nineteenth-century representations of children are thus able to obscure what seems, in adults, a permanent correlation between the idea of a self and social categories such as class or gender. For this reason, children—especially children in danger—can represent very particular subject positions while still laying claim to membership in a large unified group. This sensibility is reflected in a passage from Hutton's *History of Birmingham,* reprinted as the epigraph to Florence Hill Davenport's 1868 *Children of the State:* "If I have dwelt long upon the little part of our species, let it plead my excuse to say, I cannot view a human being, however diminutive in stature, or oppressed in fortune, without considering *I view an equal.*" In summary, then, the victimized child is critical to such diverse nineteenth-century discourse because he or she can represent a more able negotiation of the rapidly changing demands of early and mid-Victorian social arrangements, imagining the possibility of an "equal" who crosses social boundaries in life and generic boundaries in discourse. Representing endangered childhood in writing is an effective mode of addressing the fixity of social determinants such as class or gender, because the "pulpy infant," in Thomas Carlyle's curious phrase (quoted below), is ever unformed.

Filthy Origins

It strikes me dumb to look over the long series of faces, such as any full Church, Courthouse, London-Tavern Meeting, or miscellany of men will shew them. Some score or two of years ago, all these were little red-coloured pulpy infants; each of them capable of being kneaded, baked into any social form you chose: yet see now how they are fixed and hardened,—into artisans, artists, clergy, gentry, learned sergeants, unlearned dandies, and can and shall now be nothing else hence forth!

Thomas Carlyle, *Past and Present*

This is not the first or the only instance in which Carlyle confuses children with food. Earlier in *Past and Present* (1843), he draws on a contemporary trial to caution that poor families will be reduced to consuming their own offspring by murdering them for burial society monies: "And now Tom being killed, and all spent and eaten, Is it poor little starveling Jack that must go, or poor little starveling Will?" (10). Social issues, food, and children perversely collide at times in *Past and Present*. Carlyle, whose stomach problems were almost as legendary as his colorful rhetorical style, might be imagined to have some uniquely Carlylean reason for making these odd connections. But in fact, food and hunger—especially the relationship of food to children—makes its way into a diverse group of nineteenth-century writings, where it plays a significant role in the conceptualization of the child victim. Dickens provides another example of the confusion of children and food in his recollection of a childhood visit to a "little greengrocer's shop," where he was taken by his nurse: "I remember to have waited on a lady who had had four children (I am afraid to write five, though I fully believe it was five) at a birth. . . . [T]he four (five) deceased young people lay, side by side, on a clean cloth on a chest of drawers; reminding me by a homely association, which I suspect their complexion to have assisted, of pig's feet as they are usually displayed at a neat tripe-shop" ("Dullborough Town" 66).

Hunger often represents the rapid social realignment characteristic of the early Victorian period. Images of hungry people alert readers to the dangers of substituting what was seen, in one recent historian's view, as "the security of a cohesive *vertical* social structure in which every individual had a formal or informal connection with those above and below" with "the uncertainty of a mass society in which a *horizontal* class structure emerged" (Fraser 5). When hunger is expressed as a threat, it usually refers to voracious adult male bodies. A sense of anxious proximity pervades the texts discussed in much of this book, anxiety organized around a life-threatening consumption of food. In an extreme but not unique example from *The French Revolution,* Carlyle specifically (though metaphorically) defines the threat as the horror of being eaten by one's fellows: "The lowest, least blessed fact one knows of, on which necessitous mortals have ever based themselves, seems to be the primitive one of Cannibalism: That *I* can devour *Thee*" (55). This "least blessed fact" is an unequal exchange between like subjects, between "I" and "Thee." What stands behind Carlyle's concern for cannibalism informs much discourse in the early Victorian period: a voracious and powerful appetite, one that can no longer be easily defined as different and separate, may devour you and yours.

The insistence on hunger as a potential threat finds its most powerful source in the work of a man Carlyle deplored. It was Thomas Malthus, whose ideas enjoyed a wide if controversial currency in the early Victorian period, who connected eating and population growth with social proximity. As Catherine Gallagher has persuasively argued, Malthus makes a historically unique connection between the *healthy* body and social disease. Because persons in health must eat, and cannot be persuaded to cease procreating, a greater number of healthy bodies means more reproduction—and less food. In other words, the healthier the individual body, the greater the threat to the entire social body. The Malthusian reformulation of the body in relation to society also reimagines social space and social divisions. In Malthus's famous calculation, population increases geometrically, while food sources can multiply only arithmetically. People are, then, closer together in simple spatial terms, living, as the English do, on an island. But they are also *closer* insofar as they are philosophically if not biologically united by unassailable and identical needs. In his *Essay on the Principle of Population,* first published in 1798, people are reduced to appetites, which are universal, for food and for passion. Like Carlyle's cannibals, the fact of hunger unifies persons who in earlier times might have seemed more obviously separate.[3]

"I think I may fairly make two postulata," Malthus famously asserts. "First, That food is necessary to the existence of man. . . . Secondly, That the passion between the sexes is necessary and will remain nearly in its present state." As a result of this conjunction of two all-consuming appetites, Malthus makes painfully obvious the inevitable presence of other devouring bodies at the social table. Hungry bodies are also persons with competing claims not just for food but for a place at the table, and finally for a position in society. Pointing out that the Malthusian concern is not exclusively for material bodies, Frances Ferguson has noted that the *Essay* "registers the felt pressure of too many consciousnesses" (106). The Reform Bill of 1832 is a legislative acknowledgement of those consciousnesses. Similarly, the new poor law of 1834 seeks to define a policy concerning hungry persons whose presence is keenly felt. In fiction of the 1830s and 1840s, Dickens, Disraeli, and Gaskell, among others, overtly concern themselves with social problems traceable to Malthusian anxieties. And these anxieties, in turn, feed the construction of a subject who is neither a social threat nor entirely socially controlled.

Although Malthus's *Essay* will be credited with influencing (or discredited by its association with) what are often perceived as harsh attitudes and laws directed toward the poor in the early part of the nineteenth century, Malthus's most threatening pronouncement is his insistence on the necessary and intimate relations between persons who were once readily separated by rank or race or gender. In his *Essay on the Principle of Population,* giving to others is always defined reciprocally, necessarily revealing a debit in some other quarter. Malthus asserts that "no possible contributions of sacrifices of the rich, particularly in money, could for any time prevent the recurrence of distress among the lower members of society" (38). In fact, most forms of relief to the poor can only exaggerate the painful exchanges between classes, as when Malthus goes on to say that "Great changes might, indeed, be made. The rich might become poor, and some of the poor rich, but a part of the society must necessarily feel a difficulty of living" (38).

In texts produced during the 1830s and the "hungry 40s," physiological appetite is often represented as a threat, especially when it is an adult male appetite. A founding text of this kind is Mary Shelley's *Frankenstein,* which was substantially revised in 1831 and which is discussed at length below. But hunger is troubling, if not actually troublesome, in much of Dickens's work, in Elizabeth Gaskell's *Mary Barton,* in Carlyle's writings, and—by way of satire on fashionable life—in Thackeray's. The overeating wet nurse, the voracious railway worker, the indolent but nevertheless hungry unemployed laborer: these figures of a destructive appetite appear outside fiction, in divergent discourses, suggesting the importance of hunger as a topic that is prominently and widely represented.

If a besetting problem of the early Victorian period is the presence of hungry bodies, a (partial) representational solution is the endangered child. Novels and social documents sometimes transform, or try to transform, the dangerous hungers of powerful adults into the blameless and pitiable needs of infant victims. Thus, factory reform finds success in advertising the labors of children rather than the hardships endured by adult workers, and doctors turn away from discussing the fear of the lower-class wet nurse's bodily fluids to focus on fear for the starving infant's life. In substituting innocent children for potentially dangerous adults, these texts might be said to manage the threat by displacing it. And certainly one effect of the turn to children in nineteenth-century culture, especially pauper children, is to transform a large and powerful Malthusian body into a petite and manageable one. In a time of uneasy turbulence, when social unrest is often characterized as the possibility of an encroaching mob, such imaginative resolution of real problems might have considerable appeal, at least for bourgeois writers and readers.

But the interposition of the endangered child at moments of social collision can have a more complex meaning. Writers at times willfully imagine the awkward yoking of different social ranks or of the sexes and frequently place a child victim at the center of such narratives. These early- and mid-nineteenth-century collisions represent the child victim in order to realign social relationships discursively, distinguishing individuals not merely by way of social position but also based upon "moral" sufficiency. Turning away from adult bodies—all "fixed and hardened" into unchangeable social shape—Malthusian anxieties provide an occasion for turning to the child-subject, whose pulpy substance can be molded into various forms. Increasing social mobility and the problem of hunger do not simply necessitate, but are deliberately imagined in order to enable, a turn to the child. Hunger arises as an issue in order to separate and distinguish individuals. Social position plays a role in this distinction, but innocent children, whose hunger can be shown to be blameless and harmless, can transcend social limits. The child-subject in early-nineteenth-century writing, then, may be associated with class and gender anxieties, but the representation of the victimized child does not serve only to reimagine class boundaries or to construct ideologies of gender. Rather, the multiply constituted child-subject also enables the production of a more mobile and malleable self who can negotiate social boundaries and subject positions.

The child victim may have origins in the discourse on hunger and social mobility that appears in the early part of the century. But *origins* is a vexed term, one that implies a causality that can never be adequate or faithful to the historical record: there can be no totalizing theory of origins. Instead, there are historical conditions that are co-implicated in the rise of the child as victim. These include the rise of the social sphere and increase in social legislation, and the relationship of social forms to the idea of an independent self; free will versus social control; and a perceived tension between individuals and social groups.

The Rise of the Social

No strict causal account of the rise of the child victim is possible, of course, yet a refiguration of the public realm is essential to his or her presence in such diverse narratives. Debates about social role, characteristic to all historical periods, increasingly turned—or were felt to turn—in the nineteenth century toward the interpenetration of public and private life. This intervention is signaled in the passage of legislation such as the Matrimonial Causes Act or the Elementary Education Act, which increased government involvement in what had been seen as a private jurisdiction. "[F]rom 1830 onwards," writes G. Kitson Clark, "a formidable governmental machine was being created in Britain which brought much of the conduct of life and the use of property under the control of the state, and provided precedents for more extensive controls when the time of need came" (130). Ursula Henriques asserts that "changes in economic and social structure produced a massive demand for the intervention of the community, local or central, to mitigate their social effects and provide for their casualties. But of course the demand developed unevenly and in many different ways" (1). The diverse determinants advancing that intervention were forming even before the nineteenth century. But it was in the early Victorian period that the relationship between public entities and private lives developed urgency.[4]

The intrusion of the sociopolitical realm into private life, or the perception among contemporaries that this was so, is not merely a history of legislation; it might also be said to reach an apotheosis in that literary form which publicly produces the most agonizing moments of private consciousness—the novel. And as private life is drawn into public discourse, it is increasingly vulnerable to investigation, legislation, and institutionalization. A friction emerges between needs fostered by the economic arrangements of industrial capitalism, one of which is to maintain the notion of a self-determined and independent individual, and the need to accommodate the increasing intervention of the social. In both literary and nonliterary writing, a familiar Victorian social riddle is phrased in this tension: how can a subject be cast both as personally sovereign and as socially enmeshed? And the answer to that riddle may be read in the following chapters: the logic of dependent selfhood is continually proved by representing the paradigmatic subject as an endangered child.

The logic (or paradox) of dependent selfhood also makes a strong appearance in debates closely related to those concerning social intervention: the tension between personal freedom of will and forms of environmental or social control. As Catherine Gallagher has pointed out, "[E]xtended narratives normally contain a tension between freedom and determinism regardless of their subject matter," adding that the tension "is particularly pronounced in nineteenth-century novels, for although most nineteenth-century critics of the novel expressed a bias in favor of the primacy and irreducibility of 'character,' the social formation of character, its contextualization, was also a necessary subject for the novelist" (*Industrial Reformation* 34). A lengthy study of this theme in nineteenth-century writing is John Reed's encyclopedic *Victorian Will*. Reed argues that Victorian perceptions of the self encompass two basic concepts: the first is a "Rousseauistic assertion of the subjective self," and the second is an approach traceable to Goethe and Hegel, among others, in which the self is subject to control by way of association with a social or philosophical ideal (15). Thus, Reed says, "To some degree, the social conflicts of the Victorian period are grounded in contending images of the self" (19). Nineteenth-century writers of fiction as well as nonfiction prose, from Carlyle and Dickens to Eliot and Mill, vigorously exploit this theme. When writers interpose the figure of the child in the midst of debates about self and social, as is frequently the case in Victorian narrative, these "contending images" give way to a productive and coherent account of self, equally capable as an independent agent and as a socially determined subject.

In addition to philosophical debates concerning free will, and the changing role of legislative bodies in private life, rising tensions traceable to social convergence and separation call forth the child victim. For example, during the controversy over the 1834 new poor law, anxieties mounted concerning the relationship between the "indolent poor" and the gainfully employed ratepayers of the parish. Participants on both sides of the debate deployed the figure of the helpless child to advance their arguments. Such conflicts are also represented in fiction: Frances Trollope's poor law novel, *Jessie Phillips* (1844), demonstrates the disastrous mingling of ranks in the sexual union of the gentry and the servant class. The result, enabled by what are seen as the cruelties of the poor law, is a murdered child. These and other nineteenth-century narratives of victimized childhood implicitly address the ruptures of public configurations and the more predictable disunities of private life. Thus, the stories of "factory cripples," children whose deformed bodies testify to the horrors of child labor, are narratives about the failure of the family to provide for itself; but at the same time they direct our attention to the industrialization that pushed children into the factory in the first place. *Jane Eyre* provides another example: the novel surely details familial strife, but it speaks as ardently to the liminal social status of its protagonist. These texts criticize social upheaval throughout England but also point out personal failure.

At times the appeal to the child produces, in the face of social conflicts, what seems to be an imaginative resolution. These discourses may achieve an apparent coherence and authenticity, and thus naturalize the social configurations they in fact help to create. In other instances, the child enters discursive play to expose the internal instability and artificiality of dominant ideological conditions. But the ideological outcome of these debates, discursively waged over the bodies of victimized children, is subordinate to the fact that, whether these narratives expose or reinstate particular social and subject positions, they uniformly invite a generalized and in many ways unifying pity or outrage by producing a victimized child. Indeed, while class conflict serves as all-important background to the writings examined in these pages, the crucial ideological work these texts perform is in reimagining the self as a child in danger, an effect of writing that has no single or easily defined or expressed significance.[5]

The Child, Social Welfare, and the Novel

An examination of the novel and social welfare as coincident and intertwined discourses necessitates a revisionary history of the English novel, a reframing of the Victorian contribution to the evolution of social welfare, and a reconsideration of the historicity of the subject in the nineteenth century. To address the first of these three tasks, the literary argument of the book is that marriage, as a method of narrative closure and as a primary social concern, loses some of its cultural centrality in the nineteenth century. The Victorian novel often revises an eighteenth-century emphasis on versions, or subversions, of the marriage plot, and engages instead the story of the family, especially a family constellated around a child in distress. The "subject" of the novel evolves: the beset maiden on the road to marriage—or worse—is often replaced by the beleaguered child.

It has long been taken for granted that the driving force behind the novel is the marriage plot.[6] This was assumed in early criticism of the genre, but has received an extra and more recent boost from feminist critics who have found the problems of love and marriage to be a useful way of reading nineteenth-century fiction.[7] But if it has almost gone without saying that marriage motivates fictional plotting, literary critics have not hesitated to state directly the importance of the child in nineteenth-century literature. As early as 1957, Peter Coveney asserted that "within the course of a few decades the child emerges from comparative unimportance to become the focus of an unprecedented literary interest, and, in time, the central figure of an increasingly significant proportion of our literature" (ix). Coveney understands the child as a significant figure for exploring the tensions of society. The problem to which nineteenth-century artists respond, he says, is "the maintenance of individual integrity with the search for the security of universal order" (x). But for Coveney this tension is a purely artistic one, a strictly "literary phenomenon" (xiv). James Kincaid's recent book *Child-Loving: The Erotic Child and Victorian Culture* is concerned, in contrast to Coveney, with the social and cultural necessity of constructing an innocent, asexual child, and with our cultural investment in inveighing against the categories that oppose this construction, as well as the social figures, such as the pedophile, who maintain them. The erotic child is a critical feature of nineteenth-century writing; and the sexualized child, when seen as the victim of abuse, testifies to the pervasiveness of the child victim, an examination of which makes visible the rise of the domain of welfare provision and public policy so present in nineteenth-century culture, so persistent in our own.[8]

In *Strange Dislocations,* Carolyn Steedman links the child to the representation of subjectivity, claiming that between 1780 and 1930, "childhood came to be understood as a component of selfhood—perhaps, as interiority itself" (7). Steedman traces a more or less direct connection between nineteenth-century constructions of childhood and the basic theoretical formulations of psychoanalysis, in which the child is understood to be a "feeling" self of depth. Emphasizing the interiority of the feeling subject to the exclusion of other versions of subjectivity, especially in relation to the child, may offer only a partial account of the representation of selfhood in this period. Arguably, recent criticism has focused on the increasingly psychologized nature of the Victorian subject precisely because the twentieth century, even in its ambivalent relation to Freud, has resolutely—if at times unwittingly—adopted this notion of subjectivity most forcefully. But for much of the nineteenth century, the private, interior self of depth is under construction, and is always complicated by a competing account of a self explicitly not individual and not psychologized.[9]

All discussions of nineteenth-century childhood share in the insights of recent debates in social history that describe a roughly constructivist view of childhood. "In the late seventeenth century a new social attitude towards children began to strengthen," writes J. H. Plumb (65), restating and extending a position first put forward by Philippe Ariès in his influential *Centuries of Childhood*. The child is no longer viewed as the "miniature adult," but rather as an *essentially* different and discrete biological and social category. At the same time, and perhaps in direct relationship to these changes, the child becomes the repository for certain valued and post-Enlightenment traits such as innocence, liberty, and naturalness.[10]

This refiguration of childhood has roots in Romantic culture, especially in writers such as Rousseau, and in much of the poetry of the period. Figures of children are common to Romantic poetry, of course, but the Victorian child can be distinguished from Romantic conceptions of childhood in important ways. Victorian writing tends to consider the child not merely as a symbol but as a subject, focusing in greater detail and at length on his or her interior state and physical well-being. Victorians tend to cast the child as victim rather than as a triumphant representation of the transcendent self. There is more than a little distance between the Wordsworthian account of the child "trailing clouds of glory" and the starving Dickensian waif. Little Nell, for example, is an object of nostalgic reflection, but the circumstances of her existence are not idealized.

Clearly, not all Romantic portraits of childhood idealize the infant self—consider Blake, to name an obvious example. Even Wordsworth, whose nostalgic relation to childhood is manifest in poems such as "Tintern Abbey" and the Immortality Ode, portrayed the child differently in different poems, ranging from the sometime savagery of youth in portions of *The Prelude* to the sentimentality of "We Are Seven." But in general it is fair to say that Romantic culture focuses upon the child as father to the man, locating the germ of adult selves in childhood experience. By contrast, Victorians tend to concern themselves with the man as father to the child. Issues of child rearing, heredity, and protective custody dominate the writing of the period. This is not to say that Romantic writing ignores the victimization of children or functions monolithically to represent children as objects of nostalgia and perfect innocence, or that Victorians abandoned such accounts; it is to argue that Victorian representations of childhood are more likely to focus on childhood distress rather than transcendence, and to position their discourse in relation to social reform projects and debates. Nineteenth-century novels transform the focus on childhood already at play within Romantic culture from a partial transcendence of social institutions and physiological fact (or at least an attempt to transcend these confinements) to a necessary imbrication among them.[11]

In addition to the literary arguments outlined above, this book looks to the representation and deployment of the victimized child as a way of reading the "uneven" development of social welfare. This is not to propose an alternative version of the history of welfare; in fact, I conclude that a comprehensive account of welfare is at best an impossible venture, and at worst a misleading and obfuscatory one. "[B]ooks which have been written on the history of social welfare provision over the past twenty to thirty years have, almost without exception, linked the word 'welfare' to the word 'state,'" says Finlayson (1). They focus resolutely on the progress of the "welfare state," a term that presupposes that welfare provision and its history can rest securely in a discussion of state intervention. Focusing solely on the history of legislation and institutions, these historians consider the passage of a bill (the new poor law, for instance, or the Elementary Education Act) and the resulting birth of an institution (the union workhouse, compulsory schooling), offering a familiar progress narrative that elides the tensions inherent in the period. In doing so, they mount an implicit argument that social policy mediates or exacerbates social conflicts, placing first in importance the legislative results of public debate. Although a vast literature exists concerning the evolution of relief practices in the nineteenth century, virtually all of it is directed toward discovering these "roots" of the welfare state—as if the welfare state were a foregone conclusion, and state intervention the most important aspect of the reform of poor relief.[12]

On the other hand, revisionist historians of welfare and sociologists provide a historical narrative quite opposite to the "Whiggish" accounts discussed above. Following a roughly Foucauldian model, Jacques Donzelot and others read the legislative and social history of the nineteenth century as progress of a virulent kind: the advance of a normalizing discourse and socially controlling legislation, resulting in institutions that immure the poor while admonishing the middle classes by example. My debt to this latter model will be obvious in the chapters that follow. But I am also writing against the "disciplinary" reading that such theoretical models produce. If the history of nineteenth-century social reform legislation is not the progress narrative that many historians have described, neither is it an uncomplicated tale of social control. Indeed, the very category of "social welfare," upon which most of the historiography in this area depends, is a shaky and complex one.

Despite these disclaimers, social welfare is a term central to this discussion of the nineteenth century precisely because, by the twentieth century, it had become a largely unquestioned and defining category. Succeeding chapters will refer to and at times trace aspects of the history of social welfare. But this discussion will not chart the progress of social apparatus, the telos of which can only be the full establishment of the welfare state in the twentieth century. Changing attitudes toward public assistance, government intervention, and the public scrutiny of private lives are major features of Victorian life. But it is not specific historical events or even, to a certain extent, literary narratives that concern me here, but rather the emergence and dominance of particular social domains and discourses and their relation to specific literary genre and modes.

The most compelling accounts of Victorian novels in recent years have argued persuasively, or relied upon the assertion, that nineteenth-century fiction performs a disciplinary role in culture, representing selfhood in order to model the necessity of a voluntary submission to social control that can circumvent the involuntary imposition of institutional intervention in private life. In shifting the discussion of social welfare away from a debate about government intervention and institutional bureaucracy, on the one hand, and the production of knowledge about the wholly psychologized self, on the other, I am also employing a model for subjectivity in this period that departs from the more rigid portrayal of the disciplinary or liberal subject. I am speaking here not of theoretical models for constituting subjectivity, but of the way or ways in which persons are imagined within nineteenth-century discourse in order to demonstrate how, in spite of the micropolitical interventions of disciplinary society, a creative adaptation to the forms of discipline—in the "person" of the child victim—enables a navigation of the complex social terrain of the nineteenth century. The Victorian subject is not primarily an object of investigation for whom personal agency is a near impossibility. Nor is that subject an essentialized and psychologized self, subject to a repressive state that fundamentally opposes the "natural" freedom of the individual, a freedom that guarantees individual sovereignty and personal agency. Nineteenth-century discourse does not uniformly produce either a Foucauldian disciplinary subject or a liberal humanist one. Instead, many novels and reform discourses cannily produce a portrait of the self that functions as both at once. In reading the child victim as a fluid category, both self- and socially determined, we can reread the complex nineteenth-century response to the pressures of social structures on the idea of individual selves. It is then possible to identify the crucial, and supremely creative, construction of a rich and varied subjectivity in the nineteenth century. Indeed, what are often read as the repressive and restricting features of nineteenth-century social reform can produce a profoundly generative model for selfhood.

Nancy Armstrong argues powerfully that at some point in the eighteenth century the "gendering of human identity provided the metaphysical girders of modern culture," and that "the essential self was commonly understood in terms of gender" (*Desire* 14). My argument is that by the nineteenth century the paradigmatic subject was just as likely to be understood as a child. In the course of the nineteenth century, representing the victimized child becomes an important means of articulating an autonomous and socially indebted self, bound but self-determined. This has the new and lasting effect of linking subjectivity and social reform and, ultimately, the discursive categories of child and state. It would not be quite true to say that the endangered child unilaterally replaces the domestic woman as the only model for the self. But the rise of the victimized child can be charted in much Victorian discourse, and profoundly so in the novels and documents discussed in succeeding chapters. While other models for subjectivity continue to have an active place in and out of the novel—not just gendered subjects but subjects at least partly constituted by economic, racial, or geographic divisions, to name just a few potential factors—it is the child victim whose presence is so urgently felt, so palpably real. Before probing the precise nature of that palpable self in the close readings of chapters 1 through 4, I want to turn from history to metaphor, in order to trace one imperfect but imaginative source for the endangered child in Mary Shelley's 1831 version of *Frankenstein*.

Hungry and Hideous Progeny

"Every thing must have a beginning," Mary Shelley sensibly points out in the introduction to *Frankenstein*—only to add, "and that beginning must be linked to something that went before" (58). My discussion of fiction begins with the same equivocation over origins that shelters Mary Shelley's infant project, her "hideous progeny," from any dispute over its conception. If the origins of Shelley's fiction must remain indeterminate, the origin of the child victim as paradigmatic subject is decidedly overdetermined. As is true of *Frankenstein,* certain influences—such obvious factors as Romantic culture, Locke, Malthus, the rise of industrialism, the changing nature of social relations—spring to mind. Others are less knowable, which perhaps is only right. After all, the rise of the child victim has its source in history that, like Shelley's idea of the imagination, might seem to those of us rooted at the end of the twentieth century a kind of "chaos"; we can "give form to dark, shapeless substances, but cannot bring into being the substance itself" (58). Nevertheless, *Frankenstein* gives one form to the dark and shapeless substance of the child victim, even as it describes the (monstrous) contours of the child victim's frequent opposite: the Malthusian male.[13]

Shelley's novel is useful to this study precisely because the narrative combines the terrifying presence of a powerful male body with the diminutive outline of an abused child—and imagines both within the Monster's beleaguered frame. The novel thus graphically portrays the struggle that informs much discourse in the early nineteenth century, especially the works discussed in chapters 1 and 2. *Frankenstein* enacts a prototypical exchange between an ignorant, hungry, and potentially reproductive and destructive male, and a victimized child who is in need of social intervention (especially education), even as he or she represents the unassailable claims of individual desire. The connection is made inevitable in that both figures are framed within a single body. I revisit this exchange in my discussion of Dickens, and of railroad laborers and pauper education. Its evolution also becomes apparent in the work of the Brontës and George Eliot, and in the discourses of child custody law and infanticide. To put the link between children and monsters differently, *Frankenstein* combines familiar early-nineteenth-century Malthusian concerns with an inchoate narrative of the pitiable neglect of a child victim who signals the need for social reform, and whose presence will be increasingly important as the century progresses.[14]

Mary Shelley's Monster is many things, but one of those things arguably derives from Malthusian tensions: the Monster can be read as a pauper figure of appetite and reproduction who threatens social order. It is in "a solitary chamber," Victor Frankenstein tells Walton, that he kept his "workshop of filthy creation" (102). The phrase recalls the poorhouse, which in eighteenth-century discussion of poor relief was also referred to as a "workshop." And Shelley's Monster is, at least potentially, built of pauper flesh and bone. Although it was not until 1832 that the medical profession had legal rights to unclaimed workhouse corpses for purposes of dissection, some fear of body snatching among the poor was nevertheless abroad, and there is evidence that pauper bodies were being given over to anatomists even before the 1832 Anatomy Act. Victor Frankenstein collects the elements he uses in his "workshop of filthy creation" not only from the "vaults and charnel-houses" (99) but from the "dissecting room and the slaughter-house" (102). But whether literally constructed from the bits and pieces of poor bodies or not, the Monster recalls in other ways the threat of the Malthusian male.[15]

He is, first of all, a monstrous and potentially destructive material presence, preeminently a *body* whose physical needs are foregrounded. So great are those physical needs, particularly the creature's hunger, that the novel goes to considerable trouble to erase them, even portraying the Monster as, of all things, a vegetarian. Mary Shelley's Monster is starving, but he cannot—or will not—eat meat. He is "tormented by hunger and thirst," but he allows himself only "some berries which I found hanging on the trees or lying on the ground" (148). Turning vegetarian, the Monster makes his position as victim credible, even as his freedom to "wander on at liberty" enacts the roving threat of the houseless poor or the migrating laborer, financial liabilities who must be geographically fixed— given a "settlement"—in order to determine which parish will pay their way. The Monster represents his potential for inflicting damage in terms of the power to devour, cautioning Victor, "If you will comply with my conditions, I will leave them and you at peace; but if you refuse, I will glut the maw of death, until it be satiated with the blood of your remaining friends" (145).[16]

His rage at the De Laceys is similarly expressed as appetite, when the Monster claims he "could with pleasure have destroyed the cottage and its inhabitants and have glutted myself with their shrieks and misery" (181). This vengeful desire to consume others is in marked contrast to the Monster's earlier willingness to go hungry: "I had been accustomed, during the night, to steal a part of their store for my own consumption, but when I found that in doing this I inflicted pain on the cottagers, I abstained and satisfied myself with berries, nuts, and roots which I gathered from a neighboring wood" (157). This pacific diet dominates the Monster's mealtimes; indeed, he never touches meat of any kind.

Rather than energizing him, the foods the Monster chooses always enervate, and prepare him for peaceful engagements. The Monster's body is gentled in feeding on plants: having eaten, he is overcome by sleep. In the final volume, when the relationship between Victor and his creation is particularly tight, the connection between appetite, rage, and social destruction is partly transferred to Victor. Having destroyed the Monster's mate, and "burn[ing] with rage" (213), Victor finds it necessary to reflect in solitude and to "satisf[y] my appetite, which had become ravenous" (214). Victor's meal, however, is hardly alarming; he is satiated by "an oaten cake."

A significant form that the Monster's hunger takes is, of course, female companionship. The Monster demands a mate, introducing the Malthusian possibility that he may reproduce. (It is not the Monster who introduces this threat, we might note: he claims to have in mind only a marriage plot.) For Victor Frankenstein, marriage means the Monster's ability to reproduce himself, and thus to mass-manufacture mayhem; of course this potential for reproduction must be halted. The Monster ends his first lengthy speech to Victor, having revealed the origins of his bitter discontent, by saying, "I am alone and miserable; man will not associate with me; but one as deformed and horrible as myself would not deny herself to me. My companion must be of the same species and have the same defects. This being you must create" (189).[17]

The Monster's desire for affection is, as he insists, "reasonable and moderate." He presents himself as pacifist. But when he points out, "My food is not that of man" (191), he might just as well plead that "My food is not man," for Victor perceives him immediately as a voracious threat. The Monster goes on: "I do not destroy the lamb and the kid to glut my appetite; acorns and berries afford me sufficient nourishment. My companion will be of the same nature as myself and will be content with the same fare. We shall make our bed of dried leaves; the sun will shine on us as on man and will ripen our food. The picture I present to you is peaceful and human, and you must feel that you could deny it only in the wantonness of power and cruelty" (191).

But, precisely because this request *is* "human," Victor cannot fulfill it. The creation of a companion in the terms the Monster suggests would transform what can sometimes be an object of pity into a potential source of power and cruelty, and would imagine the Monster as having human rights. As Victor realizes in the course of his labors, a female Monster was likely to "become a thinking and reasoning animal" and "might refuse to comply with a compact made before her creation." Worse yet, "one of the first results of those sympathies for which the daemon thirsted would be children, and a race of devils would be propagated upon the earth who might make the very existence of the species of man a condition precarious and full of terror" (210). The Monster's hunger for companionship is here imagined as a "thirst" for reproduction.

Frankenstein also poses a question that will trouble many of the writers in the chapters to come, one also related to Malthusian anxieties: do "filthy origins" determine the self, or does "misery" make one a fiend? Mary Shelley's novel is concerned in the most graphic and elemental way with where persons come from; and it puzzles, too, over their social destination. The Monster seeks to associate himself with the bourgeois world as represented by Victor. He wishes to connect himself in the nearest possible way to Victor, reminding him again and again of his "duty" toward one "to whom thou art bound by ties only dissoluble by the annihilation of one of us" (145). The Monster especially seeks to learn the language of Frankenstein and the De Laceys; and by acculturating himself he hopes to secure a family.

Mary Shelley offers a *feeling* subject whose strongest drive seems to be knowledge. The pursuit of knowledge will humanize Oliver Twist and sanitize workhouse paupers, as described in chapter 1. And knowledge and education will define and redeem the self in the work of the Brontës and George Eliot, as discussed in chapters 3 and 4. But in *Frankenstein,* the Monster's keen desire for the "godlike science" of language (158) links him to Victor's disastrous pursuit of "unhallowed arts" (135). Knowledge leads to destruction: the more he knows, the more ardent his desire for vengeance. Shelley's novel thus imagines the birth pangs of a new kind of subject, one who hungers for knowledge and not blood; but finally the novel ends in uncertainty and irresolution. *Frankenstein* struggles mightily to put forward the brutish body and then to make its terrors less present by substituting a sensitive *person.* But the body itself is so unalterably monstrous that even a momentary sympathy must eventually give way to a reinforcement of the undeniably appetitive and reproductive body that first engendered that pity.

Nevertheless, this Monster *is* an object of pity. For all he represents a threat, he just as strongly makes the case for sympathetic intervention. The Monster's claims are exactly as just as they are intolerable. They are *just* because, as individual claims that bespeak genuine individual desire, they are indeed "reasonable and moderate," as the Monster phrases it. However, the individual claims of the Monster are at the same time, and with the same intensity, *intolerable* because the Monster's claims can never be viewed merely in terms of individual need and desire; they are also always social in that they have the potential to threaten others. This dilemma is, of course, the Malthusian one. Malthus highlights the interdependency of social life, the competition inherent in human existence, and the impossibility of viewing individual desire apart from a necessary social framework—concerns that gain their urgency through their association with the physiological needs of the body. Shelley's *Frankenstein* seeks to resolve this conflict between individual desire and social necessity by situating the Monster's claim to sympathy in relation to childhood, a resolution that will become a dominating plot in the early Victorian years. For lurking not far behind the monstrous form of that body is the shape of a pitiable child.

Perhaps it is no coincidence that twentieth-century representations of Shelley's creature so often picture him as if he were a gigantic baby: inarticulate, making babbling attempts at language, and stumbling like a toddler. In the novel, the Monster rapidly progresses from oversize infant to articulate and feeling subject, but he is nevertheless associated with the innocence of childhood. In his first attack on others, the Monster insists that he seeks only to capture innocence, the blankness of a Lockean subject, and hopes that somehow he can incorporate that innocence into himself. In his glimpses of Victor's little sibling William, he imagines such a possibility, as when he is "disturbed by the approach of a beautiful child, who came running into the recess I had chosen, with all the sportiveness of infancy. Suddenly, as I gazed on him, an idea seized me that this little creature was unprejudiced and had lived too short a time to have embibed a horror of deformity. If, therefore, I could seize him and educate him as my companion and friend, I should not be so desolate in this peopled earth" (187). But the existence of an individual, even a child of "radiant innocence," living outside social knowledge, is impossible. Thus, the Monster's fantasy that he might turn William into Rousseau's Emile is shattered when it becomes apparent that William is a little monster: "Ugly wretch! You wish to eat me and tear me to pieces. You are an ogre. Let me go, or I will tell my papa" (187). William recognizes the fantasy of incorporation that is a part of the Monster's desire to tutor his little captive.[18]

However, Shelley has already incorporated William into her portrayal of the Monster, insofar as the Monster is himself a species of innocent and blank Emile. William can be read as a monstrous brat whose "cannibalistic" murderer is an abused child. The innocent and monstrous are confused here, as they are throughout *Frankenstein*. The Monster is both victim and tormentor—both an all-innocent William, whom society is murdering, and the transgressive, resentful, murdering wretch whose anger at his treatment has turned him into a perpetrator. The picture of the Monster as an abused child is, of course, complicated by the fact that this victimized infant is always imprisoned within the body of that fearsome figure. For this reason, the physical hunger that testifies to the body's power must be converted in the novel into the need to be emotionally satiated. It is a conversion that "humanizes" the Monster, for if his desire for food draws attention to the potential power of his all-too-able body, his desire for companionship makes him more like the sentimental heroes and heroines of Dickens. Moreover, his craving for food is mediated by the fact that the Monster eschews the predatory connotations of the carnivore.

The sensitive nature, conscience, and interior consciousness of this creature, the qualities that shape his resemblance to the protagonists of later Victorian novels, are manifested in the quickness with which a gnawing physical desire is transmuted into a hungering after human companionship. It is signaled also in the way in which that companionship is just as quickly naturalized as standing specifically for the domestic comforts of the family. The rapid disappearance of physiological hunger, and of the body that requires an energizing fuel, protects him from becoming fully, or at any rate only, a Monster. Shelley's Monster painfully—not to say pathetically—testifies to the greater importance of nurturing comforts over the requirements of nature. In *Frankenstein,* minimizing the material claims of the body expands the possibilities for a self. But having introduced the body as the grounds upon which a claim to selfhood is based (the Monster denies physical need to seek what is phrased as a kind of psychological nourishment), the novel cannot completely extinguish the *idea* of the body, which presence is registered in the enduring unease with respect to that body. It is a thing too awful to look upon, even in the Monster's final, most sympathetically engaged, moments. The reader must look through Walton's eyes, who sees "a form which I cannot find words to describe—gigantic in stature, yet uncouth and distorted in its proportions" (260–61).

The hideous subject of *Frankenstein* is split between a monstrous appetite prepared destructively to reproduce at will, and an innocent victim subject to the horrors of an oppressive social world. Did misery make him a fiend? Or is this being inherently evil? The Monster's final speech articulates his peculiar position as both victim and perpetrator. The Monster suggests, quite accurately, that he is a victim who can only be seen as a brute, and that as such he is—in his words—an aborted child: "I did not satisfy my own desires. They were forever ardent and craving. . . . I, the miserable and the abandoned, am an abortion, to be spurned at, and kicked, and trampled on. Even now my blood boils at the recollection of this injustice" (263).

This "abortion," could he have been born a pitiable child, might have received the sympathy accorded, for example, William; he might even have become Oliver Twist. Shelley's Monster recalls, at last, not so much the innocence of childhood as the horrors of childbirth gone wrong. Mary Shelley's project to humanize this rejected flesh miscarries, but all the same it inaugurates an effort that will continue throughout the early Victorian years. What is missing in *Frankenstein* is the evocation of a social *outside* against which the Monster might be defined. Victor rejects the Monster, and presumably so would all society. One implicit justification for that rejection is the fact that, in the novel, the Monster's misery is traceable to no larger social forms.

In *Frankenstein,* the social field is incoherently represented. In Dickens, by contrast, the social is always not just present but highly visible in the form of the workhouse, the school, the prison, and so on. In Anne and Emily Brontë's novels, social forms other than the family are conspicuously absent, for reasons explored at length in chapter 3. And in *Adam Bede,* as shown in chapter 4, the dismantling of social solutions is an explicit subject.

In *Frankenstein,* the social realm is tentatively present, but its relationship to the action of the novel is unclear. The law functions as a purely authoritarian presence in Justine's trial and Victor's arrest, but still its judicial arm cannot reach the central crimes of the book. The school is the place where Victor practices his unhallowed arts, but it turns out to be largely beside the pedagogical point. Government appears as an ancien régime form.

Only the institution of the family seems to be evolving in *Frankenstein* toward something recognizably Victorian. The 1831 revision, among other things, lays particular stress upon Victor's childhood. In the revised edition, the position of parent and child is made to seem socially determined and dependent. In the Victorian rewrite of Victor's early years, parent-child relations are not just formative; they are formed around notions of duty, gratitude, and debt. Victor's father is transformed from an agent of patrilineal reproduction to embody a cozier familial figure. Family is no longer neatly analogous to government; it is less a means of transferring title and inheritance, more an affective and purely domestic space.[19]

Frankenstein, then, contains many of the elements that will dominate Victorian novels—the pedagogical family, the victimized child, the Malthusian male—but presents them inconsistently. What will turn out to be effective in *Oliver Twist,* and complicated in later novels discussed here, is the introduction of a social sphere in concert with the family. The victimized child is most effective in writing of all kinds when the social sphere is shown to circumscribe the individual's (child's) freedom, and also becomes the agent for demonstrating the necessity for that freedom. For the successful articulation of such a subject we must turn to the close of the decade, specifically to the young victims of *Oliver Twist,* and to the pauper children whose education in poverty will force them to take the infamous "workhouse test."

I

Hideous Progeny Made Clean:
Heredity and Pedagogy in the
New Poor Law Writings of James Kay
and in *Oliver Twist*

AT A PARTICULARLY LURID MOMENT in the complex history of what
protesters called "The New Starvation Law" of 1834, the public was
asked to digest the news that inmates of the Andover workhouse "employed in crushing bones were in the habit of eating the marrow and
gristle from the bones they were breaking."[1] In 1846 the London *Times*
published an extract from testimony in Parliament in which a poor law
guardian reported the results of his questioning of some of the men at
that workhouse: "They said that when they found what they called a fresh
bone, one that appeared a little moist, they were so eager to get it that
they were almost ready to fight over it; and that the man who was fortu-
nate enough to get it was obliged to hide it, that he might eat it when he
was alone" (4 May 1846). The problem arose with the sometime workhouse practice of demanding that inmates grind both "bones of commerce" (those already boiled for soups or soaps) and "green bones" (those
with marrow and meat still clinging to them). The widely reported scandal outraged the public and led to a lengthy inquiry into workhouse conditions.[2] But the most interesting aspect of the Andover scandal is not the
sensation it created, but rather the sympathetic response it evoked with
respect to the one figure that writers on both sides of the debate over the
new poor law of 1834 had either actively despised or fastidiously avoided:
namely, the healthy laborer who, claiming to be unable to find work,
found himself living instead off the "rates." The able-bodied male pauper
was not only the representative figure for the failures of the old poor law,

he was also largely unavailable as an object of pity—and therefore as a platform for protest—among opponents of the new one. Championing the male who failed to produce, but who was nevertheless capable of reproduction, could find no strategic or political purchase in the early decades of the nineteenth century.

If Andover represents a rare moment in this period during which consuming male bodies could be looked upon with sympathy, it was a sympathy mainly enabled by the disabilities of these particular bodies: incarcerated, emaciated, and asexual, the Andover paupers were incapable of diminishing the food supply and feeding Malthusian anxieties. Indeed, in their feeble condition the paupers seemed perpetually in danger of themselves becoming food; descriptions of the scandal darkly intimated that the starving pauper was gnawing the remains of fellow inmates. Among a parcel of bones sold to the Andover guardians were those unearthed at a local burial ground; "The attention of the porter was directed to the subject: he went and saw they were human bones."[3] Though these remains were imported from outside, the distinction between living and dead skeletal workhouse bodies was blurred. All too soon the bone-crusher could be tossed onto the pile of decaying matter himself, so nearly did he resemble it.

The story of Andover was reassuring in at least two ways. Publicized in the press and Parliament, it engendered a momentary sympathy for adult men otherwise ignored or excoriated in debates over the new poor law. Furthermore, the Andover scandal obliquely hinted at cannibalism. This imaginary recirculation of flesh suggested that the poor man's supply of food came from, and was contained within the boundary of, the workhouse. At the same time, the incarceration of the unemployed able-bodied male in quarters where, separated from women, he could not possibly swell the population, spoke to that other looming threat: reproduction. Malthus's famous "postulata"—that men must eat and procreate—were overturned. The circulation of the Andover story in the press and in Parliament served to diminish the devouring male. It was a retelling of Mary Shelley's story—another tale of big brutal men whose monstrosity is lessened only in proving their starvation and utter isolation.

The Andover scandal buried, but only briefly, the Malthusian male whose presence is so formidable in early Victorian writing. His shape was glimpsed in Mary Shelley's novel, and it appeared quite openly in the

1834 poor law *Report* discussed in the following pages. This chapter examines the sympathetic figures who replaced the Malthusian male—the literally diminished and diminutive figures through whom debates about what Disraeli called "The Two Nations" were carried out. The child victim emerged in opposition to figures of brutal masculinity; this opposition was important in fiction and nonfiction writings, as well as among both the opponents and the advocates of the new poor law. Dickens's 1838 novel, *Oliver Twist,* and the debates over pauper education that reformer James Kay pushed forward at the same time, are polemical and public discourses that stand in apparent opposition to one another. Nevertheless, each produces a victimized child, and each places that child in a position of social or institutional indebtedness, as well as one of sovereign independence. Further, Kay and Dickens do this in ways that are surprisingly similar, given the very different positions these men occupied on the political spectrum. Both men represent the origins of "filthy" pauperism by way of a simplified biology lesson: children "inherit" their condition. And second, among the pauper educators and in *Oliver Twist,* the cure for a hereditary taint is education, a schooling that must be combined with a separation from the physiologically dangerous family. However, Dickens and Kay not only seize upon similar polemical strategies when they enter into the controversy over the new poor law, they also find at last that their arguments founder on the same ground: work.

Disinheriting Pauperism

James Kay: Those instances are not numerous, but there are instances in which the children are allowed to take a walk with the master or mistress.
Chairman: Beyond the boundaries of the workhouse?
Kay: Yes.

Minutes of Evidence, Fourteenth Report from the Select Committee on the Poor Law Amendment Act

James Phillips Kay (he became Kay-Shuttleworth in 1842) has achieved a minor place in the history of education and of Victorian government since his death in 1877, but he has gathered few fans to himself with his fame. Not surprisingly, given Kay's public and ardent support of Benthamite legislation like the new poor law, Dickens despised him along with what he called Kay's "supernatural dreariness" (qtd. Paz 187). But even his closest political allies judged him harshly. E. C. Tufnell, whose name was often coupled with Kay's in discussion of pauper education, remarked, "For a long time I worked with Kay-Shuttleworth at education; but he was of so jealous a nature, that he was always afraid of having his merits lessened by others, and it was only possible to work with him by keeping constantly in the background" (qtd. Paz 187).

It is ironic that James Kay, who proposed "classification" as one cure for social ills, was himself so difficult to categorize; attempts to fit him to a hardened utilitarian mold or to dress him as an unwitting radical are equally doomed to failure. On the one hand, Kay had a relatively distinguished civil career. He was a doctor, an assistant poor law commissioner, and was appointed first secretary to the Committee of Council on Education. He authored, among other pamphlets, *The Moral and Physical Condition of the Working Classes of Manchester in 1832,* helped found the influential Manchester Statistical Society, and initiated a plan for training teachers that long served as a pedagogical model. But Kay dabbled in literary pursuits even as he worked diligently as a bureaucrat. Although he authored poetry in his youth and published novels in his dotage, Kay was only able to enter literary history when he introduced Charlotte Brontë and Elizabeth Gaskell to one another.

The divided nature of Kay's life is registered with some force in the outspoken stance he took with regard to one aspect of poor law administration: the treatment of children. Neither the poor law advocates nor the anti–poor law movement fully supported his efforts to reform pauper education. Yet Kay held fast to his elaborate plan for, as he put it in *The Training of Pauper Children,* "eradicating the germs of pauperism from the rising generation" (3–4). Kay has been dubbed an advocate of class control, and he has been seen as a guarded proponent of less-hierarchical social relations. However, no simple classificatory resting place can be found for Kay—not as a firm supporter of either social mobility or social control.[4] Instead, Kay's anomalous position with regard to pauper education exposes the contradictory cultural logic unavoidable in a philosophy that so emphasizes the Malthusian threat of the able-bodied unemployed, particularly in an age in which social relations are in flux. In his efforts on behalf of children, James Kay urged that young paupers be separated from their families and educated by the state beyond the minimal skills required for basic pecuniary support. In doing so he encountered resistance from all sides; in fact, it would be another thirty years before the spirit of Kay's intent was fully implemented in parliamentary endorsement of compulsory schooling.[5] The unspeakable question Kay's plans evoked was a simple but important one, since it challenged the fundamentals of social relationships of the time: what happens to these "innocent" paupers when they grow up and out of the workhouse? Are they to be released from pauperdom altogether and absorbed into "productive" society?

Before examining Kay's proposals at greater length, it will be useful to define the relationship of educational reform in the workhouse to the larger topic of poor relief. Briefly, the background is this: in 1832 a parliamentary commission was appointed to examine poor law administration in response to a widely held belief that the poor rates were spiraling out of control, and a sense that the present methods of relieving the poor were ineffectual. In addition to the infamous recommendation to apply a principle of "less eligibility" in all matters of poor relief, and to universally invoke the "workhouse test," the *Report for Inquiring into the Administration and Practical Operation of the Poor Laws* (put together by the appointed commissioners, Edwin Chadwick and Nassau Senior chief among them, and published in 1834) urged a centralized administration and a uniform policy and practice with respect to the relief of the poor.[6]

Among the most crucial effects of the *Report* is a redefinition of the pauper, and what some writers called the "pauper host."[7] "We believe," Chadwick said, "that modern history scarcely furnishes an example of verbal ambiguity by which greater mischief has been done, than by the ambiguity of the word 'poor'" (500). Reflecting on the history of the law, and defending it, Harriet Martineau in *History of the Peace* (1858) articulates what was a necessary background to this change in thinking about the nature of the poor: "To thoughtful observers it is clear that the same grave aristocratic error . . . [—]that of confounding in one all ranks below a certain level of wealth—was at the bottom of much poor-law abuse. . . . Except the distinction between sovereign and subject, there is no social difference in England so wide as that between the independent labourer and the pauper. . . . This truth . . . forms the very foundation of the measure" (375–76). Differences in social status, then, are not to be perceived from the perspective of the "aristocrat," an obviously wrongheaded position that Martineau believes will yield only "grave errors." The "thoughtful observers" to whom Martineau refers must be those, like herself, with a strong sense of what ails society, and a suspicious attitude toward the landed and their paternalistic approach. In Martineau's view, the "very foundation of the measure" wisely distinguished the component parts of the poor.

The 1834 poor law *Report* achieves this distinction largely by foregrounding the able-bodied male who is not employed, drawing a sharp line between those who are unable, and those who refuse, to labor.[8] Acknowledging that "circumstances will occur in which an individual, by the failure of his means of subsistence, will be exposed to the danger of perishing," the *Report* insists, "It has never been deemed expedient that the provision should extend to the relief of *poverty;* that is, the state of one, who in order to obtain a mere subsistence, is forced to have recourse to labour" (Lubove 52). The "great source of abuse" that must be redressed, according to the *Report,* is the granting of relief to laborers who are already in receipt of wages. "We have dwelt so much at length on the necessity of abolishing out-door relief to the able-bodied, because we are convinced that it is the master evil of the present system" (67). The solution was to be found "in drawing a broad line of distinction between the paupers and the independent labourers" (64), especially through the institution and enforcement of well-regulated workhouses. Relief must be made dependent upon entry into a workhouse.

The 1834 *Report* thus reserves its sharpest criticism for those men and, to some much-lesser extent, women who refuse to labor. The able-bodied male emerges as the realization of a Malthusian nightmare, the bastard offspring of the fumbling union of paternalism and industrialism. He is the victim of his own "indolence, improvidence or vice" (Lubove 58) and, above all, he is the perpetrator of "the fraudulent impositions of undue burthens by one class upon another class" (67). The 1834 *Report* recommends a simple fourfold classification of workhouse inmates: the "aged and really impotent," "children," "able-bodied females," and "able-bodied males" (93). As elsewhere in the *Report,* this distinction makes labor, not poverty, the fact that determines status. The pauper host is categorized according to those, such as "children" and the "really impotent," who cannot labor, and those who refuse to do so: the able-bodied.

The classificatory scheme that redefines pauperdom in the 1834 *Report* can thus be glossed as a matter of "fibres, muscles, and veins," to recall Mary Shelley's (or at any rate, Victor Frankenstein's) similar reading of self as body in *Frankenstein*. What did not work for Shelley, insofar as her novel ends in destruction and without a viable subject, has better success here. In the *Report,* the ability to labor is defined in the body alone, determined, that is, in relation to the physical capability of working. Held apart, and at last adjudged insignificant, are conditions beyond the control of the laborer; wages, the availability of work, seasonal changes affecting production, and economic fluctuations of all kinds may thus be disallowed. The authors of the *Report* state with confidence that simply enforcing the principle of less eligibility "will induce many of those, whose wants arise from their idleness to earn the means of subsistence" (Lubove 64). In proof of this outcome, the commissioners cite the testimony of one Mr. Tweedy of Huddersfield, who reported that of fifteen men who applied for relief in his parish and were told they could clean the streets in return for assistance, "but one came the next morning, who said the others had got jobs elsewhere" (86).

This reclassification according to physical capability redefines not only paupers but, to a certain extent, persons. It organizes worth around work, rather than around other kinds of merit, most especially mere (inherited) wealth. The independent laborer can be drawn closer to other productive persons of greater social status. At one extreme end of the social scale are the indolent poor who take and fail the workhouse test, thus demonstrating their moral degradation. Although not specifically named in the *Report,* it is the idle rich who implicitly occupy the other extreme on the social scale and who are equally despised. These are the perpetrators of Martineau's "grave aristocratic error[s]," wealthy citizens who resemble the able-bodied unemployed in their willingness to live off the labors of others.

Among the most thoroughgoing indictments of the aristocracy in this period is, of course, Carlyle's. Although he opposes what he sees as the cruelties and absurdities of utilitarian social policy, and acknowledges forces other than the body and the will to labor in governing the capacity to work, Carlyle's *Past and Present* nevertheless does just what the poor law *Report* does when it organizes worth around working bodies. Moreover, Carlyle makes explicit the *Report*'s implicit connection between the

"Idle Aristocracy" and the "enchanted" "working body of this rich English nation" (Carlyle 9). In detailing the requirements for relief, the 1834 *Report* delineates the expectations for all: the ability to work. And to the limited extent that the *Report* recognizes a difference between the ability to work and the willingness to work, it does so entirely according to that other great nineteenth-century social determinant: moral worth. To be *able* to work is to be physically fit; to be *willing* to work is to be morally healthy.

If the new poor law was in part a matter of framing, or reframing, social relations in this period, in addition to redefining the poor, its primary method in this effort was the classification of the pauper host. Within the *Report,* the fourfold classification achieves its goal: it firmly, if only discursively, separates the able-bodied unemployed from the "really impotent" and thus serves to redefine pauperdom. But the *Report* of 1834 was, of course, only theory; however firm, its divisions were words in a blue book. Within the walls of the union workhouse, classification became anything but discourse; classification, in practice, was acted out upon the bodies of the inmates and, more immediately—and what was more important as far as public policy was concerned—upon the minds of the residents of the newly formed unions. It was not the *Report* itself, but the threatened enforcement of classification as the physical separation of family groups, that provoked the rage of opponents of the law. Anti–poor law rhetoric targeted the spatial classification written into the architectural plans for new construction of union workhouses, a separation also encouraged as practice as far as possible in existing structures. Protestors seized upon the separation of elderly couples and, especially, the removal of young children from their families. In the union workhouse, for this reason, the tangible presence of the child under the poor laws was suddenly and urgently felt. Children had hardly escaped suffering under the old law. But now, their presence in the workhouse became a rallying cry for those opposed to the law.

The actual circumstances of families in both the old and the union workhouse was, many historians now agree, likely to be quite various and unpredictable. Certainly, even in the severest unions, the total separation of families was probably rare. Nevertheless, throughout the 1830s, the arguments against the poor law play upon the themes of familial separation, starvation, and cruelty to children and the elderly. The victimized child proved a formidable weapon in part because childhood was already functioning as a powerful sentimental discourse, and protestors could join their arguments with popular notions of childhood and children. But the representation of the poor pauper child separated from his or her parents was also powerful because it played upon an inherent weakness, or at least an impossible bind, in which the poor law reformers who had crafted the legislation now found themselves. The poor law commissioners, the boards of guardians who locally enforced the new law, and those in Parliament who continued to speak in its (theoretical) favor were concerned with the separation and definition of paupers *within* the workhouse, and with distinguishing between paupers and laborers. Their writing exemplifies a shift away from imagining the poor as a single (sentimentalized or reviled) social group. But classification and the theory of less eligibility were in conflict with the uneasy reality of segments of a reclassified pauper cohort—children and the elderly, for example—who were never meant to take the workhouse test.[9] New poor law advocates could hardly soften their commitment to less eligibility and classification because, among other things, it was in this way that they had redefined pauperdom. Those theories had produced the able-bodied male as a potential Malthusian threat. Inadvertently, and with the help of the anti–poor law movement, those theories were now also producing an innocent child pauper who was a prime target for those who would demonstrate the cruelties of the new law.

Into the fray stepped James Kay, with a radical plan for dealing with youthful workhouse inmates. Kay's proposal, including architectural drawings for the new schools, budgets, daily schedules, and such useful and detailed documents as a form for recording an individual "Journal of Religious and Secular Instruction," is included in *The Training of Pauper Children,* a report written by Kay and submitted to Parliament in 1838, and published as part of the *Fourth Annual Report* of the poor law commissioners.[10] The plan urged the construction of district schools physically distant from the workhouse, and at a philosophical remove from the rigors of less eligibility. It recommended that schoolmasters and schoolmistresses of higher quality, with a standardized education, and at higher wages, be employed. In terms of curriculum, Kay's plan stressed industrial training of a thorough and practical sort, "moral discipline," a course of religious education, and the advancement of secular knowledge.

It is this last category that differentiated Kay's ideas most from that of others. Kay proposed to teach subjects such as geography to pauper children, knowledge traditionally deemed unnecessary, if not incendiary, for the laboring class. Knowledge of geography, after all, might set paupers on the move, only to become a burden in another parish. That moral or religious training was important to the education of the poor was undisputed; the same was true of industrial training. But the teaching of even rudimentary skills in writing, reading, and arithmetic was another matter. A too-thorough secular education called forth the objection that pauper children in the workhouse should not receive greater benefits than the laborer's children outside it. At the request of his board of guardians, the clerk of the Belford union wrote the poor law commissioners in 1836, asking that writing be "omitted as part of the schoolmaster's instruction in the workhouse, and that he teach *reading only*. The Board do not recommend this on the score of economy, but on that of principle, as they are desirous of avoiding a greater advantage to the inmates of the workhouse than to the poor child out of it" (qtd. in Pinchbeck 503).

Asked during testimony to Parliament to describe typical objections to secular education, Kay said: "I have heard reasons of this kind assigned, that the education of the labouring class might unfit them for the performance of their practical duties in life; that the communication of a large amount of secular knowledge was inconsistent with the practice of religious duties and the preservation of the integrity of proper religious sentiments among that class; and that, as respected industrial instruction, the ordinary course pursued in the country was preferable to any other."[11] Some thirty years earlier, when Samuel Whitbread introduced a poor law reform bill that included a provision for pauper education, the objections were more explicit. Education, it was said, would cause the poor to "despise their lot in life, instead of making them good servants in agriculture and in the laborious employments to which their rank in society had destined them; instead of teaching them subordination, it would render them fractious and refractory . . . ; would enable them to read seditious pamphlets . . . [;] would render them insolent to their superiors" (Poynter 215–16). The fear that any education of the poor would render them revolutionaries seems to have subsided somewhat by the time Kay came along in the late 1830s, but there was still considerable feeling that *education* for the laborer meant industrial and religious training.

In this context, Kay emerges as, in a limited sense, a radical. He imagined a completely separate category for pauper children, one not distinguished only in terms of a body's ability or willingness to labor, but a category essentially and fundamentally different from that of the fellow workhouse inmates. Pauper children, in fact, were to occupy a position distinct and even separate from that of their parents. Thus, while classification in the 1834 *Report for Inquiring into the Administration and Practical Operation of the Poor Laws* had been content to separate children from their (able-bodied) relatives in order to define pauperdom, Kay pressed matters much further: familial separation was the mechanism that constituted the innocent and deserving pauper child as an independent subject, rather than merely constituting the evils of the able-bodied male.

In the 1834 *Report,* children were given a separate spatial and philosophical classification within the workhouse population, but they remained a part of the parasitical pauper host. And in fact, the continued physical and symbolic presence of what the 1834 *Report* called the "truly impotent" within the workhouse served to underscore the culpability of the able-bodied. But in Kay's view, children could and indeed must be removed—literally—from the workhouse and understood as part of a larger group. In the broadest sense, that group comprised all of childhood, since for him all children were, at least theoretically, innocent of their social circumstances. But Kay drew the closest link between workhouse children and the children of independent laborers residing near them. In insisting on this connection, James Kay undid the distinction between poverty and pauperdom that was so central to the poor law reformers with whom he is associated.

James Kay's *The Training of Pauper Children* begins with the unequivocal statement, "The pauper children maintained in Union workhouses are dependent, not as a consequence of their errors, but of their misfortunes" (2). Kay expands upon this idea by stating in his report, and reiterating in the lengthy testimony he gave to Parliament based on that report in March of 1838, what he views as an undisputed fact: "A child should not be degraded in his own estimation by being a member of a despised class. A child cannot be a pauper in the sense in which that term is commonly understood, that is, he cannot be indigent as the consequence of his own want of industry, skill, frugality, or forethought, and he ought not, therefore, to be taught to despise himself" (14).

Kay emphatically and unequivocally declares a place for the youthful inmate unlike any other position in pauperdom. A child, he says, simply cannot be a pauper, thus underscoring and implicitly refuting the unspoken suggestion that "pauperism" is a moral category, not an economic one, in the eyes of his fellow reformers. However much certain utilitarian supporters of the 1834 law might voice concern for, and advocate for the education of, pauper children, they could not emphasize their support of children too strongly, because that could only damage their portrayal of pauperdom as a self-induced state of moral turpitude.

Kay links the workhouse child and the child of laborers, repeatedly refusing to distinguish poor children within the same union. He often points out the inadequacy of education among the children of laborers, suggesting that whatever their social position, education is crucial: "It is impossible to adopt as a standard for the training of [pauper] children the average amount of care and skill now bestowed on the moral and religious culture of the children of the labouring classes generally, or to decide that their secular instruction shall be confined within limits confessedly so meagre and inadequate" (*Training* 2). His insistence on this point occasioned some anxious questioning when he was called back to testify a second time before the select committee. According to "The Minutes of Evidence," Mr. Fielden asked whether "the education that you propose is for children who are put into the workhouse," and asked Kay to clarify whether or not he had stated that he "did not wish to interfere with the education of the children of independent labourers" (*Sixteenth Report* 2). In his responsive testimony, Kay repeated that "it did not appear to me inexpedient to permit that the children of independent labourers . . . should . . . partake of the advantages provided for the pauper children" (*Sixteenth Report* 2).

In the exchange between members of Parliament and Kay during that testimony of March 1838, Kay's interlocutors continually sought to return to a strict account of the workhouse as a cruel prison for children, and they focused on the necessity of giving paupers training in industry and religious instruction—not secular education. "Is it not necessary," Fielden asked, "that children who are to labour on the land should be trained in different occupations connected with husbandry, at an early age?" (*Sixteenth Report* 3). Mr. Liddell remarked, "You do not think that it is one of the most necessary and desirable circumstances in the education of the children that they should attend the parish church?" (*Sixteenth Report* 6). The chair of the committee asked whether Kay was "aware that, in one particular instance, children have been punished by diminishing the quantity of their food?" (*Sixteenth Report* 4), and Mr. Liddell asked, "And they are never whipped?" (*Sixteenth Report* 5). In the guise of a paternalistic benevolence, the select committee questioned Kay's plan for education and reasserted the popular view that workhouses serve largely to punish children and keep them from the natural affections of their parents.

Kay's questioners demonstrated a belief that the *natural* state of things is a unified, if pauperized, family; Kay suggested that in a *natural* condition, pauperism is physiologically based. If members of Parliament viewed the family as a necessary unit of great importance to a general social cohesion, Kay viewed familial relations as potentially poisonous and detrimental to society. His proposal relied heavily on the idea that parental influence is, in fact, dangerous. Pauperism was consistently represented as a hereditary condition, or as a disease that can be contracted. Thus, "it is [in] the interest of society," Kay said in his written report, "that [workhouse] children should neither inherit the infamy, nor the vice, nor the misfortunes of their parents" (*Training* 14). In Kay's view, innocent children may inherit pauperism, but strict environmental conditions can reverse the damage. He endorsed a more or less biologized account of immorality, even as he expressed the conviction that society could devise a cure.

Assistant Commissioner Edward Tufnell, who along with James Kay was a major voice in support of pauper education, was typical in insisting that "pauper parents reared pauper children. To stop this hereditary trait would be to annihilate the greater part of pauperism in this country" (qtd. Mommsen 14). Children were said to inherit a disease, the effects of which may in time be ameliorated; or they might "contract" habits that have the persistence of chronic disease. According to Kay's report, pauper children may or may not "contract" a "taint of pauperism" (*Training* 2); pauperism is a "germ" that must be "eradicated." Not only were unclassified children in the workhouse literally diseased—"infested with vermin, often covered with the itch"—but they were also "being contaminated with the vicious dispositions of the persons with whom they come in contact" (*Fourteenth Report* 3).

In Kay's writing and testimony, the workhouse was no longer merely a container for the detritus of society; instead, it was a breeding ground for indolence and, most interestingly, a reproductive disaster. Kay claimed that it was the government's role to intervene and put a stop to this by separating not just men and women who might reproduce, but separating—ultimately liberating—children. Paupers, especially orphans, were seen as a pecuniary burden and a potential social threat; it was the responsibility of the government to take a role in managing reproduction: "The state is *in loco parentis* to the pauper children, who have no natural guardians, and the interest it has in the right discharge of its responsibilities may be illustrated by supposing the Government had determined to require direct, instead of indirect service in return for education. If the army and navy were recruited by the workhouse children, it is evident that it would be the interest of the state to rear a race of hardy and intelligent men. . . . The state has . . . the most positive and direct interest in adopting measures to prevent the rearing of a race of prostitutes and felons" (*Training* 5–6). In summary, Kay cautioned, "Whether the state acknowledge its interest in the education of the masses or not, the consequences of a neglect of the pauper class evidently are prolonged dependence and subsequent chargeability as criminals in the prisons and penal colonies" (*Training* 5).[12]

This warning bears resemblance to the fear voiced by Victor Frankenstein, quoted earlier from Shelley's novel, of a "race of devils propagated upon the earth." And the sentiment was later echoed by Harriet Martineau, who defended spatial classification in this way:

> *The separation of the men and women . . . was absolutely necessary to common decency . . . required by every consideration of justice to the state, which could not rear a race of paupers within the workhouse, to the prevention of virtuous marriage without. . . . That the children should be segregated was necessary to their moral safety and educational training. No part of the new law has occasioned more complaint and opposition than this workhouse classification; and no part is more clearly defensible from every point of view, or more evidently necessary. (376)*

The family was not only diseased, it also frequently perpetuated disease by way of reproduction. In the place of the institution of family, reformers advocated a new institution, one that would prove increasingly influential throughout the decade and eventually take as its mission some of the "work" of the family: education.

Education was the all-important tool, "to be regarded as one of the most important means of eradicating the germs of pauperism from the rising generation" (*Training* 4). Kay and his fellow reformers sought to liberate the pauper child from the dangerous influence of family, and to deliver him into the cleansing environment of the school. But Kay's efforts, and those of other pauper educators, served not so much to liberate as to classify, segregate, and reaggregate children under a new label. The innocent pauper child represented a new category, but once he or she was removed from the workhouse the child was re-formed, not to say reformed, within a pedagogical grouping. However distinct James Kay's plans may have been from those of other reformers in the period, the effect was not to imagine a free and liberal subject in the "educated" pauper child.[13] In place of the workhouse, pauper children would be entered into an institution, there to join a different, but no less socially indebted, category.

Kay's plan served, then, to produce pedagogical subjects. But that subject position was based at the same time upon a notion of separation from the group, especially the family, and therefore neither did his plan constitute the child-self as a subject of discipline. James Kay's child was an individual with rights that can and should be supported by the state. No longer the "possession" of a father as economic and paternal agent, the child was to be viewed as a "person" deserving of certain rights. Of course, in the carceral realm of workhouse education, these rights were to be guarded and administered by the state. To read Kay's schoolhouse plans, complete with daily schedules and architectural drawings reminding students of their physical and social place, is on the one hand to understand the micromechanics that make "docile bodies" docile, in the Foucauldian phrase. But on the other hand, these children were not—or they were not *only*—disciplinary subjects in the Foucauldian sense. They were also the individuated selves they would become once they were freed from the workhouse. In the end, these children were neither disciplinary subjects nor liberal ones. Because they were liberated into the arms of the state, they were more than anything else "clients," and as such they were neither free nor bound, but always both at once.

Although the 1834 new poor law appeared to move away from a client class in working against massive social apparatus for poor relief, the pauper educators initiated a version of subjectivity that was like a client class in their proposed treatment of children. Liberated, yet bound by the requirement of the state-supported school, the ever-victimized child was successfully imagined in the discourse of pauper education. It is not terribly far from the version of subjectivity that dominates modern welfare, though early Victorian discourse placed greater emphasis on the supposed free subjectivity of the child. The enduring pattern, from the early Victorian period and into our own, is the representation of the child in distress, a representation that authorizes the consequent construction of a client class. It is this pattern that makes a narrative about the role of the state in family life possible. And it was state intervention, ironically, that constituted endangered children in the 1830s as independent subjects.

Kay's ideas, it must be noted, did not meet with massive approval. His plans were never implemented, and the pauper child as victim in need of education was hardly a popular concept.[14] The reasons for Kay's "failure" are complex, but one thing seems clear: Kay's plans raised uncomfortable, and perhaps historically premature, questions about the place the pauper child might or could eventually occupy in society outside the workhouse. The old system of sending pauper children out to apprentice was universally deplored, but it had at least the effect of emphasizing the youthful pauper's culpability and maintaining his position as outsider: "The pauper apprentice and the juvenile vagrant were, under the old system, brethren of the same class—outcasts," Kay pointed out (*Training* 14).[15] Early on in his evidence to Parliament, Assistant Commissioner Kay was asked a crucial question: "At what period should you say that generally [the children in the workhouse] might be sent out from the workhouse and be able to earn their own livelihood?" (*Fourteenth Report* 3). The question cast "innocent" pauper children—youthful victims or "clients" deserving of care and even education, in Kay's opinion—as workers outside the system of relief; they would grow into, and could here be briefly imagined as, able-bodied males and females. The committee member's question implicitly asked what sort of citizens these paupers would eventually become.

Kay cannily steered the discussion away from productivity and returned it to education. Pauper education is the key to remaking these persons, he insisted in his testimony and his writings. He went on to address cost practically, reassuring members that "education is chiefly to be regarded by the Poor Law Commissioners as the means of avoiding the ultimate dependence upon the rate-payers of the children" (4). In this way, an increase in institutional intervention in the lives of the poor—the advent of state organization of pauper education—was represented as consistent with the goal of less eligibility and independent labor.

But Parliament and the public were apparently unconvinced. Although some poor law advocates also supported Kay's plan, and although his plans were prepared with the initial support of men like Chadwick, pauper children were not offered his version of education with any consistency. Ironically, the production of an independent self also meant the fashioning of a subject who was unable to labor. It is precisely this problem—of work and its role in the lives of "innocent" children—that motivates, and complicates, the tale of *Oliver Twist*.

Heaven's Surfaces

> *Meat! perhaps your right to that may be pleadable; but other rights have to be pleaded first. Claim your crumbs from the table if you will; but claim them as children, not as dogs; claim your right to be fed, but claim more loudly your right to be holy, perfect, and pure.*[16]
>
> John Ruskin,
> *Unto This Last*

From the start, *Oliver Twist* was a player in the public debate over the new poor law.[17] Even as the novel was being serialized in *Bentley's Miscellany,* the London *Times* published an excerpt from it in support of its vigorous campaign against the legislation.[18] And not just any excerpt: the *Times* reprinted the famous workhouse scene in which Oliver is gullible enough to announce his hunger and plead for seconds. The hungers, and the fear of those hungers, that suffuse this period are manifestly at work in *Oliver Twist* and in the strategic use of the novel by the press. In the "Please, sir, I want some more" scene, as so often in *Oliver Twist,* Dickens melodramatizes and sentimentalizes starvation to prove the cruelties of Benthamite practice. No wonder the *Times* was so quick to reprint; the newspaper had been employing the same strategy since the law's passage, reporting (and by no means with perfect accuracy) horrifying stories of adulterated and rotten foodstuffs, meager rations, and outright starvation.[19] The story of the Andover bone-crushers would, seven years later, be published in the *Times* as part of this popular minigenre of nauseating workhouse-food tales. Dickens's novel, in many ways, can also be counted in this group, for it tells the tale of hungry souls with a gusto that mimics that of contemporary journalism.

Critics recognized the importance of food in *Oliver Twist*, but not everyone found the sentimental display of starvation palatable. One writer deplored the novel's unappetizing offering in an unsigned review, "Literary Recipes," in the August 1841 edition of *Punch*:

> *Take a small boy, charity, factory, carpenter's apprentice, or otherwise, as occasion may serve—stew him well down in vice—garnish largely with oaths and flash songs—boil him in a cauldron of crime and improbabilities. Season equally with good and bad qualities—infuse petty larceny, affection, benevolence, and burglary, honour and housebreaking, amiability and arson—boil all gently. Stew down a mad mother—a gang of robbers—several pistols—a bloody knife. Serve up with a couple of murders—and season with a hanging match.*
>
> *N.B. Alter the ingredients to a beadle and a workhouse—the scenes may be the same, but the whole flavour of vice will be lost, and the boy will turn out a perfect patter—strongly recommended for weak stomachs.*[20]

But as it turned out, the public appetite for *Oliver*, in his fat three-decker version as well as in his more elongated serialized state, was considerable: the novel did very well. The anonymous critic's distaste aside, it may be the emphasis on food and feeding that gives the novel its power.

Hunger dominates the early chapters of *Oliver Twist*, as even the most cursory reading will reveal.[21] The workhouse is a place where "juvenile offenders against the poor-laws rolled about the floor all day, without the inconvenience of too much food" (48). Baby farms are where children are locked away "for atrociously presuming to be hungry" (49). In the undertaker's shop where Oliver is apprenticed, "The very rats . . . were hideous with famine" (81). Troublesome questions are asked when parish children die, but "these impertinences were speedily checked by the evidence of the surgeon . . . [who] opened the body and found nothing inside (which was very probable indeed)" (49).

Food serves mostly to distinguish worthy persons from those who deserve the reader's loathing, especially among the poorer population.

The morally healthy are those victims who are sick unto death with starvation, such as Mrs. Mann's unfortunate charges, or little Dick, or the pitiable crowd clamoring for more in the workhouse. The deserving poor in *Oliver Twist* are usually starving, and they are almost always children—and diminutive children at that, as if to suggest that in the eyes of the cruel maladministrators of the poor laws, even a largish child would eat too much; and as if to imply that in the eyes of the reader, only the most pathetic and starved victim could garner full sympathy. True, in one instance, when Oliver visits a slum as undertaker's apprentice, it is a mother who is "starved to death" (82). But everywhere else, the hungry are underage and undersize.

And size *matters:* when Mr. Bumble admits to Mrs. Sowerberry, thinking of Oliver's ability to endure hard work, "Why, he *is* rather small. . . . But he'll grow," Mrs. Sowerberry complains that he'll do so "on our victuals and our drink. I see no saving in parish children, not I; for they always cost more to keep, than they're worth." The prospect is made to seem a distant one, since Oliver, like the Andover bone-crushers, seems more a skeleton than overfed flesh: "There! Get down stairs, little bag o' bones" (73), he is urged.

There are few adults worthy of assistance in the world of *Oliver Twist,* Nancy being the most visible exception. There *are* no visible adults, except cruel administrators, at the workhouse where Oliver briefly resides. There are no adult paupers here at all—at least, no "deserving poor." It is a workhouse swept miraculously clean of the able-bodied indolent that so dominate the poor law *Report.* In this novel the adult poor simply do not appear to be starving. The slums through which the parish boy makes his unhappy progress in early chapters are not places of hunger but of crime (Fagin's haunts) or of filth, the "air impregnated with filthy odours," the public houses occupied by "the lowest orders of Irish," and "drunken men and women . . . positively wallowing in filth" (103).

The evacuation of hungry adults from the novel is as thoroughgoing as the reproduction of an undeserving—and satiated—underclass. The devouring poor live on outside the workhouse, where they get altogether too much to eat, since food apparently feeds a thirst for crime. The awesome power that a well-fed body can muster is cruelly evident in Sikes, for instance, who might put off inflicting bodily damage for a meal, but ultimately prefers violence to vittles. His eating is sometimes associated with his brutality. "Sitch a rabbit pie, Bill" (347), exclaims the Dodger, "sitch delicate creeturs, with sitch tender limbs, Bill, that the wery bones melt in your mouth, and there's no occasion to pick 'em." Sikes finds himself "a little soothed as he glance[s] over the table" (349), but his appetite for bloodshed soon overtakes him. By the time he reaches his place of last resort on Jacob's Island, we heartily agree with the appraisal of Charley Bates, who (not unlike Victor Frankenstein as he gazed upon his vengeful creation) looks "with horror in his eyes, upon the murderer's face. 'You monster!' " (448).

Despised members of the underclass, that is to say, are figures who enact the imagined dangers of Frankenstein's Monster: they overeat or are vicious. They can be fully grown and physically capable, not to mention covertly sexualized, like Sikes, or they can be young and lazy and somewhat asexual; but in *Oliver Twist* they are always male. Noah Claypole, the "charity-boy" who delights in taunting the innocent little Oliver, represents the worst of the morally corrupt recipient of public aid. It is Noah who is "hungry and vicious" (86), who eats the "nice little bit of bacon" Charlotte saves for him from the "master's breakfast" (77), while Oliver nearly starves. Noah's slide toward total moral collapse is signaled in his indolence and his luxurious and excessive ("intoxicating") eating: "Mr. Noah Claypole lolled negligently in an easy-chair, with his legs thrown over one of the arms: an open clasp-knife in one hand, and a mass of buttered bread in the other. Close beside him stood Charlotte, opening oysters from a barrel: which Mr. Claypole condescended to swallow, with remarkable avidity. A more than ordinary redness in the region of the young gentleman's nose . . . denoted that he was in a slight degree intoxicated; these symptoms were confirmed by the intense relish with which he took his oysters" (251). Noah Claypole's general degradation is demonstrated in the devastation he wreaks upon food. Oliver's meek and pitiful hunger stands in contrast to Noah's intense relish; in starving, Oliver remains, to use Ruskin's phrase, "holy, perfect, and pure."

In this way the novel seeks to manage the violent hungers that lurk behind Shelley's Monster or the pauper men of the new poor law *Report*. Dangerous appetites are evoked only to be mocked or minimized in diminutive victims, or displaced onto diseased others, or criminalized among laboring men and charity boys. That these appetites require curbing, even in the safely edited world of Dickens's novel, is made evident in the aroma of meat that lingers even about innocent Oliver, and the dangerous, if partly comic, suggestion that *even Oliver* is subject to the animalistic impulses demonstrated by the Andover men, and warned against by Ruskin. Oliver exhibits, for instance, a surprising canine ferocity at times, a willingness to claim his rights precisely as a dog would. Instructing Charlotte to bring out "some of the cold bits that were put by for Trip," Mrs. Sowerberry guesses correctly that "the boy isn't too dainty to eat 'em":

> *Oliver, whose eyes had glistened at the mention of meat, and who was trembling with eagerness to devour it, replied in the negative; and a plateful of coarse broken victuals was set before him.*
>
> *I wish some well-fed philosopher, whose meat and drink turn to gall within him . . . could have seen Oliver Twist clutching at the dainty viands that the dog had neglected. I wish he could have witnessed the horrible avidity with which Oliver tore the bits asunder with all the ferocity of famine. . . .*
>
> *"Well," said the undertaker's wife, when Oliver had finished his supper: which she had regarded in silent horror, and with fearful auguries of his future appetite: "have you done?" (74)*

Oliver's "horrible avidity"—suggestively reminiscent of Noah Claypole's "remarkable avidity"—would seem, in Dickens's satirical context, to mock the dangers of hunger seemingly so present to those who would reform the poor laws along Malthusian lines. But in doing so, Dickens forges a quiet connection between Oliver and the hated Noah, and also admits a peculiarly animalistic side to Oliver's character. This is not unlike the effect of the endless stories of starvation and spoilage reprinted in the London *Times,* which betrayed a nervous interest in what, and how much, paupers ate.

When Oliver exhibits "the violence of his rage, till his teeth chattered in his head" (88), the Beadle knows where to assign the blame: " 'It's not Madness, ma'am,' replied Mr. Bumble, after a few moments of deep meditation. 'It's Meat! . . . You've overfed him. . . . You've raised an artificial soul and spirit in him, ma'am. . . . What have paupers to do with soul or spirit? It's quite enough that we let 'em have live bodies' " (93). In the first half of *Oliver Twist,* Dickens plainly means to raise a "soul" in pauper children and to reverse the Beadle's notion of the poor as just so much flesh. But whenever Oliver comes near to being fed, the carnivore in him comes out. In this admittedly limited way Oliver resembles Victor Frankenstein's Monster: Oliver's meat-maddened body cannot be made to disappear, however much Dickens might wish to substitute a soul for that "live" flesh. This is to say that even diminutive and purified creatures nevertheless remain live bodies, and therefore are mindful of the social problems with which hunger, in the 1840s, is intertwined.

The smell of meat lingers about Oliver because, for one obvious reason, he is hungry. But the novel further suggests that as a poor youth who can be bought and sold, he also *is* a piece of meat. His bones, like the dead flesh consumed at Andover, are "bones of commerce." The novel makes this clear in its repeated return to Smithfield meat market, a mention that is superfluous to the plot but nonetheless very deliberately included. At Smithfield, "food," especially meat, is an ambulatory commodity inseparable from the crowd of undifferentiated and roaming human bodies. Smithfield is a threatening place of "gloom" and "discord," loud with the "roar of sound and bustle" (203). Not surprisingly, it is also a place of blood and gore:

> *The ground was covered, nearly ankle-deep, with filth and mire; and a thick steam, perpetually rising from the reeking bodies of the cattle . . . hung heavily above. All the pens in the centre of the large area . . . were filled with sheep; tied up to posts by the gutter side were long lines of beasts and oxen. . . . Countrymen, butchers, drovers, hawkers, boys, thieves, idlers, and vagabonds of every low grade, were mingled together in a mass. . . . [T]he crowding, pushing, driving, beating, whooping, and yelling . . . and the unwashed, unshaven, squalid, and dirty figures constantly running to and fro, and bursting in and out of the throng . . . rendered it a stunning and bewildering scene, which quite confounded the senses. (203)*

The scene confounds not only the senses but also the distinction between those (persons) selling and those (animals) being sold.

Sikes drags Oliver through Smithfield not once, but twice, and each time Oliver's befuddlement is emphasized. This confusion serves to prove that he remains uninfected by the gore that surrounds him, untainted by the market operations that define the bodies of cattle and—outside the meat market—the bodies of laborers whose lives are equally determined

by the market. Although there can be little mistaking their location—
there "were pens for beasts, and other indications of a cattle-market"
(158)—"it might have been Grosvenor Square, for anything Oliver knew
to the contrary" (159). Oliver is paraded through the display of meat as if
to establish with an absolute certainty his own distance from this scene
not just of gore, but of commerce.

On his second trip, Oliver is "astonished" and "filled . . . with
amazement" (203), as if it were possible for him to be held distant from
the economic aspects of hunger and the insistent and determining demands of the marketplace. In these scenes of meat and money, Dickens
reinforces, even if inadvertently, the fact that the poor do not simply want
or need meat. In fact the poor *are* items for sale at market, insofar as it is
not only the needs of their bodies, but the use of their bodies as labor,
that matters. The economic value of poor bodies is thus paramount,
whether it concerns the cost of food or of labor. The spectacle of the
Andover paupers brought them into relationship with the "bones of
commerce"—animal remains being sold for profit. In Oliver's associations with meat, he comes also to be associated with the market, and
with the economic value not just of livestock but of human bodies.

In this way the seemingly incidental portrayal of Smithfield Market
clarifies the significance of the many instances of Oliver's body being
made to have a cash value. Just as how one eats distinguishes one's social
place—one has either a "bad" (devouring) appetite or one is a victim of
"good" starvation—whether or not one sees pauper bodies in terms of
their cash value also determines one's merit. The novel does not attempt
to dispute the resale value of poor or pauper bodies. Instead, Dickens
makes a lesson out of whether or not persons choose to capitalize on the
value of children, and whether they associate youthful bodies with the
cash nexus.

Oliver is repeatedly connected to financial gain, beginning with the
posting of the bill on the workhouse gate, "offering a reward of five
pounds to anybody who would take Oliver Twist off the hands of the
parish" (58); and looking toward the Brownlow offering of "Five Guineas
Reward," which "will be paid to any person who will give such information as will lead to the discovery of the said Oliver Twist" (174).
"[T]he boy's worth hundreds of pounds to me" (240), says Fagin. And of
course Monks's great crime is that he recognizes Oliver's economic value
and understands the child strictly in cash terms.

In fact, Oliver's relations to almost everyone in the novel are defined economically. The (felonious) labor Oliver can perform for Fagin; the fortune he can preserve for Monks; the work he can do in his apprenticeships; the money that can be saved by starving him—all of these relationships turn upon his economic price or cost; in other words, upon what the market must or will bear. As Toby says, he's "an inwalable boy" (209). Reinforcing Oliver's potential value, the Dodger says, "You've been brought up bad. . . . Fagin will make something of you, though, or you'll be the first he ever had that turned out unprofitable" (183). And in countless other moments during Oliver's "progress" through the carceral underworld, he is seen not just as an "item of mortality" (45) but as an agent of profit. Mr. Sowerberry finds a way to translate Oliver's face into immediate profit, and thereby recoup the loss of the meager rations Oliver is allowed: " 'It's only about young Twist, my dear,' said Mr. Sowerberry. 'A very-good-looking boy, that, my dear.' 'He need be, for he eats enough,' observed the lady. 'There's an expression of melancholy in his face, my dear,' resumed Mr. Sowerberry, 'which is very interesting. He would make a delightful mute, my love' " (78–79).

Despite his avowed sympathy for the poor, which is expressed through this emphasis on cash value and poverty, Dickens distances himself from the lazy nonlaborer. The able-bodied male is criminalized in Sikes; or else he is possessed of an overactive appetite that countermands any claim he might have on the public's pity (and pocket), as is the case with Noah Claypole. Like James Kay, Dickens places his sympathy with the "innocent" poor, though for him only certain children are innocent. Meanwhile, the pervasive anxieties we have seen in *Frankenstein* and in the new poor law concerning the indolent but hungry poor are mirrored at the other end of the social scale by a portrayal of the indolent and avaricious upper class. The Malthusian male is repressed in *Oliver Twist,* except in the portrayal of the vicious and sexualized Sikes.

At the same time, Dickens offers the vicious (and also sexualized) Monks as a portrayal of the idle rich, who are the subject of an implicit critique in new poor law discourse and deplored directly by Carlyle in *Past and Present.* Monks's able male body is indolent because he is a member of the decadent upper class. He is like Sikes in his malevolence, and like the Monster in *Frankenstein* in his (literal) relation to the little boy he seeks to destroy. In Monks, the novel names a more vicious appetite, one that it combines with that of revenge: hunger manifests itself in Monks as a desire to acquire. But Monks's need for money is not unrelated to the pauper's need for food; after all, the necessity of feeding the poor is finally an economic issue, and it was the tremendous cost of that food, in the form of increasing parish rates, that partly gave impetus to the poor law reforms in the first place.

This correlation between Monks and dangerous elements among the poor forges a relationship between the idle and decadent upper classes and the idle and decaying poor, not unlike Harriet Martineau's distinction between "the independent labourer and the pauper." The pauper and the idle rich are more like one another than not. Monks says he wants blood, but what he seeks just as ardently is cash. The desire for "blood" refers obliquely to family, inasmuch as it is an inheritance Monks seeks to secure. But blood, in the traditional sense of primogeniture, is not enough in *Oliver Twist;* indeed, it is worth almost nothing. As the legitimate son, Monks is already in possession of the "blood." Inheritance, the mere passing on of fortune, is not to be condoned.

Oliver Twist turns a story of inheritance—a marriage plot—into a narrative of family and heredity; it turns the passing on of fortune into the transmission of disease, and in this way mirrors Kay's account of familial relations.[22] The important fact about Monks is not that he has the "blood" as the firstborn son, but that he has his mother's blood—that he "inherits" her morals: *maternal* heredity and the physiology of inherited traits matters here. Illegitimate Oliver is cleansed of the stain of his birth to become "an innocent and unoffending child . . . although the offspring of a guilty and most miserable love."[23] The economic structure that underlies the marriage plot is undermined in the story of Oliver and Monks's father, who was forced to endure "the misery, the slow torture, the protracted anguish of that ill-assorted union" (435). Leeford Sr.'s marriage for money is disastrous, redeemed only in his loving, if guilty, embrace of Oliver's mother.

Oliver's "filthy origins" are obscured and rendered unimportant not because he is the legitimate heir but because he is the rightful and righteous one, shown in the fact that he "inherits" his mother's innocence. In other words, it is not the marriage plot, but a bourgeois version of the family romance, that matters. *Oliver Twist* ends not with Rose Maylie's marriage—and certainly not with Oliver's—but with the family tableau pathetically captured in Cruikshank's drawing for the final number: Rose and Oliver stand looking at Agnes's empty tomb inside the village church, consolidating their togetherness in a purified family grouping that might satisfy the child's wish to discover his "real" (and loftier) family. But that loftier elevation owes its greatness not to the revelation of royal origins, but rather to the recovery of an unknown heritage of moral purity.

The contamination and disease that defines family life in the workhouse writings of reformers appears in *Oliver Twist* in the aristocratic decadence of Monks. He represents not only the rejected world of the father (governed by primogeniture and legitimacy), but introduces the immoral heredity of the mother's quasi-aristocratic line. For Monks is the victim of some virulent, apparently degenerative, disease, simultaneously suggestive of syphilis and a congenital defect. Even as he wishes infection upon Oliver ("black death upon your heart, you imp!" [298]), he betrays his own bodily infirmity; unable to aim a blow at the child he instead "fell violently on the ground: writhing and foaming, in a fit" (298). Doubtless, Monks is a horrid fellow, almost certainly a former slaveholder who lounges on his "own estate in the West Indies—whither, as you well know, you retired upon your mother's death to escape the consequences of vicious courses here" (438), says Brownlow. But he is also a sick one; lest we think Monks's foaming fit is mere evidence of emotion, the novel wastes no time in making certain we understand the thoroughgoing, apparently congenital and probably sexualized, nature of Monks's defects. As Brownlow, judgelike, intones: "you, who from your cradle were gall and bitterness to your own father's heart, and in whom all evil passions, vice, and profligacy, festered, till they found a vent in a hideous disease which has made your face an index even to your mind" (439).

Meanwhile, from his "weak and erring" mother Oliver inherits his moral purity, a fact that Mr. Brownlow underscores as he reviles and excoriates Monks, telling him that his father divided the bulk of his property between Agnes Fleming and his unborn child: "He did this, he said, to mark his confidence in the mother, and his conviction—only strengthened by approaching death—that the child would share her gentle heart, and noble nature" (458). Nobility is redefined as it is shifted away from notions of social caste and moves toward bourgeois notions of virtuous behavior—all this in spite of the fact that Oliver's mother is without question a "fallen woman." Inheritance is made a condition of moral character, proven through deeds and intrinsic interior qualities.

The "noble" nature that Oliver proves to have inherited from his mother secures his future, if not his fortune. The fortune, in fact, dissipates; Oliver's reward is not to be his inheritance but his heredity. And Monks suffers under his own hereditary hatred combined (like Kay's chronic paupers) with pedagogical poison; Monks learns to despise the father he had been "trained to hate" (458).[24] He robs his mother, who was found to be "sinking under a painful and incurable disease" (459), perhaps the result of her "continental frivolities" (435). Among her sins was her destruction of the will, her careful husbanding of the proofs of Oliver's illegitimacy, and in addition to the hatred and disease she gives her son, she offers them: "she bequeathed these secrets to me, together with her unquenchable and deadly hatred of all whom they involved—though she need not have left me that, for I had inherited it long before" (459). With such a legacy, it is no surprise that Monks, his father's seriously diminished fortune split between himself and Oliver, soon squanders it and "at length sunk under an attack of his old disorder, and died in prison" (476). For James Kay, the cure for hereditary disease is separation and education. In Dickens, no such newfangled ideas are entertained. Monks's hereditary flaws cannot be corrected in spite of his education. And Oliver is, of course, born with his purity complete, and his innocence remains intact regardless of social forces that seek to educate him in crime.

In spite of the fact that Oliver is, for all practical purposes, ineducable, his tutorials at the hands of the Maylies and with Mr. Brownlow have been made much of. In a Foucauldian reading of the novel, Oliver's admission into the bourgeois world of Brownlow would transform him from a source of income to liberal subject. In joining Brownlow's "little society," Oliver might be said to enter into "liberal society," the private domain of individual freedom, whose boundaries are usually familial. Furthermore, Oliver is provided with a "story," a narrative that, in constituting Oliver as an object of knowledge, would also make him a subject of discipline. The point of so carefully separating carceral confines from domestic comforts, in this early novel at least, would be to show the absolute necessity of a bourgeois self-discipline that can keep the carceral institution at bay. In such a reading, little Oliver must become the liberal subject whose complex education succeeds most importantly in schooling him in bourgeois behavior, a discipline he "internalizes."[25] But it is a discipline to which he can only submit if he is assumed to possess "depth" of self, an interiority that at a later historical period will be called psychology.

The assumption of psychologized depth, and the constitution of self as object of knowledge, must be questioned, since these notions lurk implicitly beneath the concept of disciplinary selves. In the case of *Oliver Twist,* at least, the transition from Fagin's carceral family to Brownlow's liberal one does not mark the start of Oliver's inner life. Instead, Oliver's entry into the Brownlow world marks a shift from purely economic "value" to the abstract "value" of truth. Both sorts of value are organized around a single, decidedly superficial, "object" to which the readerly eye is drawn again and again. The many travels the novel records—from Fagin's den to his death-house cell, from the country to London and back again, across Smithfield Market and onto Jacob's Island—revolve around one fixed point: poor little Oliver's face. If Monks's face is "an index even to your mind," it is Oliver's *face* that quite specifically convinces the Maylies he cannot be a thief, his *face* that so enrages Monks and turns Nancy toward truth. Oliver's facial features arrest Brownlow and alarm Grimwig. Oliver remains "a face" even in middle-class London. He is no more than an abstraction; specifically, his "heavenly surface" represents truth. When Brownlow observes Oliver's face, he finds it is "impossible to doubt him; there was truth in every one of its thin and sharpened lineaments" (130). "Bless his sweet face!" says Mrs. Bedwin, "I can't bear, somehow, to let him go out of my sight" (151). In these instances, Oliver becomes less individual subject than "liberal object"—not a "self," but a surface displayed publicly to ornament the "little society" that closes the novel. And not just to ornament: Oliver's face is the occasion for chains of signification that reveal not character but plot, largely the familial and hereditary relationships that constitute the mystery of family in this novel.[26]

Thus, Oliver is transformed not from a carceral to a liberal subject, but rather from cash value to face value. This is merely another superficial accounting of the self; it is not a change that allows the authorities to "produce and possess a *full account* of Oliver," as Miller suggests (*Novel* 9). To put it another way, *Oliver Twist's* accounts remain largely economic ones, rather than the novelistic "accounting" for the self necessary to the disciplinary novel. The thoroughgoing focus on Oliver's face is explicitly about the *surface* of the body, inviting no interest in interior states. Dickens offers a philosophy of facial features, in which he bemoans the changes in faces, not selves, marked by experience: "Alas! How few of Nature's faces are left alone to gladden us with their beauty! The cares, and sorrows, and hungerings of the world, change them as they change hearts; and it is only when those passions sleep, and have lost their hold for ever, that the troubled clouds pass off, and leave Heaven's surface clear" (223).

It is the unchanged face of innocence, which the narrator identifies with childhood and sees in death, that is worth noting. Faces, the narrator goes on to tell us, return in death to the perfect innocence of childhood, and allow us to "see the Angel even upon the Earth." While all countenances in this novel can signal abstractions, Oliver's is most exemplary. And this is interesting because modern culture preserves the face as a marker of individuality, evidence of at least a physically distinct self. The face is said to reflect what is within; it can be read as if it were a map to feeling. Not so Oliver, whose angelic features are especially generic. Oliver's face says nothing of what's within; indeed, it invites the reader to assume that—like the stomachs of little paupers opened at an inquest—there is *nothing* within.

Facial resemblance defines the self's superficiality; resemblance also clues the reader to the importance of maternal heredity and the biologizing of persons that establishes worth in *Oliver Twist*. Convalescing in Mrs. Bedwin's chamber, Oliver "recognizes" his mother's features: "What a beautiful, mild face that lady's is" (128), he says of the portrait conveniently hanging above him. Mr. Brownlow also recognizes Oliver and his mother when he enters the room, for "the old idea of the resemblance between [Oliver's] features and some familiar face came upon him so strongly, that he could not withdraw his gaze" (130). Focusing on Oliver's and his mother's face allows Dickens to posit a theory of heredity without necessarily suggesting depth of self. It also allows him to acknowledge the physiology of heredity without too explicitly calling up the inevitability of corporeal matter.

For in *Oliver Twist,* the face opposes the body, rather than the mind or the spirit—bodies decay while faces endure. Soon after meeting Oliver, Mr. Brownlow calls up "before his mind's eye a vast amphitheater of faces" (119): "There were the faces of friends, and foes, and of many that had been almost strangers peering intrusively from the crowd; there were the faces of young and blooming girls that were now old women; there were the others that the grave had changed to ghastly trophies of death, but which the mind, superior to its power, still dressed in their old freshness and beauty, calling back the lustre of the eyes, the brightness of the smile, the beaming of the soul through its mask of clay, and whispering of beauty beyond the tomb, changed but to be heightened, and taken from earth only to be set up as a light" (119). Bodies are earthy, redolent of food and decay. Faces, even the worst of them, are heavenly, and reflect in memory a childlike innocence. Dickens asks the reader to consider the surfaces, the angelic topography that speaks to soul and not psychology.[27]

Faces not only *reflect,* but they do so with perfect accuracy, as when Mr. Gamfield, the horrible master of chimney sweeps who would sentence Oliver to a life of servitude and misery, is said to have a "villanous countenance [that] was a regular stamped receipt for cruelty" (65). It is not just Brownlow who understands that one's outside, especially the face, is determining. When Fagin searches for Monks at The Three Cripples, he employs the same knowledge: "It was curious to observe some faces which stood out prominently from among the group." There are those "whose countenances, expressive of almost every vice in almost every grade, irresistibly attracted the attention" (237). Among the women there are those "with every mark and stamp of their sex utterly beaten out, and presenting but one loathsome blank of profligacy and crime" (237).

That is how the novel can, in chapter 30, formally separate the sentimental confines of the cradle and the melodramatic terrors of robbery, producing (as does James Kay) an innocent subject out of the filth of the carceral underworld. Oliver is delivered into the loving hands of a maternal embrace, when by all appearances he should be delivered into the hands of the authorities. This happy chance is made possible specifically by way of Oliver's face, when the novel stages a literal unveiling of the criminal face to the eyes of bourgeois domesticity, thereby turning the terrifying housebreaker into pitiable victim innocently asleep in bed. This scene, in which his face is interpreted "correctly," secures Oliver's safe passage back into respectable society; in other words, it is his looks and not his inner self that leads to Oliver's acceptance among the bourgeois coterie that establishes normative behavior in the novel. After the robbery, Dr. Losberne, "with much ceremony and stateliness," leads Rose and Mrs. Maylie upstairs: "Motioning them to advance, he closed the door when they had entered, and gently drew back the curtains of the bed. Upon it, in lieu of the dogged, black-visaged ruffian they had expected to behold, there lay a mere child: worn with pain and exhaustion, and sunk into a deep sleep. . . . 'What can this mean?' exclaimed the elderly lady. 'This poor child can never have been the pupil of robbers!'" (267–68). The scene clears the way for the child to become the pupil of mothers, and fathers, in the foster family that will rescue him.

Even the appropriately named Mr. Grimwig must admit that, while all boys' faces reflect some connection with food and consumption, Oliver's is of the less dangerous sort:

> *"He is a nice-looking boy, is he not?" inquired Mr. Brownlow.*
> *"I don't know," replied Mr. Grimwig, pettishly. . . . "I never see any difference in boys. I only know two sorts of boys. Mealy boys, and beef-faced boys."*
> *"And which is Oliver?"*
> *"Mealy. I know a friend who has a beef-faced boy; a fine boy, they call him; with a round head, and red cheeks, and glaring eyes; a horrid boy; with a body and limbs that appear to be swelling out of the seams of his blue clothes; with the voice of a pilot, and the appetite of a wolf. I know him! The wretch!" (148–49)*

Oliver's face reflects hunger, according to Grimwig, but it is innocent, apparently not the appetite of a "wolf."

Indeed, his face is a tonic, for "the sight of the persecuted child has turned vice itself, and given it the courage and almost the attributes of virtue" (440). It is interesting that the "vice" that has been "turned" happens to be Nancy, whose maternal feelings toward Oliver have caused her to risk her life, and whose own face will haunt Sikes to his death. Oliver's face turns Nancy (almost) to a maternally inflected virtue; Monks's face is an index to vice that we must also read back to a mother, namely his own—who, once the "clanking bond" of her marriage to Leeford is loosened, is "wholly given up to continental frivolities, [and] had utterly forgotten the young husband ten good years her junior" (435).

Given this family history, it is not surprising that in *Oliver Twist*, as in the poor law discourse, family separation is crucial. The family is toxic—and physiologically so. Oliver is separated from his wealthier family, and travels through a series of lower-class "families," from the unfortunate clan at Mrs. Mann's, to the undertaker's establishment, to Fagin's den, demonstrating the obvious truth that a child is never capable of being outside social structures of one form or another. He cannot be imagined as a fully psychologized and free agent, because—to put it one way—someone has to feed him. In other words, while the creation of the child is necessary for imagining free subjectivity in the Victorian novel, in *Oliver Twist* that free subjectivity is continually fenced around, just as it is in the poor law writings on the necessity for pauper education. If the paradigmatic subject of the novel is a child, that subject must be understood as one without legal subjectivity *from the outset,* and always in the position of client. The child was never, properly speaking, a judicial subject, and cannot become a disciplinary one. Also, as in the writings of Kay and other pauper educational reformers, family separation is here viewed as necessary because biology dictates that families can be toxic. Natural families can be contagious and hereditarily tainted. Precisely like the pauper educators, the conclusion of *Oliver Twist* works to occlude inheritance as an economic category, and to replace it with heredity as a biological category that proves worth.

The foster family of *Oliver Twist* is like Kay's institution: a place to reaggregate as the pedagogical subject. It is pedagogy, not bourgeois domesticity, that is championed. Family would appear to be as toxic as James Kay suggests, only for Dickens the rich are as disease ridden as the poor. The remedy is a foster family where appropriate education can take place. However, the bourgeois pedagogy that Mr. Brownlow trots out from time to time is not—quite—sufficient to secure Oliver's purity.[28] Bourgeois pedagogy founders in *Oliver Twist* because pauper education must sooner or later encounter the topic of work. The conflict concerning work can be seen in the nervous collision of literacy and labor in a scene between Oliver and Mr. Brownlow:

> "How should you like to grow up a clever man, and write books, eh?"
> "I think I would rather read them, sir," replied Oliver.
> "What! wouldn't you like to be a book-writer?" said the old gentleman.
> Oliver considered a little while; and at last said, he should think

it would be a much better thing to be a bookseller; upon which the old
gentleman laughed heartily, and declared he had said a very good thing.
Which Oliver felt glad to have done, though he by no means knew
what it was.

"Well, well," said the old gentleman, composing his features.
"Don't be afraid! We won't make an author of you, while there's an
honest trade to be learnt, or brickmaking to turn to." (145)

The lesson here, as in the pleas for pauper education written by James
Kay, is to avoid too closely associating paupers and work. The market
from which Dickens has attempted to carefully distinguish Oliver can
never be fully obscured. In the above passage, laboring is set at odds with
the middle-class enterprises of reading and selling books.

Something similar happens as Fagin attempts to "educate" Oliver in
the ways of thieves. Leaving Oliver alone in the near-dark, Fagin urges
him, "[H]ere's a book for you to read"—"a history of the lives and trials
of great criminals; and the pages were soiled and thumbed with use"
(195–96). Work, we see, can just as easily be thieving as bricklaying.
Dickens's protagonists are not destined for either labor, of course; they
are more likely to resemble Mr. Brownlow himself, whose ambitions for
Oliver will be realized by Dickens at last in *David Copperfield*. If not professional writers, then certainly these protagonists are slated to be professional liberals, which is just what Oliver is trained to be in relation to the
laborers in this novel—the *only* laborers in this novel, we might note.
During his sojourn in the country, Oliver and his happy "little society"
make "many calls at the clean houses of the labouring men" (292).

Like the new poor law writings on pauper education, *Oliver Twist*
must constantly grapple with, and fend off, the all-important topic of
work. Oliver, like the innocent workhouse pauper, can thus be made
clean only by maintaining a relationship to the contamination of the past.
In their confessional encounter, Mr. Brownlow directly confronts Monks
with his victim, thrusting Oliver before him to represent him with fervor:
"This child . . . is your half-brother; the illegitimate son of your father."
But Monks is having none of it: "Yes," he corrects, "That is their bastard
child." Mr. Brownlow goes on, "He was born in this town," and once
more Monks corrects him, "In the workhouse of this town" (457). Monks
attests to the impossibility of Oliver's ever leaving the workhouse. If Oliver

ever truly abandoned that past, he would have to, quite simply, get to work.

It is for this reason that childhood and domesticity are so very crucial. Even as Fagin's domestic circle is an opposite version of familial bliss, and a mockery of the domestic, it also represents an alternative version of the workhouse in which Fagin is more pauper educator and pedagogue than mother. Fagin's plans would seem both to mock and to mirror the idea of pauper education and industry. He puts the boys through their paces in a catalogue of criminal activity; he educates them in the finer points of felonious activity. They are "pupils," and a model of what pauper education can accomplish. Here, at last, are able-bodied young men who do not refuse to labor and who, having been separated from the awful influences of their past, may now be more properly schooled: "At length [Oliver] . . . took many occasions of earnestly entreating the old gentleman to allow him to go out to work. . . . Oliver was rendered the more anxious to be actively employed . . . by what he had seen . . . of the old gentleman's character. Whenever the Dodger or Charley Bates came home at night, empty-handed, he would expatiate with great vehemence on the misery of idle and lazy habits; and would enforce upon them the necessity of an active life, by sending them supperless to bed" (112).

The novel loses no opportunity to make this connection between work and thievery, or of enlarging on the "industriousness" and "independence" of the criminal children. "Have they done work, sir?" Oliver asks; and Fagin quickly responds, "Make 'em your models, my dear. Make 'em your models" (111). It is the Artful Dodger who catechizes Oliver in the importance of hard work: "'Go!' exclaimed the Dodger. 'Why, where's your spirit? Don't you take any pride out of yourself? Would you go and be dependent on your friends?'" (182).

Work thus represents a problem for Dickens, for the "value" of work cannot be denied, but neither can it be fully embraced; to do so would begin to chip away at the portrait of innocence that has been so carefully crafted in Oliver. The world of work is an adult one; or else, when it involves children, it is viewed by men like Dickens as a fate worse than the workhouse, ample evidence for which can be seen in the child labor discussions of the period. Work is not just an adult world, but increasingly, at this relatively advanced state of industrialism, must be understood as a male one. That masculinized and grown-up world has almost

no representation, other than Fagin's province, in the novel. In the gen-
teel and feminized spaces of Brownlow's "little society," there may be
servants, but there is, properly speaking, no labor. Oliver rejects the
criminal schemes of Fagin, which had been fed to him partly through his
confinement among thieves, partly through a kind of apprenticeship, and
partly through Fagin's literary offerings. But when, in Brownlow's book-
laden world, Oliver rejects the idea of authorship in favor of more practical pursuits, we hardly find it persuasive—Oliver is not meant to be a
brickmaker.

Like the pauper innocents offered up by Kay and Tufnell, Oliver
must always remain a child, or risk losing his status as victim and client.
There can be no apprenticeship for Oliver, for he would then be in danger of growing to an able-bodied adult. *Oliver Twist* engineers a socially
acceptable, and socially indebted, self. Agnes Fleming gives birth to the
innocent Oliver out of the filthy world of the workhouse; Oliver's origins, unlike those of Mary Shelley's Monster, can be obscured. These
novels, along with the debates of 1834–38 that we have examined, forge
a connection between production and reproduction, and seek resolution
in a story of revised inheritance—in heredity. If Kay and Dickens seek
to resolve their problems similarly, they also founder on the same ground:
their infant subjects are unable to labor. Dickens is linked to the story of
the child, doomed to reproduce literary progeny of his own, children
who can never grow up to become "clever men." It is plausibly this requirement that keeps little Paul Dombey, in Dickens's 1846 novel (the
one to which we now turn), from maturing. For if Paul lived, he would
have to inherit his father's business. It may be the problem with work,
then, that causes Dickens to change the gender of his child protagonist,
and to make the switch from a focus on mothers and their boy children
to a focus on child mothers, in *Dombey and Son*.

II

In the Bosom of the Family: *Dombey and Son* and the Wet-Nursing Debates of William Acton and C. H. F. Routh

WANTING TO APPEAR CAPRICIOUS, one could hardly do better than to suggest a necessary relationship between the wet nurse and the railroad laborer in the mid-nineteenth century. Of course, Dickens made the connection first, but in *Dombey and Son* the link between the rails and the nursing mother is defined, in the Toodle union, as marriage. Suppose you wanted to insist on such a relationship outside the boundaries of the novel, and to argue for a connection less random than matrimony? One might turn to John Francis's 1851 *History of the English Railway, Its Social Relations and Revelations.* Francis views the railway worker as the primitive and wildly reproductive source of a spreading (anti-) social epidemic: "impetuous, impulsive, and brute-like; regarded as the pariahs of private life, herding together like beasts of the field, owning no moral law and feeling no social tie, [the railroad laborer] increased with an increased demand, and from thousands grew to hundreds of thousands. . . . There were many women, but few wives; loathsome forms of disease were universal" (67).

The navvies—unskilled migrant laborers who performed the heavy work of railroad construction—are literal and figurative appetites out of control: "The waste of power which their daily labour necessitated, was supplied by an absorption of stimulant and nourishment perfectly astounding. Bread, beef, bacon, and beer, were the staple of their food. . . . They devoured as earnestly as they worked. . . . If they caught a fever, they died; if they took an infectious complaint, they wandered in the open air, spreading the disease wherever they went. . . . Their presence spread like a pestilence" (67).

Place this monstrous Malthusian image alongside that of the poor woman in C. H. F. Routh's medical treatise *Infant Feeding and Its Influence on Life,* and some likenesses emerge. Dr. Routh's paid laborer is unable to fulfill her duties and provide sustenance because, interestingly enough, she eats too much. She may suffer from *"hyperoemia or plethora,"* a variety of lactation problem the doctor has

> *chiefly observed among* hired wet nurses *selected from among the poorer classes, and admitted into wealthier families. It is a peculiarity of many of our London poor, indeed of domestic servants generally, that when obliged to support themselves, or put upon board-wages, they live as it were upon the smallest quantity of food possible; but when feeding at the expense of a master or mistress, the amount they devour often surpasses all moderate imagination. They, in fact, gormandize. If . . . a wet-nurse is given all she asks for, she will be found to eat quite as much as any two men with large appetites; and as a result she becomes gross, turgid, often covered with blotches or pimples, and generally too plethoric to fulfill the duties of her position. (56)*[1]

In their different ways these two dangerously hungry types are socially destructive, literally eating their betters out of house and home. The navvy's appetite contributes to the failure of social ties; the wet nurse's gormandizing can mean death for the child she is charged with keeping alive.

The wet nurse and the railroad laborer are figures of appetite, like Victor Frankenstein's Monster, Dickens's Sikes, or the Andover paupers; and they also represent the threat of a greater social fluidity. The wet nurse circulates her body fluids upward; in the doctor's words, they flow from the "poorer classes" and are "admitted into wealthier families." The railroad laborer represents the socially leveling effects of the expanding railway system as it constructs a circulatory network of arteries and veins throughout the geographic and social body of England. Each of these figures is tensely poised over a fissure seen as necessary but dangerous. It is critical that there be milk for an ailing child because "artificial feeding" represents a grave risk. And the increased traffic in goods and in people that the railroad makes possible is desirable, even necessary from a certain economic vista, but the necessity foregrounds the stark reality of social change. In Dickens's portrait of the railroad, the bourgeois passenger comes into tangible contact with the machine, not to mention an all too casual contact with lower-class passengers; the railway is the place where Dombey encounters the masses. Similarly, in hiring a wet nurse, parents must turn their child over to a servant whose interests may not coincide with their own.

Taking on the drama of social fluidity, *Dombey and Son* extends the developing narrative of the victimized child-subject in critical ways. The upwardly mobile acquisitive male who threatens to victimize reappears in Dickens's 1846 novel in the form of the orally aggressive Carker. Like Monks, Carker represents an upper-class threat of destruction. But in *Dombey,* there is no Sikes to match Carker's Monks. Instead, Dickens not only gentles and sanitizes the poor, he turns comic in his portrayal of them.

During this period of Chartism, in which the working man was a subject of some concern, it is interesting to see how Dickens turns Francis's voracious and migrant beast of railway construction into a stable laborer: the thoroughly domesticated Mr. Toodle is no navvy and presents little threat. Polly Toodle is surely a match for her mister in benignity; she is hardly a gross and turgid wet nurse. Far from exhibiting the unquenchable hungers of the wet nurse, she is herself a source of food to the Dombey family. In *Dombey and Son* Dickens complicates the picture of a pure and yet socially dependent child developed in *Oliver Twist,* where adulthood and the world of work presented difficulties. Both Oliver and little Paul Dombey must remain nonlaboring children in order to maintain their place as client-subjects. Engaging with the sentimentalizing influence of domesticity, Dickens's narrative in *Dombey* invents a story of motherhood, in Florence, that is also always a version of childhood.

It was not only Dickens's fiction that moved beyond a simple model of contamination to employ the more useful concept of "influence." A woman's influence, carefully used within her domestic circle, was said to be as important as any governmental controls. Sarah Stickney Ellis voiced the most popular version of this idea, arguing that wives have the power to curb men's minds in a noble direction: "The first thing to be done in the attainment of this high object is to use what influence you have so as not to lower or degrade the habitual train of your husband's thoughts; and the next is, to watch every eligible opportunity, and to use every suitable means, of leading him to view his favourite subjects in their broadest and most expansive light" (101–2).

Meanwhile, the idea of womanly influence took an important turn in the newly established medical journals, which published contentious arguments concerning breast-feeding practices and, even more specifically, the wet nurse's body fluids. Like Dickens's novel, debates over wet-nursing had something to do with social fluidity. And also like Dickens's novel, these debates distinguished contamination from influence through an emphasis on gender. The result, in both medicine and fiction, was a rearticulation of child endangerment. In chapter 1, I argued that the emergence of a pedagogic subject was signally important in *Oliver Twist* and in the writings of the pauper educators. This chapter considers the strategic use of gender, particularly the nurturing, nursing mother, in the developing and uneven narrative of the Victorian child.

Immoral Milk

Breast milk is at the heart of circulation in *Dombey and Son*. It describes a circumfluent path from Polly Toodle through the Dombey family, and from there, by way of the novel's emphasis on the transformative power of maternal love, the woman's milk metaphorically gains an even wider circulation. The nursing mother, or her unfeeling substitute who brings her victim up by hand, is a recurring Dickensian image, often testifying to the health or disease of a family, even a class or social group.[2] Although it is highly elaborated in Dickens, the portrayal of breast-feeding is not unique to Victorian novels. Eighteenth-century writers, for example, engaged the topic of the breast and nursing with some enthusiasm. But the female breast of pre-Victorian writers is frequently imagined as conjugal property. When the breast is put to its maternal use, it is likely to be portrayed as a force for strengthening or eroding the bonds of husband and wife, rather than feeding an infant.[3] Victorians, on the other hand, tend to represent the breast in ways that redefine the nature of the family and the place of the child in it.

In 1748 the doctor William Cadogan, writing about the need for breast-feeding, perceived the infants of the mid-eighteenth century as inherently strong, imperiled mainly by the practice of "babying" them. Insisting that infants "bear Pain and Disease much better" than grown persons (6), he claimed that "the puny Insect, the Heir and Hope of a rich Family, lies languishing under a Load of Finery . . . abhorring and rejecting the Dainties he is cramm'd with, 'til he dies a Victim to the mistaken Care and Tenderness of his fond Mother" (7). By contrast, Victorian medical manuals almost universally portrayed infancy as a time of dependency and danger, requiring swift intervention and greater medicalization, as in T. H. Tanner's *A Practical Treatise on the Diseases of Infancy and Childhood* (1861): "The most striking picture of perfect helplessness and weakness that can possibly be imagined, is exhibited by the infant at birth. Incapable of making any regulated movements, or of employing its organs in any way, it requires assistance of every kind; and if left to itself quickly perishes" (108).

Such dependency authorized a greater bond between a mother and her child, and consequently the father's role was seen as less significant. Mother and doctor must intervene to prevent the worst possible calamity, for "there is distinct evidence to prove that in the present day more than one-fourth—in the unhealthy districts of some large manufacturing towns not less than one-third, and even a greater proportion—of all the children ushered into the world, and born to endure for three-score years and ten, are cut off within the first five years after birth" (1).

Victorian handbooks brought mortality directly into the middle-class home. Although they were written as Victorians began to investigate in detail the private lives of the poor, especially children, they are not documents of social investigation. There is scarcely mention of a slum-dweller, and infant death is not imagined as the inevitable consequence of poverty. In titling his opening chapter "Introductory Remarks on the Great Mortality of Children, and the Consequent Duty of Mothers," Thomas Bull provided a clear lesson for the middle-class mother who failed to heed sound medical counsel. The bond between husband and wife is of diminished importance here; now there is to be a relationship between mother and doctor, maintained in the name of the helpless child. The theme was sounded in Andrew Combe's *Treatise on the Physiological and Moral Management of Infancy* (1846) as well: "In no point of view . . . is it possible to defend the prevailing error of leaving out what ought to constitute an essential part of female domestic education. . . . Even in the best regulated families, it is rare to meet with a mother, who, before becoming such, has devoted the least attention to the study of the infant constitution, to the principles on which it ought to be treated, or to the laws by which its principal functions are regulated" (35). The mother had an evident duty to become expert in infant constitution—or risk her child's death.

This moral imperative to nurse one's child turned a mother's care into a matter of training, not just of mother but of the child, too. Breast-feeding was crucially about—to use the word that would be employed throughout these manuals as well as in novels and conduct manuals—influence: "[T]he infant is to be trained to become a man; its moral as well as its physical nature is to be cultivated; parental influence is to be the means of doing this, and Providence may have wisely determined that the infant shall for months be dependant on its mother for support, in order that her instinctive feelings may lay the firm foundation of that love which causes her to cling to her little one with a fondness that surpasses all other affection, and [makes] . . . her the child's best guardian, friend, and teacher, during its early years" (West 409).[4] The middle-class woman must nurse her child in order to inculcate the appropriate values, not simply to keep him alive.

Pediatric texts argued vociferously for maternal breast-feeding, and invoked a portrait of the mothers of the day as too lazy or "nervous" or "fashionable" to care for their children. These doctorly lamentations continued to appear in handbooks and manuals, even though it is unlikely that many English women—of any class—routinely employed wet nurses in this period. According to Valerie Fildes, "the great majority of British infants were breast-fed at home by their mothers" (*Breasts* 98).

Why, then, should breast-feeding practices have come to take so prominent a place in nineteenth-century manuals for mothers? Certainly, nursing instruction offered doctors an expanded opportunity for inserting themselves into family life, making the alliance between pediatrician and mother appear inevitable. But the role of the wet nurse, as it was hotly debated in the medical journals among doctors, had as much to do with social differences as it did with either medical authority or gender. The debate was carried on during the 1850s, primarily between William Acton and C. H. F. Routh. Their discussion turned on the question of whether the wet nurse was a victim of the upper classes, being "eaten" by those with money, literally milked for her vital fluids, as Acton would have it; or whether this corrupt servant was feeding grossly off the riches of her betters, her immoral behavior crudely turned into an undeserved financial gain.[5]

Among doctors, the wet nurse was always understood to be the mother of an illegitimate child. Not all women who chose to offer their services as wet nurses, of course, were necessarily the mothers of bastards (Polly Toodle is an example of the married wet nurse in fiction), but both Acton and Routh located the stain of illegitimacy at the center of their arguments. The debate was for this reason a natural topic for Acton, whose most widely read work in the twentieth century is his mid-Victorian essay on prostitution. Acton saw wet-nursing as a socially acceptable employment alternative to prostitution. Should society, an anonymous doctor asked in *The Lancet* in 1859, extend "an avenue back to the world from which they are cast out to those who have fallen[,] through the very functions by which that fault has originated"? That is, should "organized means . . . be used to employ women of this class as wet-nurses" ("Medical Annotations" 113)? Routh's response was swift and unequivocal: "I believe these benevolent intentions, if fully carried out, would be attended with some of the worst consequences that could be conceived, both socially and morally" (Routh, "Selection" 580).

Routh offered an organized, if not always medically defensible, argument. First, fallen women are by definition corrupt. "I know from experience," the doctor said, "that where you have to do with a woman of bad character (particularly if she has been confirmed in her vicious habits—if she be a harlot in taste and habit), do what you will, you cannot obtain from her reliable information" (*Infant Feeding* 119). Second, there is a concern that the nurse's own child will suffer, perhaps with the willful consent or desire of the mother: "*We are, perhaps, encouraging murder, at least, authorizing the death of the nurse's child*" (112). And third, wet-nursing is said to encourage vice and promote a course of sin: "If fallen women are preferred to married . . . if we pass over their fault lightly . . . we are favoring the passions of the frail sisterhood" (111).

In Routh's argument, the wet nurse is duplicitous and dangerous, and the reader is forced to confront the inevitable fact that she must maintain such intimate contact with the household. Routh hints, if only by insisting so vigorously upon the opposite view, that a wife's mind might be poisoned, even her chastity assailed: "As to the effect upon a mistress of a household in a country where the purity of our wives is unimpeachable, and their virtue proverbial, the tendency to corruption by conversation with such women is fortunately very rare, and I believe that it seldom, if ever, occurs. To dwell on this point is therefore unnecessary. Still all will admit that too frequent association and companionship of the better classes, even with virtuous domestic servants, is nearly always prejudicial" (110).

We are not allowed to forget the lure that the fallen woman must present even to the most faithful husband. "She is generally attractive. Her attractions have been her snare; and the vanity which has caused her to fall once, and the difficulty of curbing strong passions once roused, make her an easier prey" (108). The more comfortable, and therefore dominant, danger is that the wet nurse will encourage other servants in a life of rewarding vice, for it is "chiefly among the women servants in an establishment . . . that the danger is greatest. . . . 'What a difference in wages! What superior food is given her! She rides in the carriage as a lady visitor. She is more considered than any other servant in the establishment. What prevents my doing likewise?'" (110–11). Everyone in a household, it is clear, stands to be corrupted.

But no one is more at risk than the infant who receives unmediated and intimate contact. If the wet nurse's speech might destroy her mistress or her fellow servants, if her body might lead to her master's destruction or that of some other servant, it is the fluids of her body that threaten to contaminate her infant charge. The risk is not just to health but to the moral fiber of the child, for "if a nurse of confirmed vicious and passionate habits suckles a child, that child is in danger of having its own morality tainted likewise" ("Selection" 580). The contagion of the wet nurse is longlasting—lifelong, in fact: "[O]nce the morbid cell has been developed, it will impart its nature to surrounding parts, and poison the whole blood . . . it is possible to sow a seed in the infant which shall contaminate the life of the man, taint his whole constitution, and influence his psychical power" ("Selection" 581).

Routh's aim is to encourage a woman to nurse her own child or, if that is not possible, to employ methods of artificial feeding. (To this end, Routh eventually invented and patented the "Mamma" bottle, one of the first reasonably safe infant-feeding bottles.) The servant's body fluids should be avoided not only because they may taint the child, but because to use them would be to relieve a mother of her natural duty. Routh's polemic distinguishes between classes of women, insisting that the working-class woman be left to her servant status and that the middle-class family

fulfill its own domestic duties. Like the governess, the wet nurse cannot
be secured above or below stairs. But unlike the governess, whose wages
signify servant status but whose education provides her with an ambigu-
ating superiority, the wet nurse is unambiguously lower class. It is the
resulting potential for contagion that most troubles Routh.

Espousing the minority view that would eventually prevail, William
Acton establishes a liberal discourse of reform in concert with a Benthamite argument for greater "use" of the socially discarded fallen woman.
Acton begins by mocking Routh's medical assertions: "[A] cry was attempted to be got up about the influence of *immoral* milk. I thought this
had been for ever silenced by the many recorded instances of children
having been reared on asses' milk, without manifesting any of the stub-
bornness of the foster mothers" ("Child-Murder" 184).

Acton speaks as the voice of modernity, claiming both reason and
science as his supports. But perhaps his most modern role comes in his
quick adoption of social reform as a goal. Taking precisely the position
opposite that of Routh, Acton views the working-class woman with a
sentimental fondness. She is, in his vocabulary, "falling" and not "fallen";
to employ her as wet nurse is first of all to help her. Acton tells a tale as
novelistic as it is medical:

> Remember, it is not street-walkers nor professional prostitutes we
> are speaking of. We are speaking of the young house-maid or pretty
> parlour-maid in the same street in which the sickly lady has given birth
> to a sickly child, to whom healthy milk is life, and anything else death.
> With shame and horror the girl bears a child to the butler, or the police-
> man, or her master's son. Of course she is discharged; of course her se-
> ducer is somewhere else; of course, when her savings are spent, she will
> have to take, with shame and loathing, to a life of prostitution. Now,
> she is healthy and strong, and there is a little life six doors off, crying
> out for what she can give, and wasting away for the want of it, and in
> the nursing of that baby is a chance, humanly speaking, of her salvation
> from the pit of harlotry. ("Unmarried" 175)

Proximity is no longer a horror; on the contrary, it conveniently makes
the working-class girl's services more readily accessible. Acton invites
readers to join him in paternal benevolence, constructing those readers as
middle-class professional men with a social conscience.

But these must be men, also, with a sense of business and an understanding of the exigencies of supply and demand. The language of the market soon merges with Acton's vocabulary of reform: "No accoucheur in extensive practice can shut his eyes to the demand for wet-nurses. He has to meet that requirement every day; and I ask him . . . if he has ever been able to supply it from the ranks of married women? There is the demand, already largely supplied by the very class that most wants help. We only ask that the supply be enlarged and regulated" ("Unmarried" 175). To reform the servant woman is to market the fluids of her body.

Like Dickens in *Oliver Twist,* the social reformer Acton recognizes the value of poor bodies on an open market. But unlike Dickens, the doctor promotes exchange as a social good. It may be the gender of this lower-class person that makes the promotion of market forces possible. Acton merges the portrayal of the sentimentalized female with an argument for the enlargement and regulation of the market. The commodification of the servant-class woman's milk is masked by the sentimental psychologizing of her plight, at the same time that it is made available in the marketplace. And it is also important that the wet nurse is no child. James Kay, advocating for the education of pauper children, avoided the relationship that had previously held between little bodies, labor, and the market in the system of apprenticeship. William Acton, by contrast, brings his adult servant-class women into direct relationship with market demands; indeed, he largely imagines the "law of supply and demand" for milk as a way of supporting his argument for reform. Acton's representation of a woman whose presence in the market is welcomed helps position his reader as a liberal father who can take advantage of her resources at the same time that he reforms her. Charles Dickens, as will be seen shortly, uses a woman who is both mother *and* child to achieve the same end.

This interchange between social conscience and the market makes it as necessary for Acton as it is crucial for Routh that the wet nurse be a *fallen* woman. Acton relies upon associating the social reform of the fallen with the demands of the market. This leads the doctor to a curious reversal in which he must recreate purity in the defiled body of the fallen woman, and simultaneously represent moral corruption in the "conjugal solicitude" that is sanctioned in marriage. Acton elevates his "honest" fallen wet nurse over the married one: "A married woman who voluntarily leaves her own child for money may not be much better than the girl accidentally seduced, who nurses another's child for bread. . . . It is not wise to be too acute in your inquiries about the husband, and the nature of the conjugal solicitude that keeps him eternally hanging about your area steps, or lounging in the back kitchen. . . . You certainly know the best of the married wet-nurse, who hawks about her breast of milk . . . but you know little else" ("Unmarried" 175). The married vendor of milk seeks profit, and for that reason may be reviled. Meanwhile, the hawking of milk among the lower classes can be sanctified so long as it is associated with the rhetoric of reform.

Acton reserves for himself the powerful voice of liberal father, the moderate paternal figure that we encounter formidably in Dickens. The sentimentalizing of the fallen wet nurse serves to discursively separate classes just as firmly as does Routh's anxious fears of contamination. Two rhetorical modes—Acton's reformist stance and Routh's rejection—contend in the medical journals. While these models may superficially oppose one another, ultimately they are eminently compatible. On its own, Routh's rhetorical extremity is self-betraying, often medically illogical, even in 1859. The reader is unlikely to see himself as the husband tempted by the servant girl's meager charms, and his wife is not likely to imagine herself in tender companionship with her child's nurse. Routh's text merely sets up an absolute boundary; it imagines an extreme—a syphilitic drunken nurse destroying a household; a weak family that cannot control its impulses or its servants—that is hardly cautionary. If anything, Routh is reassuring, in that he offers a narrative tale from which the paternal bourgeois reader may easily distance himself. In this respect he bears some relation to Mr. Dombey, whose disgust and fear of Polly Toodle helps form the reader's more moderate response.

Routh's discourse has a special function in relation to Acton's more balanced view: it reinforces Acton's position as socially responsive. Acton's liberal stance, bolstered by the hysteria of extremism, becomes the reasonable position. It invites the danger to approach and assures us that proximity is harmless, the potential for contamination negated by the reformative generosity of the liberal father, a generosity mirrored in ourselves. This gesture of inclusion works, of course, to distinguish and exclude, as such paternal gestures almost always do. It is the very gesture we encounter in Dickens's novel. Routh and Acton busily feed on the "wet-nursing dilemma," debating the perils and profits of social fluidity. Meanwhile, the debate as a whole reinscribes the social differences between classes. It also reinforces the importance of avoiding the fallen woman's body fluids, which can be done only by maintaining family health. This is the implicit lesson in the second chapter heading of *Dombey and Son,* "In which Timely Provision is made for an Emergency that will sometimes arise in the best-regulated Families." While dire need will make itself felt, the best defense is an ordered family. If Acton represents an eruption of the liberal father's voice in medicine, it must be said that the novel adopts this voice first and most forcefully. Not only in Dickens, but perhaps in Dickens especially, a grand space is created for a simultaneous reform and use of the family, for a complex, and literary, formulation of class and gender issues, generated over the body of the distressed child. This is only possible, however, once the infant has been imagined as in desperate need of care. Little Paul Dombey is utterly dependent, in his first and in his last needs. So, too, the unnamed infants imaginatively called up by nineteenth-century medicine, who had become the helpless dependents of mothers, doctors, and hired servants.

Body Politics and Body Fluids

Dickens reverses the usual portrait of the hungry: in *Dombey and Son* the poor are literally food for the rich. The railroad laborer and the nursing mother are viewed as solidly useful members of society, joined together in a marriage not only happy but extraordinarily fruitful. The Toodle brood, in its numbers and outrageous vigor, contrasts sharply with Mr. Dombey's slim reproductive output. Dickens reads the railway worker not only as socially palatable but as, well, edible: "Miss Tox escorted a plump rosy-cheeked wholesome apple-faced young woman, with an infant in her arms; a younger woman not so plump, but apple-faced also, who led a plump and apple-faced child in each hand; another plump and also apple-faced boy who walked by himself; and finally, a plump and apple-faced man, who carried in his arms another plump and apple-faced boy, whom he stood down on the floor and admonished, in a husky whisper, to 'kitch hold of his brother Johnny'" (63–64).

It almost makes one hungry just to hear of them. Disease is out of the question entirely: as Miss Tox tells us of the Toodle's home, "the cleanest place, my dear! You might eat your dinner off the floor" (64). Mr. Toodle is no home-wrecker; in fact he is a solid, if simple-minded, bulwark of the family. Far from spreading pestilence, the railway laborer and his kin exude the kind of health only possible in Victorian novels among those whose morals are as clean as their kitchen floors. *Dombey's* emphasis on the wet nurse and the railroad puts a unique spin on a much-debated Victorian worry: who is being fed, and who is being eaten alive?

Circulation, across class lines as well as within social categories, structures the world of this novel, first of all in a universal insistence that social circulation is unavoidable. When Sir Barnet Skettles urges Florence, "My dear Miss Dombey, are you sure you can remember no one whom your good Papa . . . might wish you to know?" (418), he is expressing a fact of the novel no less true for its baleful consequences: people must gather. London society demands fluidity, both in the social and in the business worlds. Sir Barnet Skettles, in his call to mingle, comically underscores the urge to circulate. Edith Dombey introduces the importance of coupling in its more realistic, and most malevolent, manifestation. On the prowl for a suitable mate for her daughter, Mrs. Skewton has brought her "to a great many places. To Harrogate and Scarborough, and into Devonshire. We have been visiting, and resting here and there" (362). Edith's refusal to put herself into active circulation does not stop her being "hawked and vended here and there" (473) on the marriage market. Mr. Dombey, pacing on the railway platform as he awaits the train upon which he will try to escape his unpleasant memories and (above all) his daughter, demonstrates how, in modern life, there is no escape from what he sees as the "vulgar herd" (351). However eagerly they might try, characters in this novel discover that it is impossible to go it alone. Far from suggesting that a *cordon sanitaire* must separate rich from poor, Dickens virtually celebrates—certainly, he explicitly acknowledges—the necessary intermixing of the classes in industrializing society.

Further, lest we imagine that the potential dangers of social circulation might be avoided by seeking refuge in a purely financial, and therefore less complicated, exchange of currency, the novel insists that the financial cannot function without the social. Mr. Dombey's perfect economic plan is profitless in the face of his sterile home life, where he is unable to produce an heir. His best efforts gain him only little Paul, a son too sick to inherit, and too "old-fashioned" to care about the proper distribution of property. And there is Florence, "merely a piece of base coin that couldn't be invested—a bad Boy—nothing more" (51). Meanwhile, the abundant fantasies of social mobility that flow from Sol Gills's shop, and the social transgressions of which Captain Cuttle is so blithely capable, cannot pump up an obviously hopeless economy within this otherwise thriving family: "[C]ompetition, competition—new invention, new invention—alteration, alteration—the world's gone past me," Sol says (93), and then astutely identifies his problem as lacking a proper inheritance to offer his perfectly appropriate heir, Walter. These opposing worlds—one financially solvent but morally bankrupt and without heir; the other boasting the model youth, but economically moribund and outside the capitalist loop—of course must merge, and in doing so at the novel's end enact one of its chief messages: Be morally scrupulous (defined in part as playing the role of the good family man), but at the same time be certain your business is shipshape.

Everywhere in the novel, the isolation for which these characters yearn is made a virtual impossibility, reiterated when Mrs. Chick clucks of Mr. Dombey, "It's of no use remaining shut up in his own rooms. Business won't come to him. No. He must go to it" (930–31). The need to traffic in goods, of course, is most aptly proven in the Firm itself, which hinges upon continual circulation in that the business of import and export is responsible for circulating goods all over the world. And of course, Mrs. Skewton's circulation of her daughter's body qualifies as a necessary economic move quite as much as it is a socially strategic one. The world of *Dombey,* then, is vastly different from the divided realms of *Oliver Twist,* where even though (or perhaps because) the carceral and bourgeois so often resemble one another, they must be kept strictly separate. If this novel demonstrates the importance of separating economic from domestic spheres, it also proves the interdependency of these two realms and, at times, the fact that they are indistinguishable from one another. However, unlike later Dickens novels in which that interdependency is taken for granted, in *Dombey and Son* "circulation" is the explicit subject, especially in the novel's portrayal of Mr. Dombey himself, who finds social fluidity deeply threatening.

Having established the critical impossibility of avoiding either social or economic circulation, the novel goes about demonstrating that such contact carries with it the threat of danger, particularly the possibility of infection. Most notably in the case of Mr. Dombey, this fear reveals a personal lack or flaw. Traffic between people is a mock-scary thing, liable to result in a violent collision or supreme personal discomfort. Physical contact can be disconcerting, as when Mr. Chick gives "Mr. Dombey his hand, as if he feared it might electrify him," and Mr. Dombey takes it "as if it were a fish, or seaweed, or some such clammy substance" (110). These fears, in fact, are not confined to interactions across class lines, and more often hint at contagious or infectious contact when the participants are *not* poor. "There may be such contagion in me; I don't know," Carker the Junior says (248), fearful of infecting Walter Gay. When Edith imagines that her mother bears infectious malice toward Florence, and Mrs. Skewton shrieks, "am I to be told . . . that there is corruption and contagion in me, and that I am not fit company for a girl" (514), Edith anticipates her own anxious avoidance of Florence's touch. This avoidance is manifest later when Edith, in flight, "crawl[s] by [Florence] like some lower animal" (754). That physical proximity might prove infectious, or at any rate abhorrent, is implied in Harriet Carker's "recoiling" from Alice Marwood: "Remove your hand! . . . Go away! Your touch is dreadful to me!" (848).

The exception to the general rule that it is the middle and upper classes who stand to contaminate each other, or occasionally their underlings, occurs in Florence's abduction by "Good Mrs. Brown." The episode enacts the fears of working-class contamination Mr. Dombey had had concerning Polly's nearness to little Paul, which had led him to believe that "a great temptation was being placed in this woman's way. Her infant was a boy too. Now, would it be possible for her to change them?" (71). It is not Paul, however, who is altered or contaminated by contact with the poor. Mrs. Brown, releasing Florence after her ordeal, "conducted her changed and ragged little friend through a labyrinth of narrow streets and lanes and alleys" (131). Florence emerges from this maze of slums the perfect picture of a street urchin. Here Dickens departs from his otherwise comic portrayal of contact across the social ranks; and he also clues us, in substituting Florence (of no concern to her father) for Paul (whose welfare so consumes Mr. Dombey), that it is Florence's relations that are and will be central to the novel.

But wherever one travels in the *Dombey* world, physical proximity is altogether too likely to spell trouble. Bunsby, failing to take careful note of Captain Cuttle's warnings, is ensnared in Mrs. MacStinger's matrimonial net. It is in part Edith's nearness to Carker, that is to say his tracking of her—"not a footprint did she mark [upon her 'dangerous way'], but he set his own there, straight" (736)—that ensures her fall. Mr. Dombey's stiff reserve might reflect an anxiety about getting too near. Mr. Toots comically reverses that stance; his passive-aggressive behavior toward Florence brings him into a constant contact with her that only pries them further apart. Susan Nipper—and perhaps this is what makes her the perfect foil for Toots—charges forth with enviable strength of purpose. But her assertive conviction leads to violent and inevitable eruptions, typified in her "struggles with boys, . . . for, between that grade of human kind and herself, there was some natural animosity that invariably broke out, whenever they came together" (401).

Things break out when people come together; yet in *Dombey,* isolation, no matter how often attempted, is just as often interrupted. Having created this drama of necessary circulation, the novel takes matters further and specifically addresses class when it imagines the rich as painfully dependent upon the poor. For all his riches and power, Mr. Dombey's finances are never the thing that can rescue him in his need. While the novel defines personal and professional relationships of all kinds as crucially necessary, by far the most necessary forms of circulation in the novel are those that take place between the classes, particularly between the Dombey and the Toodle families.

It is no shock to learn that the working class is utterly dependent upon the upper class. But, surprisingly in this novel, the wealthy are powerless in the face of a humiliating need to seek out the assistance of the poorer classes, either in ways that are demeaning (such as augmenting a child's nutrition with hired milk) or in places that degrade (as in Good Mrs. Brown's den). Mr. Dombey reels with disgust in discovering that his hopes "should be endangered . . . by so mean a want; that Dombey and Son should be tottering for a nurse, was a sore humiliation." He views with "bitterness the thought of being dependent . . . on a hired serving-woman" (67). Polly and her family, of course, have much less complicated feelings about the financial interactions here; dependency, or at least economic exchange, and the lofty behavior of the better-off is old news.

An even more horrible (and filthy) reliance on the poor comes much later in the novel when Mr. Dombey must descend into the slums to receive "secret intelligence." Good Mrs. Brown relates Dombey's initial abhorrence, followed by eagerness: "T'other day when I touched his coat in the street, he looked round as if I was a toad. But Lord, to see him when I said their names, and asked him if he'd like to find out where they was!" (817–18). Once again Dombey is humiliated to find that all his power has failed him, and it is the poor and dirty alone who can help him: "'Woman! I believe that I am weak and forgetful of my station in coming here. . . . [H]ow does it happen that I can find voluntary intelligence in a hovel like this,' with a disdainful glance about him, 'when I have exerted my power and means to obtain it in vain?'" (818–19).

We might expect the traffic between the Toodle and the Dombey families to be especially troubling, because Polly and her husband exemplify unmediated encounters between classes. In the employment of each, consumption and production are unavoidably simultaneous.[6] There is no factory or slum separating social groups in *Dombey*'s representation of the Toodle family; because the "point of production" in the wet nurse and the train is the "market" itself, contact is nearer. When Mr. Dombey makes use of Polly's services, he must have *Polly* as well, since her body is the factory from which her tangible self cannot easily be separated. The prospect of sending Paul out to nurse, to the slum itself—the Continental solution, and one that may account for the greater endurance of wet-nursing there, as opposed to England—is more abhorrent because it raises even scarier prospects of social proximity.

In the novel, the threat of social proximity and fear of the working-class woman's body fluids is embodied largely in Mr. Dombey, who wants nothing more than to disassociate himself and his son from her. The best Mr. Dombey can do is to rename Polly "Richards," remove her from her working-class surroundings, and redefine the maternal role as "a question of wages, altogether" (68). Needless to say, Mr. Dombey would prefer that the relationship between Polly and her charge be contained as merely financial, and thus he tries to enforce Polly's breast milk as a commodity in spite of her presence in the house. And, of course, Mr. Dombey's insistence on the language of the market, and his attempt thereby to impose control on the nursing relationship, can only convince the reader of the impossibility of his project. Mr. Dombey's attempts to keep Polly at a distance have the effect of reinforcing the intimacy of the very connection he hopes to deny.

The rails, like Polly, might be expected to be a particularly threatening site for interclass relations. Even as the railroad was a place where the gap between the bourgeois subject and the machine was narrowed, the railroad even more controversially limited the distance between the middle-class passenger and the working-class as a social group.[7] Most obviously, the railroad tangibly represents the demise of the coach and the rise of more egalitarian transport along the rails. Those who had once been separated in private coaches now found themselves following in the tracks of their lesser fellows. Not surprisingly, first- and second-class coaches were made to seem as rich as possible. Unlike the American railroad cars, the English compartments were modeled on coaches rather than canal boats. But however elaborate the furnishings, the truth of the matter was only reinforced by the lavish appointments: third-class passengers were simply in the next car, or down the line. As Constantin Pecquer rather gleefully pointed out, "It is the *same convoy*, the *same power* that carries the great and the small, the rich and the poor; thus the railroads most generally provide a continuous lesson in equality and fraternity" (qtd. Schivelbusch 74–75).

In Dickens's novel, it is Mr. Dombey who expresses horror at "equality and fraternity." The more vigorously Mr. Dombey tries to separate himself, the more proximity arises as an issue. The more firmly he works to insist upon a financial basis for relations between classes, the more that financial relation is denied. While Dombey tries hard to reduce matters to economic exchange, the poor keep insisting on an intimacy that transgresses purely financial limits. "Do you know of nothing more powerful than money?" Alice Marwood asks Dombey (819), and then makes sure he knows that anger and revenge—not his monetary reward—are her motivation in giving him her "secret intelligence." Mr. Toodle denies the strictly financial basis of his relationship to the family when he meets Mr. Dombey at the train station. Dombey is enraged to note that "this presumptuous raker among coals and ashes" wears mourning crape to memorialize the death of little Paul Dombey (353). And at the close of the novel, Polly arrives to nurse the father, as she had done the child, this time offering her services, if not her body, without any pecuniary consideration: "In the dusk of the evening Mr. Toodle . . . arrives with Polly and a box, and leaves them, with a sounding kiss, in the hall of the empty house. . . . 'I tell you what, Polly, me dear,' says Mr. Toodle, 'being now an ingine-driver, and well to do in the world, I shouldn't allow of your coming here . . . if it warn't for favours past. . . . To them which is in adversity, besides, your face is a cord'l'" (932). For Dombey, there is always the troubling fact of social proximity. Worse

for him, he is made to seem humiliatingly in need of the poor, who refuse to allow that dependency to be reduced to a strictly financial arrangement.

Dombey and Son insists upon circulation—of finances, of "intelligence," of milk, of passengers. Dickens quite deliberately renders Mr.
Dombey indebted to the poorer classes, and in continual intercourse with
them. Thus, in constructing socioeconomic circulation as absolutely necessary, and deeply degrading for the (wrong-headed) well-to-do, *Dombey
and Son* would seem to make matters impossibly complicated. The novel
insists on asking a provocative question, a question familiarly central to
Victorian socioeconomic debate; that is, how does one maintain profit-
able circulation while avoiding personal pollution? Then Dickens dismisses, or at least diminishes, the question by making it the concern of
the most unsympathetic character in the novel.

The fear of the laborer as contaminating is embodied largely in
Mr. Dombey, and to that extent it is limited by the reader's conception
of Mr. Dombey as a far from sympathetic figure. Yet Mr. Dombey represents a familiar early and mid-Victorian voice; indeed, he very closely
resembles the voice of C. H. F. Routh. It is one with which the reader is
simultaneously invited to identify and to reject—thus enacting the training in class relations for which the novel presses. Mr. Dombey occupies a
relatively extreme position, but one with which we may briefly sympa-
thize, certainly recognize, only to ultimately reject it in adopting the
more complicated negotiation of class relations offered in the text's representation of gender. The novel thus incorporates the same strategic action we examined in the rhetorical interplay between Acton and Routh.
Dombey and Son includes both sides of the debate—the liberal father and
the archconservative—in its own gesture of inclusion.

Dickens insists on the question by persisting in representing the rich
as needing the poor. The novel restages the problem, virtually obsesses
on it, in fact, in order to suggest a powerful answer, one found in embryo
in the medical rhetoric of William Acton. Just as Acton rejects Routh in
making fun of the fear of asses' milk, Dickens uses satire to dismiss social
issues in the Toodle realm. To the extent that Dickens is in conversation
with an ambient discourse about the devouring poor, Mr. Toodle is a
satirical response that makes anxieties about appetite seem absurd, just as
Oliver's absolute emptiness answers to doubts about whether or not to

feed the hungry in *Oliver Twist*. And in Mr. Dombey, Dickens provides a realist account (which functions in a parallel relation to the Toodle satire) of the misguided nature of bourgeois anxieties. The result, as is the case in the wet-nursing debates, is to reinforce the novel's position as socially responsive. Dickens's liberal stance is enhanced by Dombey's harshness and the comic mode in which the Toodle family is represented, thus defining the reasonable position.

For these reasons, the novel focuses on and returns repeatedly to the Toodle family as the center of circulation problems; like the railroad itself, the Toodles turn up everywhere. In Dombey's first need, to ensure Paul's survival, it is Polly and her family who arrive to fill the gap. It is Polly for whom Paul asks as he nears death, and for whom the mad search about London for Staggs's Gardens proceeds. At the train station, it is Mr. Toodle who intrudes on Mr. Dombey's grief. And in Mr. Dombey's dismal hours of repentance, it is Polly who comes to nurse him. And finally, Rob the Grinder's peripatetic and almost sinister presence— showing up, through his own blundering or by someone else's design, at most of the central encounters in the text—is a hyperrealized circulatory body. He is the working-class auditor to events in the novel great and small.

If the Toodle family seems to circulate too freely toward the Dombey family, and if they offer an impossibly sanitized and perfected version of the railway laborer and his wet-nursing wife, they also seem a bit too dramatically to represent circulation problems between classes. Literally marrying the railroad laborer and the wet nurse, two figures viewed with some suspicion by Victorians (as seen in Francis and Routh), allows Dickens to structure his portrayal of the working-class family, and from thence his portrait of interclass conflict, along the lines of circulation. The novel stages the dilemma of proximity by way of a working-class family that emblematizes, not to say overdetermines, anxieties about Victorian social fluidity. The railroad and the wet nurse, as Dickens styles them, but also as they are represented in cultural discourse outside the novel, are signally about the circulation of necessary commodities. These two figures are also about the economic value of (poor) bodies, a theme familiar from *Oliver Twist* and the new poor law debates, as well as the wet-nursing debates of Acton and Routh. In the navvy especially, as seen in Francis's

History, the relationship between food eaten and labor expended is critical to anxieties represented about the laborer. The same is true of the wet nurse, whom Acton, like Mr. Dombey, turns into an economic equation, noting, "There is the demand [for breast milk]. . . . We only ask that the supply be enlarged and regulated."[8]

The railroad, represented in *Dombey and Son* both in the locomotive itself and in Mr. Toodle, emphasizes the increased circulation of commodities and bodies at midcentury; very likely it was the most visible and powerful sign for the increase in traffic between people and in goods. The "impact of this railway development is beyond dispute," says one historian: "The railways accomplished a transportation revolution by reducing transportation costs and by broadening local markets. Even as it produced these economic changes, the railway stimulated social change, resulting in the interpenetration of town and country, and the blurring of social distinctions" (Lubenow 109). But we need go no farther than *Dombey* itself to perceive the railroad as evidence of a new, mobile society: "To and from the heart of this great change, all day and night, throbbing currents rushed and returned incessantly like its life's blood. Crowds of people and mountains of goods, departing and arriving scores upon scores of times in every four-and-twenty hours, produced a fermentation in the place that was always in action. The very houses seemed disposed to pack up and take trips" (290).

The railroad and wet nurse both signal social fluidity, but no matter how closely they might be linked in Dickens's text, the discourses surrounding the two of them outside the novel have different cultural weight. For the railroad and the railroad laborer were likely to have been far more focal in the average mid-Victorian mind than the largely medical debate over the wet nurse. In addition to the constant parliamentary debate authorizing new rail lines, the economic fervor and anxiety over "railway manias" in the 1840s, and the relatively rapid change in temporal and spatial relationships within England, the railroad represented a fundamental and *visible* change in the Victorian landscape—literally so, in the massive street clearances of London.

These street clearances connected the railroad with the opening of a social wound, for they revealed to the middle-class eye the slums that had been obscured in small alleyways and tiny streets.[9] The "pestilential alleys" were described by social reformers as "ill-ventilated culs de sac and dens of wretchedness in the vicinity of Shoe Lane and Saffron Hill—the nurseries of vice, the nuclei of filth and disease" (Dyos 13). The clearances contributed to a notion of the railroad as, if not the agent, then at least the revealer of filth and poverty. The railroad was thus imagined as, and to a certain extent held responsible for, bringing lower classes into closer relationship with the bourgeois world, insofar as it brought the filth and dirt into open view. For "much of the rest of the century, the opinion persisted that morality was intimately connected with the free circulation of air and exposure to 'public gaze'" (Jones, *Outcast* 180). Meanwhile, of course, this sense of the railway as ruthlessly anatomizing social ills was in competition with the economic gains it had also made real and visible to the middle classes.

The visibility of the railroad, and its importance during the period in which *Dombey* was being serialized, raises a question about its relationship to the wet-nursing debate. The two social issues are linked in an emphasis on circulation and in their tendency toward social leveling, but they had entirely different effects on the lives of Londoners. Why, then, does Dickens bind them so securely, indeed formally, in *Dombey and Son*? One answer may be the problem with work associated with *Oliver Twist*. Mr. Toodle's work is not only far from threatening, it is made secondary to Polly's labors, which in the novel come to be equated with the act of mothering itself. The male laborer, and the machine with which he is associated, steps to the background as domesticity comes to the fore. The threat of the railway is, finally, not social at all. Instead it is entirely personal; it represents the possibility that one may be lost in the whirl of industrialized society.

Dombey and Son does not ignore the leveling aspects of the train or completely avoid the subject of street clearance. But in Staggs's Gardens, the revelation of poverty is not handled by being made the subject of a renewing reform, a strategy frequently in use outside the novel. Instead, the novel rather weirdly offers only two possibilities. There is, on the one hand, a dirty and distressing slum, the only alternative to which is an antiseptic terrain rewritten by the railroad. All sense of community—except the thematic unity suggested in calling every business the "Railway" something or other—is thoroughly erased. The first effect of what is described as the "earthquake" of railway intervention is a domestic chaos that competes with the industrial, wherein "frowzy fields, and cow-houses, and dunghills, and dustheaps, and ditches" sit at the "very door of the Railway" (121). Once the railroad arrives, Dickens implies, there is no longer any *there* there. Dickens views the railway's "mighty course of civilization and improvement" with suspicion, remarking, "Nothing was the better for it, or thought of being so" (122).

Dickens ignores, in Staggs's Gardens, the fact of the many who would have been made homeless by this construction, and gives us a slum transmuted into a characterless appendage of industrialism:

> *Where the old rotten summer-houses once had stood, palaces now reared their heads, and granite columns of gigantic girth opened a vista to the railway world beyond. The miserable waste ground, where the refuse-matter had been heaped of yore, was swallowed up and gone; and in its frowzy stead were tiers of warehouses, crammed with rich goods and costly merchandise. The old by-streets now swarmed with passengers and vehicles of every kind: the new streets that had stopped disheartened in the mud and waggon-ruts, formed towns within themselves, originating wholesome comforts and conveniences belonging to themselves. (289)*

The neighborhood is now clean, and it quite firmly supports an increase in circulation. But the cost of massive renewal is in its absolute loss of *individual* character. In place of the slums and filth that had been its little identity before, Staggs's Gardens no longer has a name, no longer properly exists. Now it is a series of "railway hotels, office-houses, lodging-houses, boarding-houses; railway plans, maps, views, wrappers, bottles, sandwich-boxes, and time-tables; railway hackney-coach and cab-stands" (290).

The loss of identity the rails produce in Dickens mirrors the effect of the train on the middle-class passenger; for he, too, suffers a disorient-ing dislocation of self at the hands of the train. Mr. Dombey's famous train ride is the signal for a potentially fatal loss of self. The equalizing properties of the train are associated with death and monotony, which are to some extent identified with one another. The train is pictured as socially levelling, "dragging living creatures of all classes, ages, and de-grees behind it" (354). It democratizes and monotonizes the landscape itself, for "onward and onward ever: glimpses of cottage-homes, of houses, mansions, rich estates, of husbandry and handicraft, of people, of old roads and paths that look deserted" (354). And as it rushes onward, fearless and invincible, it brings Mr. Dombey to a deathlike monotony.[10]

The train anatomizes the slums, and Mr. Dombey holds it responsible: "As Mr. Dombey looks out of his carriage window, it is never in his thoughts that the monster who has brought him there has let the light of day in on these things: not made or caused them" (355). The progress of the train, of industrialism, is a force that cannot be controlled, which "rolls and roars, fierce and rapid, smooth and certain" (354); it is "resistless to the goal" (355). The train becomes inextricably confused with the equalizing force going on everywhere around it and in it. The train station is the territory of the vulgar herd, the place where, encountering Mr. Toodle, Mr. Dombey is horrified at the suggestion of any sympathy between himself and this raker among coals: "To think that this lost child [little Paul] . . . should have let in such a herd to insult him with their knowledge of his defeated hopes, and their boasts of claiming community of feeling with himself, so far removed: if not of having crept into the place wherein he would have lorded it, alone!" (353).

On the train, there is nothing but "monotony" (354). The locomotive travels "not through a rich and varied country, but a wilderness of blighted plans and gnawing jealousies" (354). Mr. Dombey's internal state is pathetically reflected in a landscape that greets him from the window. He is "pursuing the one course of thought" and finds "a likeness to his misfortune everywhere" (355). In the train, as it is represented in *Dombey,* dislocation and loss of self are the inevitable result of a leveling circulation.

Similar troubles are reflected in Carker's mad fugitive ride. Although he is propelled by coach, he is pursued in his thoughts and more urgently pushed forward by the train, for even as he rushes away there is "Some visionary terror, unintelligible and inexplicable, associated with a trembling of the ground,—a rush and a sweep of something through the air, like Death upon the wing" (863). The railroad is the agent that avenges without passion and ends Carker's life. If Mr. Dombey's mind is reduced to a single thought, one that pursues him as insistently as the railroad pursues Carker, then Carker is reduced to being unable to think at all. He is "tormented with thinking to no purpose," troubled by the "monotonous ringing of the bells and tramping of the horses; the monotony of his anxiety . . . the monotonous wheel of fear, regret, and passion" (867). When Carker does at last arrive at the railway, a waiter mistakes him for a railway traveler, and in a sense the waiter is right to do so: Carker has as good as been traveling by rail. "Very confusing, Sir," the waiter says. "Not much in the habit of travelling by rail myself, Sir, but gentlemen frequently say so" (871). The train represents the most frightening, and least resolved, threat of the text—that one's self will be lost entirely in the disorienting world of public travel.

Dombey and Son radically obscures this unresolved threat by representing the railroad in Mr. Toodle, and by linking him to Polly. And the text doubly seeks to ensure against the properties of the train by emphasizing that it is Mr. Toodle, a comic figure, who becomes so closely identified with the machine that he loses himself. We see him "in the bosom of his family," "shovelling in his bread and butter with a clasp knife, as if he were stoking himself" (619). The devouring appetite of Francis's navvy laborer is made over as mechanical speech. When Toodle talks it is the language of the locomotive we hear: "If you find yourselves in cuttings or in tunnels, don't you play no secret games. Keep your whistles going, and let's know where you are" (619). His thoughts, as Mr. Dombey's threatened to do, are governed by the movement of the train: "'I comes to a branch; I takes on what I finds there; and a whole train of ideas get coupled on to him, afore I knows where I am, or where they comes from. What a Junction a man's thoughts is,' said Mr. Toodle, 'to-be-sure!'" Mr. Toodle becomes the train, just as his son, Rob the Grinder, is named after it ("The Steamingine was a'most as good as a godfather to him, and so we called him Biler, don't you see!" [70]).

As others have noted, the novel maintains an ambivalent attitude toward the railway. While the narrator shares Dombey's feelings about the railway, particularly its connection with loss of social and personal identity, he is not in sympathy with Dombey's feelings about the Toodle family. *Dombey and Son* rejects a simplistic fear of social proximity, demonstrating instead that it is not physical touch but emotional bondage or liberation that matters most. As in the wet-nursing debates, it is the idea of *influence* that comes to dominate. And in his portrayal of influence, Dickens reverses the notion of class contamination upon which Routh insists.

Male contagion, or working-class appetite, is nowhere evident. There is no Sikes, no Noah Claypole, in *Dombey*. Instead, the most tangible evil in the novel is Carker's negative "influence," which defines his power in the novel. That power extends to everyone, but works with special energy upon Dombey. Carker influences Mr. Dombey to do his will, and of course he attempts to manipulate Edith, in order to advance his own complicated plot. His influence extends even to Florence, for he "had assumed a confidence between himself and her . . . a kind of mildly restrained power and authority over her—that made her wonder, and caused her great uneasiness" (476–77). Wherever Carker goes, he demonstrates a masterful control over others. And in his deployment of Rob the Grinder, Carker achieves an almost supernatural power over the young working-class male: "Rob had no more doubt that Mr. Carker read his secret thoughts . . . than he had that Mr. Carker saw him when he looked at him. The ascendancy was so complete, and held him in such enthralment, that, hardly daring to think at all, but with his mind filled with a constantly dilating impression of his patron's irresistible command over him . . . he would stand watching his pleasure" (676–77).

Thus is aggression translated into a matter of influence. Carker's power lies in his ability to cunningly manipulate others, not in his physical force. It is Carker, not Toodle, who is seen as the underling who wants to "gormandize," to take (to eat) everything his master has put away. Those prominent teeth signal his voracious desires, as when he "approaches Edith, more as if he meant to bite her, than to taste the sweets that linger on her lips" (525). He is ever displaying his "two unbroken rows of glistening teeth, whose regularity and whiteness were quite distressing. It was impossible to escape the observation of them, for he showed them whenever he spoke; and bore so wide a smile upon his countenance . . . that there was something in it like the snarl of a cat" (239).

Carker's unprovoked and excessive cruelty (particularly his treatment of Alice Marwood) is only matched in its intensity by Florence's unprovoked and excessive beneficence. In the domestic realm, contagion becomes influence, and the powers of Carker's acquisitive aggressive are toppled by the gentle influence of the home.[11] *Dombey and Son* demonstrates that the influences contained in the world of money are transformed by embracing a positive (female and middle-class) value of "influence." Polly translates the dangers of labor into working-class service, and in turn, the (maternal) services Polly provides become the basis of Florence's encompassing—not to say smothering—sympathy.[12]

Florence takes over as the novel's most important governing force.

The feminine values Polly embodies are gradually incorporated into the representation of Florence. In their first meeting Polly and Florence establish a correspondence: "In the simple passage that had taken place between herself and the motherless little girl, her own motherly heart had been touched no less than the child's; and she felt, as the child did, that there was something of confidence and interest between them from that moment" (81).

And, indeed, there is, for the best of Polly is soon passed on to Florence. Florence replaces Polly as Paul's surrogate mother: "We'll go home together, and I'll nurse you, love" (267), Florence tells Paul. She becomes his world and all after Polly's dismissal; and repeatedly in the scenes between the siblings, Florence appears more mother than sister. She is seen, in fact, at least by Mr. Dombey, as the new wet nurse, and one who has overstepped her limits: "Florence would remain at the Castle, that she might receive her brother there, on Saturdays. This would wean him by degrees, Mr. Dombey said; possibly with a recollection of his not having been weaned by degrees on a former occasion" (205).

Florence not only replaces Polly as nursing mother; she also replaces little Paul as the novel's central representation of the distressed and victimized child. In the early chapters of the novel, Paul, like Oliver, maintains a purity established by way of his helplessness, and a dependency ensured (as is Oliver's) by his mother's death at his birth. Paul Dombey, again like Oliver, cannot grow up: to do so would engage him in the world of work. In *Dombey and Son,* if not in Dickens generally, female children can function as both child and mother. The substitution of Florence for Paul as the most egregious example of a victimized child is thus strategic. She need never enter the world of work, and she can luxuriate among the spoils of *her* inheritance: domestic harmony. But *Dombey and Son* does not end with conjugal domesticity, or in a comedic pairing that promises happiness in marriage. The novel closes with a picture of childhood yet again: it is only in the renewal of the child couple that begins the novel—and not in conjugal felicity—that closure can be achieved. The final paragraphs portray Florence and her two children (little Paul and little Florence) with their fully reformed grandfather. The voices in the waves, associated with (the first) little Paul, end the novel; those voices not only constitute the world of the novel as the province of childhood but urge that innocence on the reader as well, for in the last lines we are told to hope that the sea voices whisper of "the unseen region on the other shore," and do so "in our childish ears" (976).

It is Florence, with her limitless goodwill and gentle charity, and her perfect merger of childhood and maternity, who gradually becomes the governing influence of the novel. "The constitution of the household is more entirely representative than even that glorious constitution of which we all have heard so much, and which keeps our ship of state afloat. . . . [I]f any one will tell us that the nursery is less important than the Exchange, or that it is a more dignified business to vote for a county member than to regulate a Christian household, we will grant that the woman has an inferior range of duty," Margaret Oliphant said in 1856 (382).[13] Florence becomes what Sarah Ellis conceived of as an influential trainer of the thoughts of others, conversant as she is in the authoritative arts of the nurturer. Walter "preserve[s] her image in his mind," and it "restrain[s] him like an angel's hand from anything unworthy" (288). Florence maintains a special influence over Paul, as Carker does over Rob the Grinder; only she, with a mother's skills, can truly reassure him. And she is the only one who touches Edith's heart. Everywhere we look in the novel, particularly as Florence grows older, testimony to her selfless devotion is brought to the fore—so much so that nothing less is asked of the reader than that he, too, must cling like Diogenes in helpless canine devotion: "Di, the rough and gruff[,] . . . his dog's heart melted[,] . . . put his nose up to her face, and swore fidelity. . . . When he had eaten and drunk his fill, he went to the window where Florence was sitting[,] . . . rose up on his hind legs, . . . licked her face and hands, nestled his great head against her heart, and wagged his tail till he was tired" (324). So we, too, come to worship at Florence's feet.

Florence becomes her brother Paul's nurse, and by the end of the novel she has also become her father's. Florence is aligned, as the nursing mother, with Polly Toodle. And she is opposed to two other nursing mothers in the novel: Alice Marwood received no benefit from her mother's poisonous milk, for she was "born, among poverty and neglect, and nursed in it." Mrs. Skewton reminds Edith, just before dying, "For I nursed you"; but her body fluids, while they contain no tangible pollution, are implicitly as poisonous as that of her lower-class double, "Good" Mrs. Brown.

Florence's ability to nurture and to nurse Paul is aligned with Polly and her world—that is, with the world of the good, caretaking mother. She stands in opposition to Mrs. Pipchin, who compared to Polly Toodle is a bitter apple, for "all her waters of gladness and milk of human kindness, had been pumped out dry" (160). Like the mean Dickensian mother-substitute who has preceded her, Mrs. Mann, and one who will come after, Mrs. Joe (both aptly named), Mrs. Pipchin makes certain she gets fed, while the children may go hungry.

It is Florence who officiates alone at Mr. Dombey's moment of redemption, and she holds him as a mother comforts her child: "Upon the breast that he had bruised, against the heart that he had almost broken, she laid his face, now covered with his hands, and said, sobbing: 'Papa, love, I am a mother'" (940). The important transformation by this point (and even in this passage) is not the emotional reconstruction of Mr. Dombey, the narrowing of his pride, but rather the gradual but sure canonization of Florence as the breast-feeding mother who simultaneously remains the victimized child. The more thoroughly her influence governs events, the more possible it is for any threat from elsewhere to be reduced. The emphasis in the novel has shifted from the workplace, where economic and social disputes ignite, to the family, where the milk of human kindness drowns all fires before they can explode.

The possibility of a beneficent domestic sympathy that can overcome all with its love is first suggested in the representation of Polly Toodle. As the novel progresses, that positive influence becomes the defining property of Florence Dombey. The focus shifts radically from the laborer and the incendiary possibilities of the workplace. The important sphere of influence is not Mr. Dombey's office but his home (not the Exchange but the Nursery). The very idea of economic exchange is transformed: value will not refer to consumables and the price the market will bear. Rather, value refers to the interiority of the subject, specifically to Florence's inner being. The importance of redefining female worth in this way has, of course, been emphasized in the representation of Edith, whose *value* has been so carefully defined according to false values.

No longer merely a piece of useless coin, Florence's very presence is remunerative: the Skettleses "would have valuable consideration for their kindness, in the company of Florence" (398). Or, more pertinently, as Susan Nipper later says to Mr. Dombey, "there ain't no gentleman, no Sir, though as great and rich as all the greatest and richest of England put together, but might be proud of her and would and ought. If he knew her value right, he'd rather lose his greatness and his fortune piece by piece and beg his way in rags from door to door . . . than bring the sorrow on her tender heart that I have seen it suffer in this house!" (704).

Florence is elevated from a useless currency that can never be invested to the embodiment of the true *value* of the novel. That value is in part her soothing influence, and in part her reproductive function. Overtly, Florence's body becomes, as she produces a new little Paul, a factory for the future of business, a business now to be presided over by the enterprising Walter Gay. Florence's covert value lies in the power of her middle-class motherhood to obscure social conflicts outside the family. Her domestic sphere becomes a locus for power by novel's end; it has become the center stage for novelistic struggles, while the slums, the poor, and the workplace are kept at a distance. Into Florence's ready lap the moral center of the novel has arrived; thus, we come to value her sphere of influence above all else, to rest our trust in the bosom of the family.

In *Dombey and Son* the narrative voice of the liberal father guides us across the minefield of social relations, across class lines, in order to obscure them at last in a reliance on Florence Dombey's motherhood. *Dombey* uses Polly Toodle just as Acton uses his pretty housemaid who resides just down the street; each sentimentalizes the working wet nurse as a rich and necessary subject for their separate narratives. And those narratives, in their turn, serve to stabilize a bourgeois identity. *Dombey and Son* abandons the Dickensian plot of mothers and their boy children to find a victimized child-subject in the little mother. And the novel ends, as does *Wuthering Heights,* in the appearance of a child couple. But in *Wuthering Heights* and in *The Tenant of Wildfell Hall,* the domesticity that defines Florence's power becomes the jail that circumscribes the lives of Brontëan female characters.

III

Tender Tyranny: The 1839 Custody of Infants Act and Custodial Incarceration in *Wuthering Heights* and *The Tenant of Wildfell Hall*

The laws—always so occupied with property and so little with persons, because their object is peace not virtue—do not give enough authority to mothers. However, their status is more certain than that of fathers; their duties are more painful; their cares are more important for the good order of the family. . . . There are occasions on which a son who lacks respect for his father can in some way be excused. But if on any occasion whatsoever a child were unnatural enough to lack respect for his mother—for her who carried him in her womb, who nursed him with her milk, who for years forgot herself in favor of caring for him alone—one should hasten to strangle this wretch as a monster unworthy of seeing the light of day.

Rousseau,
Emile

IN *Dombey and Son* Dickens comically affirms the need of a barrier against an appetitive underclass when he demonstrates the eagerness with which family servants yearn to destroy the pantry. The above-stairs celebration of Dombey's second marriage is mimicked in a certain "giddiness" among those who "have been breakfasting below. Champagne has grown too common among them to be mentioned, and roast fowls, raised pies, and lobster-salad, have become mere drugs" (530). This alimentary abandon is short-lived, however, for as night closes in, the breakfast is "denuded of its show and garnish. . . . Mr. Dombey's servants moralise so much about it, and are so repentant over their early tea, at home, that by eight o'clock or so, they settle down into confirmed seriousness; and Mr. Perch, arriving at that time from the City, fresh and jocular . . . ready to spend the evening, and prepared for any amount of dissipation, is amazed to find himself coldly received, and Mrs. Perch but poorly, and to have the pleasing duty of escorting that lady home by the next omnibus" (532).

Although repentance may be the natural last course of debauched feasts in all social classes, contrast this scene with a later one in which the servants, having learned that "master's in difficulties," make it their first task to "perform perfect feats of eating" (926). Mr. Towlinson allows that "in the first place, he would beg to propose a little snack of something to eat; and over that snack would desire to offer a suggestion which he thinks will meet the position in which they find themselves. The refreshment being produced, and very heartily partaken of, Mr. Towlinson's suggestion is, in effect, that Cook is going, and that if we are not true to ourselves, nobody will be true to us. . . . Boxes are packed, cabs fetched, and at dusk that evening there is not one member of the party left" (927–28). Under the influence of a relaxed supervision, the servants have their way with the larder; a now unrepentant appetite is followed by a rapid decamp. With "master" no longer dominant, self-control, not to mention the bourgeois moralizing that the servants evidently imbibed along with the intoxicating lobster salad, goes the way of the little snack.

The question of abandoned appetites is of substantial concern in the 1830s, as I have argued in discussion of the new poor law, and in *Frankenstein* and *Oliver Twist,* in the introduction and chapter 1. Appetite is also an organizing trope throughout the "hungry 40s," as was clear in the wetnursing debates examined alongside *Dombey* in chapter 2. Mary Shelley and Charles Dickens associate hunger with threatening bodies, devouring bodies. Their narratives seek compromise with or protection against the literal hungers that suffuse their fictions, and the Malthusian and social appetites those hungers bring to mind. In the scene from Dickens's *Dombey* quoted above, the "raised pies" and "roast fowls" represent, just momentarily, an uncontrolled appetite, but one that is quickly dismissed in a collapse into comedy. Seldom can hunger be imagined in this period without undergoing such a transformation into comedy or without being redefined, through metaphor or analogy, as a purely acquisitive, and therefore corrupt, desire. The novels and nonfiction writing discussed thus far provide examples of the displacement and dismissal of hunger.

The Tenant of Wildfell Hall and *Wuthering Heights* are significant in the 1840s for the way in which hunger remains both literal and figurative. Hunger remains a presence, if only a spectral one (in the ghostly sightings of Heathcliff and Cathy), even at novel's end. The satisfaction or denial of bodily need in Dickens distinguishes the bourgeois family from hungry outsiders. In the Brontë novels, however, hunger invites, rather than deflects, anxieties about domestic enclosures. Indeed, in these novels, hunger becomes an agent of revelation in disclosing domestic spaces *as* enclosure. Not only does hunger remain literal in Anne and Emily Brontë, but the Gothic dangers of the family that are displaced in *Dombey*—the imprisoning home, the threat of kidnapping, or, what abduction often represents, the loss of (social) identity—endure as imminent threats. In *Wildfell Hall* and in *Wuthering Heights,* these dangers cannot be dismissed as the fate or responsibility of insatiable others, for they emerge from needs that originate in the family itself, and they persist as a private menace.

In the Brontë world, hunger can be transformed into an unspecified desire, always ready to consume the self. *Wuthering Heights* closes with Heathcliff's extended fast, a literal starvation figured as devouring desire: "I have a single wish, and my whole being and faculties are yearning to attain it. . . . I'm convinced it *will* be reached—and *soon*—because it has devoured my existence—I am swallowed in the anticipation of its fulfilment" (354). Meanwhile, Anne Brontë's novel demonstrates with a single-minded ferocity the quickness with which want becomes addiction. While a failing Heathcliff puzzles that "I'm animated with hunger; and, seemingly, I must not eat" (358), Arthur Huntingdon, speaking of various sensual attractions and the spiritual law that would deny him pleasure, cannot put off his feast: "I am hungry, and I see before me a good substantial dinner; I am told that, if I abstain from this to-day, I shall have a sumptuous feast to-morrow. . . . I should be loath to wait till to-morrow, when I have the means of appeasing my hunger already before me" (219).

In both novels "hunger" represents desire of *all* kinds. In *Wuthering Heights* desire is an independent force that has no specific or attainable object that can be represented in the novel, and serves only to reproduce itself in fiction. The word offered in *Wildfell Hall* for the play between hunger and desire is "appetite." Exploring appetite shows the instrumental connection the novels forge between hunger and pedagogy or, to put it another way, between desire and restraint.

It is in making this link that *Wuthering Heights* and *Wildfell Hall* pursue a vision of the endangered child-subject. For example, Arthur Huntingdon's overweening needs are traced, by his wife, to a failure in training: "[H]e has no more idea of exerting himself to overcome obstacles than he has of restraining his natural appetites; and these two things are the ruin of him. I lay them both to the charge of his harsh yet careless father and his madly indulgent mother. If ever I am a mother I will zealously strive against this *crime* of over-indulgence—I can hardly give it a milder name when I think of the evils it brings" (238). Helen Huntingdon defines her husband's desires as a family problem, as a problem of training. She redefines law ("this *crime* of over-indulgence") as a private affair. Hope for curbing hunger lies, this passage suggests (and the rest of the novel bears out), in the rigors of child rearing. In Emily Brontë's novel, a similar resolution is reached when the self-consuming desires of Cathy and Heathcliff are repaired in the aftermath of their emaciation by a taming of Hareton Earnshaw's appetite and its redirection toward literacy.[1]

In the two Brontë novels discussed here, appetitive desire constructs a self whose desires threaten disincorporation, whether through an excess of appetite (Huntingdon) or through starvation (Heathcliff, Cathy). Restraint can maintain a stable self, but in these novels that control is possible only in children, and it is for that reason the child-subject becomes the prized individual. In *Wuthering Heights* and *The Tenant of Wildfell Hall,* it is possible to forge a self in the inherently violent enclosure of the family, but it is only possible to maintain that self in Rousseauesque fashion, combining the primitive savagery of childhood with the defining limits of pedagogy. The Brontës, like Dickens before them, produce victimized children. But these novels are interesting in that they do not sentimentalize family as safe haven for the liberal subject. Their fiction by no means serves the immediate ends of disciplinary society.

These novels attend to the child and to child rearing, directly in Anne Brontë and implicitly in *Wuthering Heights,* in a focus on "custody" issues. In taking up custody, these novels turn to problems of possession, incarceration, and protection as a way of resolving the tensions of appetite. Like "appetite," the word "custody" is a holding place for two significant notions that the novel maintains together: incarceration and protective guardianship. It was just this crux, between bonds and bondage, that defined the parliamentary debate over child custody in the late 1830s. The debates over the infant custody bills did for the bourgeois child what the new poor law did for the pauper infant at the beginning of the decade: they redefined the child from property to person. The subject thus produced was, however, preeminently a legal subject; the individual is mediated by the judicial apparatus that surrounds him. The emergence of the child-subject in legal writing, and the developing narrative of children's right and interests, intersects in interesting ways with the familial story told in the Brontë novels.

Of Tender Years

Session after session we are amplifying the province of the legislature, and asserting its moral prerogatives. Parliament aspires to be the pater patriae, *and is laying aside the policeman, the gaoler, and the executioner, in exchange for the more kindly and dignified functions of the father, the schoolmaster, and the friend.*

London
Times, 4 May
1847

In his *Commentaries on the Laws of England,* William Blackstone asserts that "children will have a perfect *right* of receiving maintenance from their parents," but he is also quick to acknowledge that, as far as the enforcement of this right is concerned, "providence has done it more effectually than any laws, by implanting in the breast of every parent that . . . insuperable degree of affection, which not even the deformity of person or mind, not even the wickedness, ingratitude, and rebellion of children, can totally suppress or extinguish" (435). Blackstone thus construes a natural basis for the law of parent and child, implying that the judiciary merely codifies what is an intrinsic "right," even for a rebellious and wicked ingrate. At the same time that he absorbs filial obligation into the law, however, Blackstone places parent and child relations *outside* the judicial, for he acknowledges that it is finally feeling, that "insuperable degree of affection," that truly legislates parental duty. Indeed, Blackstone goes so far as to suggest that the natural duty of parents to protect their children is "rather permitted than enjoined by any municipal laws: nature, in this respect, working so strongly as to need rather a check than a spur" (437).

Blackstone's recognition that the state of the law in 1765 did not strictly insist upon parental "duty" is important, for English law governed parent and child relations only in certain instances. The *Commentaries* describe a legal world in which the "best interest" of the child, and in fact family law as a category, did not yet exist. The minor child became available for legal interference primarily when property was involved. This was true even with respect to the most basic considerations, including custodial rights. Before the passage of the Custody of Infants Bill of 1839, it was the existence and disposition of a minor's estate that made the concern of the law possible. When parents separated or, much more rarely, divorced, the father's right to custody of his progeny was largely unquestioned and legally absolute. Under the law of custody, even though it governed the body of the child, the court acted only upon his effects. Adjudicating a well-known case in 1827, Lord Eldon cited precedent for the theory that "this Court has not the means of acting, except where it has property to act upon" (qtd. Forsyth 13). It was not legally impossible for the Court of Chancery to act in *parens patriae,* but it was highly improbable. Paternal custody right was maintained by a reluctance to interfere with the private matters of the family, which were thought best governed by the father.

Custody law and precedent historically defined a child's relationship to his family as financial. The mother's role was made secondary, or ignored altogether. In 1850 the English barrister William Forsyth looked back on the earlier era with dismay: "The general rule of law in this country is, that the legal power over infant children belongs to the father and that during his life the mother has none. In the words of Blackstone, 'a mother, *as such,* is entitled to no power, but only to reverence and respect' . . . [;] the father has, at common law, a right to the exclusive custody of his child even at an age when it still requires nourishment from its mother's breast" (11). Custody rights in preindustrial England supported the primacy of property and status in legal relations of the family, and the enduring importance of primogeniture. The child himself was in effect a form of property and so, like all other wealth in the marriage, belonged more or less exclusively to a husband. For the most part, of course, the law treated all persons in relation to property. But in the judicial code and in legal practice, the father, as the marker for property and status, was understood to be the paradigmatic individual, a category emphatically understood to be a social one.

In the course of the nineteenth century the social representation of the family was retooled, and the father's absolute right over his offspring, not surprisingly, received critical comment. The family was transformed from an analogue for rigid patriarchal control to a "correlative figure of parliamentary democracy" (Donzelot 4).[2] In this context the state of custody law began to seem troubling as an unchallenged legal fact. Forsyth "admits" in *A Treatise on the Law Relating to Custody of Infants* (1850) that

> *the application of this law which enforces with such jealous care the*
> *rights of the father, has often been extremely harsh. He might be a man*
> *of the most immoral character, and his conduct towards the mother such*
> *as to render it impossible for her, without all sacrifice of dignity and self-*
> *respect, to live with him; and yet, provided only that he was cautious*
> *enough not to bring his children into actual contact with pollution . . .*
> *he had the entire control over and disposition of them, and might embit-*
> *ter the life of the mother by depriving her of the society of her offspring.*
> *And what untold suffering might she not be called upon to endure, in*
> *the mental struggle between the affection which prompted her to submit*
> *to insult and injury for their sake, and the desire to escape from such*
> *usage by abandoning her home! (12)*

Family law in the early part of the nineteenth century was subject to considerable criticism because the law did not reflect rising public sentiment about the family, particularly the role of the mother.

But even though the ideological gap between a portrait of sentimental motherhood and the law of custody only widened after Blackstone, the mother's right to custody of her child was not established for many decades. The 1839 Custody of Infants Act allowed a wife who was separated from her husband to petition the court and, provided she was of good character, to gain access to her young children and, potentially (although it was unlikely), temporary custody of children under seven years of age. The 1873 Custody of Infants Act permitted the mother to ask for access to, and in certain instances custody of, her children up to sixteen years of age. Neither of these reforms actually transferred the right of custody to the mother. The 1886 Guardianship of Infants Act for the first time appointed a mother guardian upon a father's death, provided there was no question concerning her suitability. (Prior to this act, a father could transfer his custodial rights to anyone regardless of a mother's wishes.) The 1886 legislation left untouched the father's right of custody unless misconduct on his part was alleged, in which instance a mother could sue for full custody of her child. An early-twentieth-century legal historian describes this law as "essentially a mother's Act," and quotes from the act itself, which directs the court, upon a mother's petition, to "make such order as it may think fit regarding the custody of such infant and the right of access thereto of either parent, having regard to the welfare of the infant, and to the conduct of the parents, and to the wishes as well of the mother as of the father" (qtd. Bicknell 2). But it was not until the 1925 revision of the Guardianship of Infants Act that the child's welfare took full precedence over the parent's right. Reform of custody law in the nineteenth century did not, by and large, resolve the dilemma of a legal code at odds with a cultural representation of nurturing motherhood.[3]

Nevertheless, the parliamentary debate read motherhood into the law as a nurturing domesticity vitally necessary to a child's proper development. The bill acted out opposing cultural representations and transformed the category of "woman" into "mother." Opponents (Edward Sugden in the House of Commons and Brougham in the Lords) championed the first term, "woman," in a resolute focus on the institution of marriage. In their view, a change in custody rights "would open the door to such frightful changes in the whole of this country, and in the whole of the principles on which the law of husband and wife was founded— ay, and such innovations on those laws which had hitherto been regarded as the safeguard of families" that, in short, "the floods of immorality would be sure to overflow the character of the institution of marriage."[4] The oft-repeated logic was reinforced by Mr. Sugden in the House of Commons: "The great tie which prevents the separation of married persons is their common children. A wife was, in general, glad to have that excuse for submitting to the temper of a capricious husband" (40:1115). The emphasis in the minority opposition to the Infant Custody Bill whenever it was debated was on conjugal life and its close tie to social cohesion. The parliamentary record states that "Mr. Tancred had a strong feeling against the measure," for he was convinced that "the greatest evil which could befall a wife was a separation from her husband, and, so far from doing anything to facilitate such separation, it appeared to him that the House ought to support every enactment of the law as it now stood which placed an obstacle in the way of such a separation" (40:1112).

Other opposing arguments also emphasized wife over mother. For example, Sugden later remarked that women who leave their husbands ought not to be rewarded for such behavior by being allowed access to their children. There was general concern that an adulterous or misbehaving wife would not be properly chastised if the law were reformed. One further interesting objection of Sugden's was that a reformed law would give "a right to the judge before whom the question [is] mooted to investigate the whole domestic life of the parties from the time of the marriage" (42:1050). This was repeated by Mr. Shaw, who believed women upheld the distinctly private nature of family life, for "no woman of delicate mind would submit to call upon a court to interfere." In sum, as Brougham said in the House of Lords, the bill was "destructive of the comforts, and dangerous to the purity, of marriage life" (44:787). The decided emphasis was on the unity of husband and wife.

By contrast, the majority opinion in both Houses argued for the bill in the name of the mother, insisting on the morality of such a position. Mr. Praed asserted that "this proposal was calculated to do more moral good than any measure which had been for a long time been before the House." He went on to say that "in nine cases out of ten, especially when the children were of tender years, the mother was the better guardian, and this no one would deny" (42:1052–53). In defense of his bill, Talfourd asked "what was more deplorable than that this depth of feeling [on the mother's part] should be the last link to prevent a virtuous woman from separating from her husband who ill uses her, and that only by this iron bond" was she kept in her home. The legal, even financial, bond of marriage had disappeared, only to be firmly replaced by the "iron bond" of mother and child (42:1054).

In the House of Lords, Lyndhurst argued for the mother who "might be the most virtuous woman that ever lived" but who still might not gain access to her infant child (44:773). He cited then-famous cases in which the mother's position was unambiguously wretched: in one instance, "the husband . . . got possession of the child" while the question of custody "was being agitated in Court (the child having in the mean time been delivered to the mistress of its father, who was then confined in Horsemonger-lane Gaol, where the child was carried to him day by day)" (44:774). Such examples served to elevate motherhood and to present fathers as unfeeling brutes. Lyndhurst left it "to the House to conceive what must have been [her] sufferings." He advocated taking "the matter out of the hands of the father, and plac[ing] it in the hands of an independent judge" (44:778), overturning the privacy of family life. He called attention to "the love a mother had to her offspring, the delight she received in their smiles, the interest she took in all their sorrows, and the happiness she had in the superintendency of them" (49:487). When the bill was passed, the Lord Chancellor made a statement that summed up the inchoate sensibility in which the Custody Act participated: "the great danger in the Legislature endeavouring to arrange the disputes of husband and wife was, lest they should lose sight of that which ought to be the primary object of all courts of justice—the conservation of the rights of the children" (49:493–94).

Children's rights: the Lord Chancellor's summation newly directed attention to the middle- and upper-class child's individual welfare. It made way for a judicial intervention in family life, reserving for the court the right of judging parental fitness. Such judgments might now be made based on moral grounds, as opposed to mere physical cruelty. The anecdote of Horsemonger-lane Gaol suggested that while an unsavory father and his mistress may pose no threat to his child's body, they certainly stand to contaminate the child's mind, and such contamination should be monitored and halted by authorities. In addressing the moral state of the middle- and upper-class family, the 1839 parliamentary debates introduced a new definition of the rights of children, one now potentially based on an internal state, motivated by "morality" rather than property.

The notion of children's rights did not appear for the first time during the custody debates, of course. The protection of children, and an implicit notion of rights, was integral to child labor discussions at least as early as 1802, if not earlier. And, as seen in chapter 1, the new poor law crucially separated pauper children from their parents, physically and philosophically, an idea extended by James Kay in order to produce an uncontaminated working-class subject. But these discussions of the rights and freedoms of childhood remained distinct from the custody acts in two important respects: First, and most obviously, child labor and workhouse issues, at least overtly, concerned the working and pauper classes only. Second, the discourse around child labor in particular maintained a strong emphasis on the body and tended to produce legislation that acted upon, nominatively to protect, the victimized child and his or her corporeal self. The moral welfare of working children was certainly not ignored, but there was a strong emphasis on, for example, the "factory cripples" that child labor produced.[5] Child labor concerns were frequently supported by the tangible and direct evidence—the "ocular proof"—to be found in the manufacturing districts.

The concern for the welfare of working-class children in mills and coal fields called for, and eventually achieved in a limited way, direct intervention and control. For example, the Ten Hours Act, approved in 1847, limited labor demands on workers, and evidence from and about children was crucial to its passage. These legislative mandates implied a moral position, but in practice they provided for the disposition of the child's beleaguered body. He must be returned to the home, or taken out of it to attend school.

This is not to deny that there was a strong relationship between the issues raised and the legislation passed concerning child labor, and the issues and legislation that emerged from the custody debates; most notably, both mark the dominance of a protective sensibility. But the concern for the welfare of the upper- and middle-class child in the talk about custodial rights was distinguished by a decided moral policing of the private individual, in which a judge considered the fitness of the parents in order to protect the child. The court moved beyond the public and economic space of the factory or the workhouse and invaded the "private" domain of the family, eliciting testimony about the sexual, religious, and domestic conduct of the parties. As in the pauper education debates of the late 1830s—and, for that matter, in the novels of Anne and Emily Brontë—the primary consideration was whether the indirect influence of a parent's personal behavior might contaminate a developing child.

The change meant positing a fairly complex psychology for the child. The custody acts themselves were exceptions to the general rule that the middle- and upper-class family was not regulated by the law; as D. A. Miller states in his discussion of *Oliver Twist*, "Liberal society and the family were kept free from the carceral institutions that were set up to remedy their failures only by assuming the burden of an immense internal regulation" (*The Novel* 59–60). The debates in the Houses provide especially interesting reading; they not only represent graphically the struggle between two ways of understanding the private domain of the family, but they offer a rare example of legislation that directed itself to the family with property. That is, they represent a moment when the internal regulation to which the bourgeois family willingly submitted in private was publicly evaluated and made visible.

The 1837–38 parliamentary debate exposed pedagogical motherhood in the making. The sentimentalized mother was understood to nurture and protect. It was her role to train, to raise, and to tutor the child in values. She functioned as a sign for pedagogy; like the law, she would come to hold what would be seen as an educative and benevolent position in the family. The father was associated with absolute control and willful exercise of power, as Lord Lyndhurst sought to prove with a lengthy review of custody case law during House discussion of the bill. Confined to prison or, more commonly, conspiring with his mistress to do the children harm, the father of the custody reformers was unfeeling and immoral. Having reimagined the father as a potential tyrant, the state would eventually find it possible to usurp his role and to take ultimate responsibility over the family, especially the poor family. The mother was thus allied with the state as instructress and benevolent guardian. It would be her task to keep the family out of the carceral realm.[6]

The early Victorian shift seen in the parliamentary debate moved from the father's absolute right to a more complicated concern over the mother; the shift significantly refocused the subject for whom custody negotiations were taking place: the child. The sentimental mother provided the foundation for a subject who was no longer merely a piece of family property. These changes helped construct not only a more fully psychologized individual but one constantly open to, in fact whose vulnerability invited, intervention. There would now be a self in family law "of tender years," one who would require benevolent guidance to determine his "best interests." His value was no longer linked to property; now he was understood to be the *priceless* center of the family.[7] The child-subject of the custody debates was created within the constraining structure of the judiciary, but was imagined, like the workhouse pauper, to be capable of transcending that confinement.

Emerging domestic law, in its connection with a gradually emerging system of welfare, both created and contained the subject, but it did so specifically in scrutinizing and redefining the child. The mother's rights need not be literalized, though they must be invoked, in order to mediate the tension over custody law; the introduction of pedagogy into the law was sufficient to lessen that tension. The 1839 bill was not, finally, about mother-right, although the language of nurturing and sentimental motherhood was crucial. The bourgeois child addressed in Parliament, like the pauper in the workhouse, could be created only by way of an "imprisoning" structure of marriage and family. He was imagined only within the defining limits of a legal discourse. The domestic antidote to the carceral was never fully accomplished, for the domestic continued to function, under the control of the abusive and tyrannical father, as prison. This point was literalized amusingly in the anecdote, read into legislative record, of the father exercising his custodial rights from within the confines of Horse-monger Lane jail. The disciplinary subject, in other words, is never (quite) constituted. The "free" child, the liberal subject, was here only *legally* produced. Although he had a (limited) psychology, and although he had been transformed out of property and into subjectivity, he was first introduced by way of, and filtered through, the judicial. The familial is not here separated from the carceral realm, but rather emerges from it, and maintains an important relationship to it. In *The Tenant of Wildfell Hall* and *Wuthering Heights,* imprisoning marriage and sentimentalized motherhood are reimagined in a turn to the pedagogical child couple. Unlike the fictions of Dickens, these novels resist sentimentality and the embrace of motherhood. On the other hand, like Dickens—and like the custody reformers of the 1830s—Anne and Emily Brontë recognized in childhood an answer to the dilemma of self.

Hunger, Rebellion, and Rage

Child custody looms large as a topic in both novels, overtly so in *The Tenant of Wildfell Hall.*[8] The plot concerns the flight of Helen Huntingdon from a depraved husband, a flight she risks in order to remove her young son, little Arthur Huntingdon, from the polluting excesses of his profligate father. When she finds her adulterous husband in the shrubbery with the abandoned Annabella Wilmot, the ensuing confrontation concerns the welfare of little Arthur rather than the behavior of his father: " '[W]ill you let me take our child and what remains of my fortune, and go? . . . Anywhere, where he will be safe from your contaminating influence, and I shall be delivered from your presence—and you from mine.' 'No—by *Jove* I won't! . . . Do you think I'm going to be made the talk of the country, for your fastidious caprices?' " (315). *Wildfell Hall,* set in the years before the passage of the Infant Custody Act, in one sense tells the story of what happens when paternal rights interfere with a sanctified notion of motherhood.

But if *Wildfell Hall* is explicitly about custody, it just as firmly asserts that the guardianship of home can easily collapse into imprisonment. The novel offers numerous identifications between home and prison, beginning with the Gothic description of Helen Huntingdon's refuge at her "bleak . . . asylum" (76), Wildfell Hall itself, "enclosed by stone walls, and entered by an iron gate with large balls of grey granite" (46). In narrating Helen's early history the novel moves through a series of imprisoning domestic structures: the proposed marriage to the aptly named Mr. Boarham; the constraints of life at home with her aunt and uncle; and then the literal confinements of marriage itself as it is experienced with the decadent Arthur Huntingdon. Helen evolves from imagining marriage as the state of "enjoy[ing Arthur's] society without restraint" (199), to her literal confinement in her own home where she cries out after her keys have been taken from her, "I am a slave, a prisoner" (373).

Wuthering Heights is less focally concerned with a single custodial case; it is, however, more deeply infused with the issue of custody, beginning with the alarming way in which the house itself keeps turning into a penal colony. Coming to Wuthering Heights would seem to require transforming oneself into either prisoner or ward; it hardly matters which, since they amount to the same thing. Lockwood comes under the protective custody of the house, only to have that protection turn ominous as night falls. Isabella crosses the threshold in marriage and finds her new home not just a prison, but one in which, Hindley instructs, she must immure herself: "He suddenly arrested me, and added in the strangest tone—'Be so good as to turn your lock, and draw your bolt—don't omit it!' " (176). Heathcliff, who has a long history in the custodial battles of this family, makes it clear that "you're not fit to be your own guardian, Isabella, now; and I, being your legal protector, must retain you in my custody" (189).

Custody and incarceration have been confused, and Isabella has become an infant. Heathcliff not only dismisses her to her room, but adds: "That's not the way-upstairs, I tell you! Why, this is the road upstairs, child!" (189). Even Nelly Dean cannot escape the threat of confinement under the shadow of that house: " 'I'll take measures to secure you, woman!' exclaimed Heathcliff, 'you shall not leave Wuthering Heights till to-morrow morning'" (190). At length Nelly is actually jailed at the house and held captive for several days. Meanwhile, all attempts to lock out the jailer, Heathcliff—"put the key in the lock, and draw the bolts" (211)—are spectacularly unsuccessful.

Imprisonment, readers readily admit, is dominant in Emily Brontë's novel. But just as critical is the very literal way that every child, every body, who enters the house is or rapidly becomes a problem of custody. The novel enacts a repetitive series of highly pitched custody battles, which often have a legal basis, although the requirements of the law are sometimes rejected in favor of private arrangements. This is the case, for instance, when Heathcliff "trades" his legal custody of his son Linton in order to be allowed to maintain his guardianship of Hareton after Hindley's death. The custody battles begin much earlier than this, of course. In fact, we might say that custody is the originating event of the story, for it is the unexpected introduction of Heathcliff, "starving, and houseless" (78), into the narrative and into the Earnshaw family that sets action in motion in *Wuthering Heights*. Following this inaugural act, Hindley becomes guardian to Heathcliff and Cathy after old Earnshaw dies. Hareton becomes Heathcliff's ward with Hindley's death, and Linton is given over to his father's custody after his mother dies, though he enjoys a very brief sojourn under the guardianship of Edgar Linton at Thrushcross Grange. Catherine Linton Heathcliff comes under Heathcliff's "care" after her marriage to Linton and his subsequent death. At the same time, her property is turned over to Heathcliff as Linton's surviving heir.

Wildfell Hall, superficially at least, constructs custody much as Sergeant Talfourd did during the 1830s: as a struggle between a tyrannical father, whose concerns are either financial or vengeful, and a loving mother, who has only the child's interest at heart. The profligate Arthur fights for his son for form's sake, while Helen appears to embrace the by now familiar idea of the child as priceless possession. Little Arthur thus serves to define a category that directly opposes property: "I am not going to sell my child for gold, though it were to save both him and me from starving: it would be better that he should die with me, than that he should live with his father" (399).

Wuthering Heights, on the other hand, while it represents this struggle in similar structural terms, locates the battle not between father and mother, but rather between a tyrannical power that would enforce its will through a punishing and often physical brutality, and a coercion evoked by way of persuasion. This novel stages its battles for custody between Nelly's disciplinary tactics and Heathcliff's torturing acts. At one time or another, Nelly and Heathcliff vie for control over most of the bodies that pass through their world, particularly in the case of the younger generation—Hareton Earnshaw, Catherine Linton, and Linton Heathcliff. In each of these "cases," Nelly pleads directly with Heathcliff to allow her to be protector to these children, and to bring them to, or keep them at, Thrushcross Grange. In each case, Heathcliff insists upon what is his right to custody.

To describe the workings of *Wuthering Heights* in this way is, of course, to gesture toward a reading of the disciplinary tactics of the novel. But it should also be to deny that those tactics, however succinctly they may be displayed in the novel, hold sway. More important than the poles of torture and discipline that the novel figures in its examination of custody is the fact that discipline is hardly triumphant; indeed, it is often subjected to a severer scrutiny than the brutalities of Heathcliff. Nelly, that is, scarcely defines the normative in this novel, and her "disciplinary" tactics are secretive and troubling. In representing Nelly as both guardian and guard, *Wuthering Heights* questions persuasion as much as it does violence; just as houses keep turning into prisons, parental figures keep metamorphosing into prison guards. When Catherine Linton says, "The Grange is not a prison, Ellen, and you are not my jailer" (275), she is reflecting a troubling suspicion, shared by some critics, that Nelly is neither innocent observer nor nurturing nursemaid. It will be important to compare Nelly's coercion in the nurseries over which she presides with the pedagogic relationship that eventually sparks and sustains the relationship between Hareton and Catherine Linton Heathcliff, one that is allowed at last to form narrative resolution.

The debunking of discipline is equally evident in *Wildfell Hall,* for that novel refuses to endorse "restraint" as resolution. Excess may lead to disaster, but too much restraint is just as disturbing, as we have opportunity to observe in the pinched and lifeless portrayal of Helen's aunt. For her, love is war, and "when the citadel of the heart is fairly besieged, it is apt to surrender sooner than the owner is aware of, and often against her better judgment" (149). Her prescription for a sterile union that ignores the appetites of the body is rejected as soundly as is Huntingdon's abandonment to fleshly appetites, for this novel will not deny the body its place. Lord Lowborough is the novel's Victorian precursor to the recovering alcoholic, viciously addicted to his "hell-broth"; but the fearsome self-control he exercises over mind and body keeps him from drinking, only to suck the vitality from him as thoroughly as dissipation kills the out-of-control Huntingdon. Alternatively, Richard Wilson leads a "temperate" existence, but he pays a price for it. His self-improvements impoverish; like the overeager student, he lives with an internal taskmaster, and must lie about even in his free hours "with a pocket edition of some classic author in his hand. He never went anywhere without such a companion wherewith to improve his leisure moments. . . . [H]e could not abandon himself to the enjoyment of that pure air and balmy sunshine[,] . . . not even with a lady by his side. . . . [H]e must pull out his book, and make the most of his time while digesting his temperate meal" (89). Richard Wilson's "temperate meal" is as much disprized as is Huntingdon's stuffing himself with sensual pleasures. It is possible, that is, not only to be taken into custody as prisoner but also to be too much in possession of oneself.

"Custody" is rapidly assimilated, as if by necessity, into a discourse about guardianship, as the legal issues of Heathcliff's or Arthur Huntingdon's rights become intertwined with the caretaking functions of Nelly Dean or Helen Huntingdon. At the same time, the novels never cease being about incarceration. They are always poised between the enforcement of punishment and the perils of a course of self-directed regulation. These Brontës make it clear that the family is the inevitable, and indeed the most threatening, site for relations of power both direct and indirect. Not surprisingly, they introduce the idea of kidnapping frequently into their texts. Scenes of overt abduction reveal the covert power relations of domestic enclosures, and in exposing the inevitably violent nature of "custody," these scenes preserve the idea of the cell in the fantasy of the home.

Those power relations are not restricted to certain individuals. It is clear in Cathy's diary that Hindley is a tyrant well before Heathcliff takes up the role. The word "tyranny" is altogether a private affair in Brontë fiction. It conjoins connotations of revolution, absolute power, violent control, and political sovereignty with a notion of the inherent and un-resolvable power relations that exist within the family, as well as the dif-ficult position of any sovereign self. Lockwood reads Cathy's narration of Hindley's behavior: " 'You forget you have a master here,' says the tyrant. 'I'll demolish the first who puts me out of temper!' " (63). When Frances grows peevish, "Hindley became tyrannical" (87), and then, later, "The servants could not bear his tyrannical and evil conduct long" (106). Per-haps the most memorable use of the word is Heathcliff's, addressed to Cathy, concerning his dalliance with Isabella: "I seek no revenge on you. . . . That's not the plan—The tyrant grinds down his slaves—and they don't turn against him, they crush those beneath them. You are wel-come to torture me to death for your amusement, only, allow me to amuse myself a little in the same style" (151). In this passage, power, tyr-anny, and enslavement are entirely personal, enabling Heathcliff to con-fuse not only the public and the private but the relationship between love and violence as well. This is only one of many instances in which Heath-cliff is named "tyrant" (214), for he "amuses" himself in Cathy's style often, as when Nelly cannot "picture a father treating a dying child as tyrannically . . . as I afterwards learnt Heathcliff had treated" Linton (291). Eventually, Linton himself becomes "the little tyrant" (306), seizing the opportunity to take up like amusements.

Similarly, Helen writes of Arthur Huntingdon: "I would not submit to be tyrannized over by those bright, laughing eyes" (173). He becomes, in their courtship, "the reigning tyrant of [her] thoughts" (181). But Ar-thur, in turn, calls her "You little exorbitant tyrant" (247) and, a bit later, "my pretty tyrant" (269). After their marriage Helen discovers that, far from being a political property, tyranny can be exerted by the force of appetite itself: "His appetite for the stimulus of wine had increased upon him. . . . I succeeded in preserving him from absolute bondage to that detestable propensity, so insidious in its advances, so inexorable in its tyranny" (272). Finally, according to Helen, Arthur's parenting problems derive from the fact that his "selfish affection is more injurious than the coldest indifference or the harshest tyranny could be" (333). In *Wildfell Hall,* as in *Wuthering Heights,* the bloody revolution literally takes place at home, but no effective resistance, and certainly no solace, is successfully imagined.

The legislative reformers during the custody debates of the late 1830s envisioned liberation in political change. In refusing to allow social remedies into their fiction, the Brontës were writing against a general current of fiction and legislation during this period. In early Dickens, by contrast, individual failures appear remediable through social reform. Although *Oliver Twist* records the moral failures of characters like Monks as much as it describes the legislative failures of the new poor law, the 1837 novel has been taken as a polemic against Benthamite practices. The novel implies that the cruelties of Bumble or Mrs. Mann can be ameliorated under a better system. Indeed, it was used as a piece of anti–poor law propaganda when portions of the novel were printed in the *Times.* In later Dickens, for example in *Dombey and Son,* moral failings must be remedied in, or recuperated by, the family; but that family always functions in an oppositional relationship to civic or social forms that are preserved in the novel, though held at a distance. The happy home exists only by way of the unhappy "political" forms that oppose it. Social forms continue to be crucial throughout Dickens's work, and they continue to be subject to narrative critique—from the world of business and finance in *Dombey and Son* and in *Little Dorrit,* to Chancery in *Bleak House,* to the factory and schoolroom in *Hard Times,* or in any number of other examples that have earned Dickens the name of social novelist.

The Brontës take up social issues such as custody and inheritance only to reduce them to the purely private. It can be said, of course, that all novels proceed in this way; and indeed, the translation of public issues to private matters is the shift that makes discipline possible, in a Foucauldian reading of fiction. But the Brontës—Anne and Emily anyway—do more than merely demonstrate the greater persuasive powers of family over political governance. The law, it is true, is irrelevant, "delayed very late" (314) at Heathcliff's order. The family does not function in oppositional relationship to a heartless outside. Heartlessness always resides in, and can never be fully separated from, the haven itself.[9]

If bold recourse to the law is not only insufficient but is proved futile, and if the existence of institutions outside the purely domestic is ignored, then we might expect that a recuperated next-generation couple could serve as solace to a shattered family, and make nice the naughty injustices of the past in a comedic pairing. But the Brontë novels reveal marriage as inherently flawed, not just unredeemed but unredeemable. *The Tenant of Wildfell Hall* suggests that violence and cruelty are an inescapable part of coupling, and critics have often pointed out the clarity with which Anne Brontë seems to understand the brutalities of marriage.[10] Her portrayal of Arthur and Helen Huntingdon's courtship and marriage is a cutting analysis of relationships, it is true, but most readings of the novel have tended to see Brontë's fulminations against the couple as a critique of brutal masculinity and the socially informed power relations that give that brutality a legal and cultural sanction.[11] But *Wildfell Hall* does not, in fact, trace a causal relation between conjugal violence and masculinity. Cruelty in couples originates within the self; it emerges inevitably as a result of the individual appetites of men *and* women, and in fact it is the generating force that makes the individual possible. Male/female relationships here and in *Wuthering Heights* are conceived of as essentially sadomasochistic, but the positions within such a system function less as a critique of gender relations than as a comment on relations more generally.[12]

As much as marriage is represented as imprisonment in *Tenant,* for example, it is a prison created out of desire rather than enforced by a straightforward brutality. Helen's interest in Huntingdon emerges first as a direct result of the restraint she is under in her aunt's household, and among the likes of that very boring suitor, Boarham. Arthur Huntingdon, in all his "wildish" glory, represents "expansion to the mind, after so much constraint and formality as I had been doomed to suffer" (153). Helen's sexual desire is apparent, whether it is expressed by way of a certain religious zeal (167), or by the betrayal of her emotions by her body (164), or in the way in which the two continually spar verbally and physically. A powerful physicality defines Helen's relationship to Arthur Huntingdon; they cannot keep themselves to themselves. "I placed my hand on the portfolio to wrest it from him; but he maintained his hold. . . . I wrenched the portfolio from his hand" (176). Soon after, we learn that he "caught me in his arms, and smothered me with kisses" (184).

Pleasure is dependent upon cruelty, as we have seen in the frequently violent nature of erotic communion. Objects of love are eroticized in terms of violence, as when a courtship moment is enhanced by Hunting-don's coming in from a more conventional hunt "all spattered and splashed as he was, and stained with the blood of his prey" (177). But if the Huntingdon marriage can be characterized as fundamentally cruel, it must be acknowledged that the pain Helen endures she generously re-turns later, when she hounds Huntingdon on his deathbed. Thus, the nature of pleasure and cruelty is not rigidly gendered, or consistent.

Every brutal act that Huntingdon can be said to have offered Helen is eventually offered to him. Particularly in Huntingdon's decline, we witness a near-perfect reversal of the power relations that dominated their courtship. The literal restraints under which Huntingdon placed Helen become his own, as he gradually knows marriage to be a prison. As much as he attempts to hold Helen and to make her a captive (212), it is increas-ingly clear that he is the captive, and that it is his own imprisonment we witness. Helen is not above physical reinforcement of her ideas: "Don't be so hard upon me, Helen; and don't pinch my arm so, you're squeezing your fingers into the bone" (218). In their first quarrel she locks herself away from him, using imprisonment to deny him her body (223). Incar-ceration, that is to say, works both ways. If it can keep her in the house, it can also keep him from having access to her. "I was determined to show him," says Helen, "that my heart was not his slave" (223). Marriage be-comes "these mutually inflicted torments" (226), or as "comfortless as a convent cell" (349).

Increasingly, Helen's sanctimonious behavior and religious zeal re-semble an especially pointed kind of torture. The question of who is in power in the relationship emerges as a central one as Huntingdon begins to deteriorate and Helen preys upon his very body. In his feverish ram-blings, not unlike Cathy's in *Wuthering Heights,* Huntingdon himself seems to recognize, and recoil from, the source of his disease: " 'It is I, Arthur—it is Helen, your wife,' I replied. 'My wife!' said he, with a start—'For heaven's sake, don't mention her!—I have none.—Devil take her,' he cried, a moment after,—'and you too! What did you do it for?' " (428).

The man who had sought to satisfy every appetite is now unable to eat: "It is enough to poison one—eating such a disgusting mess!" (265). Nothing can help him, for he has "an infernal fire in [his] veins, that all the waters of the ocean cannot quench" (265). Overtaken by his appe-tites, Huntingdon's body deteriorates, and Helen presides somewhat gleefully over this process, making her statement, "I mean to stay with you" (429), sound more ominous than charitable. Like Cathy Linton, Huntingdon disincorporates, a victim of "mortification."

It would not be far wrong to say that, with Huntingdon imprisoned in bed, Helen virtually proselytizes him to death. She says that he makes a slave of her, in her caretaking capacity, but of course he is enslaved *by* her (438), reversing their relationship of earlier times. He is now a captive kept from seeing and owning his child. Asking for his son, Huntingdon is instructed that "you will not see him till you have promised to leave him entirely under my care and protection, and to let me take him away whenever and wherever I please. . . . I must have a written agreement, and you must sign it in presence of a witness" (431). The absolute power of male privilege and legal sanctions is not just overturned here; in addition, it is almost as if maternal custody is an established, even legal, fact. It is *Helen* who maintains control over the child and wields custody as a weapon; Helen who threatens and imprisons; Helen who tyrannizes over a helpless victim. And it is Arthur who will be made subject to a "written agreement."

Although novelistic closure is suggested in Gilbert's marriage to Helen, it is a qualified and conditional marriage made possible by the radical class difference. It is a union that barely manages to take place, and does so only after a protracted separation between the lovers, and a period of penance on Gilbert's part. And, as I argue in the conclusion of this chapter, Gilbert's marriage to Helen is more crucially concerned with establishing him as stepfather then marking him as husband.[13]

Gilbert Markham's likeness to Arthur Huntingdon is often elided in order to read into Brontë's ending a conditional conjugal equality, in order to make Anne Brontë's novel a protofeminist one. This understandable gesture—understandable because the novel *is* very much in contention with the social arrangements of its time and does bring gender into question in significant ways—does not always do service to the complexity of the narrative. Gilbert Markham is certainly opposed to Arthur Huntingdon. Gilbert is a farmer whom we often see bucolically at work in the fields or among his livestock, in contrast to Huntingdon's indolent lounging or aristocratic leisure pursuits (hunting animals, for example, rather than tending them as livestock). But Markham has throughout the novel maintained an undercurrent of volcanic fury that is often eroticized; he is not, after all, so different from Huntingdon. (This comes under some revision in the novel's ending, however, as we shall see.) Gilbert says of his younger self that he "had not acquired half the rule over my own spirit" (35) that might be wished, some evidence of which we have already seen. But he never fully achieves that rule. He is prone to outbursts, he spies on "Mrs. Graham" (124), he is vicious to his horse and physically abusive to Lawrence (whom he suspects of consorting with Helen) (134–35). As he himself says of his behavior toward Helen, "I secretly exulted in my power, [and] I felt disposed to dally with my victim like a cat" (143).

Even the love scene in which Markham and Helen are reunited after a long separation is another vision of torture, promising only "one long fever of restless terror and impatience" (487). Their "romance" suggests only a self-denying union with the other's body: "It would not be a separation: we will write every day; my spirit shall be always with you; and sometimes you shall see me with your bodily eye" (486). This kind of union had been prophesied earlier, in this couple's most charged and eroticized moment, which unsurprisingly is the moment of separation. Impassioned speeches escalate into a discussion of the possibilities for an otherworldly love that defies at least the corporeal boundaries of selfhood: "'We shall meet in heaven. Let us think of that,' said she, in a tone of desperate calmness; but her eyes glittered wildly, and her face was deadly pale. . . . 'It gives me little consolation to think I shall next behold you as a disembodied spirit. . . .' [I replied]. 'No, Gilbert, there is perfect love in heaven!'" (409). "One moment I stood and looked into her face, the next I held her to my heart, and we seemed to grow together in a close embrace from which no physical or mental force could rend us. A whispered 'God bless you!' and 'Go—go!' was all she said; but while she spoke, she held me so fast that, without violence, I could not have obeyed her" (411).

This episode recalls the famous one in *Wuthering Heights* in which Cathy and Heathcliff merge entirely, issuing in her death and their perpetual union in the grave and, in the supernatural sightings that close the book, out of the grave. Like *Wildfell Hall*, *Wuthering Heights* sees only the possibility of disincorporation in adult desire: "An instant they held asunder; and then how they met I hardly saw, but Catherine made a spring, and he caught her and they were locked in an embrace from which I thought my mistress would never be released alive" (197).

That this kind of coupledom does, in all its appetitive action, establish a kind of subjectivity in the novels is certainly arguable. Desire produces a self, it is true; the energy of *Wildfell Hall* provides us with the kinetic figures of Helen and Arthur Huntingdon, just as desire works to distinguish as well as to merge Heathcliff and Cathy in *Wuthering Heights*. But these appetitive selves show an alarming tendency to consume themselves. Heathcliff and Cathy disincorporate in their desire and, like the separation scene in *Wildfell Hall,* are disembodied spirits. Cathy is right when she tells Nelly, "I am Heathcliff," but it would be just as true to say that "Heathcliff is Cathy," and that neither of them is fully realized as a distinct self. If *Wildfell Hall* reveals that desire is at its most intense at the prospect of substituting the pleasures of the "bodily eye" for those of the body, and in reaching toward death and a "perfect love in heaven," *Wuthering Heights* focuses more closely on the devolution of the couple, as a result of appetite, into uncivilized, animalistic *consumers*. These beings ultimately can do little but cannibalize one another.

Heathcliff and Cathy lose themselves in turning into each other, as we have seen. But selves everywhere in the novel demonstrate a dangerous potential for devolving into animals, as when, in the merger scene quoted above, Catherine "made a spring," and soon Heathcliff "gnashed at me, and foamed like a mad dog" (197). Heathcliff is less and less a man in the aftermath of Cathy's death, as Isabella aptly notes when she insists, "He's not a human being" (209). Even Catherine Linton turns animal as she bites Heathcliff (302), and of course Hareton's uncivilized nature is animalistic, while Linton is no more than a "perishing monkey" (304). The kind of energy unleashed in these novels is sufficient to produce selves, but they are unstable and devolutionary. Heathcliff and Cathy are imagined as subjects mostly in relation to their merger with one another, their submission to desire; just as, by a converse but structurally similar logic, the hottest moments in *Wildfell Hall* are moments of separation. But when characters submit to their desires, those desires are likely to overtake them.

This produces in *Wuthering Heights* a literal disincorporation; Heathcliff and Cathy must die to be together. In *Wildfell Hall,* Anne Brontë produces a union desirable only in its unattainability. Once accomplished, it pales into platitudes, represented only in Gilbert's offhanded and terrifically bland epistolary account: "As for myself, I need not tell you how happily my Helen and I have lived and loved together, and how blessed we still are in each other's society" (490). Blessed, indeed: this is hardly the electrified atmosphere we witnessed earlier. But, perhaps by this time in the novel, if not in the history of the Novel, we do not need to be reminded that there is hardly any life, and certainly no liveliness, after marriage.

Thus, *Wuthering Heights* and *Wildfell Hall* would seem to demonstrate the impossibility of fully imagining independent selfhood. The world outside the familial enclosure has been erased: there is no school or church on the threshold of which a subject might form itself, or define itself against, in the way that, for example, the workhouse functions as a defining threshold in *Oliver Twist*. The institution is curiously but nevertheless entirely absent in Anne and Emily Brontë.[14] In other novels, the *outside* that makes the *inside* (by inside I mean both the self's interiority and the interior of the home) both safe and possible at last, in fiction like that of Dickens, is denied. The enclosure that is (all too) present—the family—has been identified as the site for the production of only devolutionary selves. Having made the training of desire, or the control of hunger, a purely private or familial affair, these novels would seem at last to have arrived at a dead stop.

How, then, do these Brontë fictions locate a stable subject in a world of self-consuming, self-destroying appetite? What being can register the importance of appetite and need but yet is not consumed by it? Who can be contained without revealing that containment as an unregenerated incarceration? Ultimately, both novels turn to the child-subject, abandoning hope in marital pedagogy in favor of child training. Childhood is narratively prized because it can resolve, even as it exposes, the problem of custody and appetite. Custodial care can be imagined as pedagogy, and desire as a hunger for knowledge. The child can be a desiring subject of a kind, but one who is also always in need of training. It is therefore true that while adult selves burn out, children are sustained by the necessity of remaining ever in training. Innocent of dissipating desire and elevated from the primitive through pedagogy, the client-subject represents a solution to the puzzle of subjectivity in the Brontës.

But by "children" these novels do not refer to the very young, or simply primitive. As if having taken the lessons of Rousseau's *Emile* in hand, *Wuthering Heights* especially distinguishes between the savagery of childhood and the later states of trainability. Cathy and Heathcliff, of course, are themselves always children, a child couple like the one that will finally replace them in the novel's conclusion. But Cathy and Heathcliff are ferociously hungry children who, in their perennially primitive state, never stop devouring. It is this savage and primitive version of childhood, continued in adult selves who were never properly reared by their custodial guardians, that is apparent in both novels as an unrestrained spirit that destroys matter as it defies it.

As desire disincorporates bodies, humans become animals or corpses. But they also come to resemble savage children. Huntingdon, for example, is represented as a product of mismanaged mothering, as when Helen says fairly early in their marriage that "his wife shall undo what his mother did" (191). The lack of training is evident when Huntingdon is seen as "lusty and reckless, as light of heart and head as ever, and as restless and hard to amuse as a spoilt child" (238). When Huntingdon looks upon his infant son, he sees in the baby what the reader sees in him, "a little selfish, senseless, sensualist" (255). In *Wuthering Heights,* adults never quite differentiate themselves from their savage childhood selves. Cathy pinches and hits Nelly in her young womanhood, and Nelly warns Edgar of her untrainability: "Miss is dreadfully wayward, sir! . . . as bad as any marred child" (112). Cathy can "beat Hareton, or any child, at a good passionate fit of crying" (125), and even in her last illness she is "no better than a wailing child" (162).

Linton cannot carry on, and must die off, too, because he is untrainable. Linton may be tortured into submission, but he is essentially and unchangeably defective. Heathcliff points this out, and asserts that Linton's value lies only in how he might be appropriated for the purposes of revenge. He has no "true" value, which comes to reside in Hareton, valued for his capacity to evolve, to learn, to become. This "evolution" happens without benefit of genetic contribution on the part of Heathcliff. Linton remains an infant—"writhing in the mere perverseness of an indulged plague of a child" (273)—who cannot develop or grow because he is a "defective character" (297). He is full of rage, and his breeding cannot keep him from a powerful fury that spends itself, turning him into a devolutionary problem. Catherine urges him uselessly, "Rise, and don't degrade yourself into an abject reptile—*don't*" (299). It is only a few pages later that he is described as "a perishing monkey" (304). Linton is certainly the most distressed of the needy children in these novels, but (like

Heathcliff when he first arrives at *Wuthering Heights*) his need is countered by his refusal or inability to be transformed into a victimized child-subject.[15]

Catherine and Hareton are children capable of appetite, but rather than devolving into uncivilized savages, or animals, or simply disincorporating, they are trained into selves that manage appetite. The importance of this capacity is reflected in the emphasis on child rearing throughout the novel. Heathcliff's treatment of Hareton entirely concerns Hareton's "uncivilized nature," and the possibility of demonstrating how thoroughly "nature" can be thwarted or proven wrong. Heathcliff prevents or artificially alters Hareton's progress: "Now, my bonny lad, you are *mine*! And we'll see if one tree won't grow as crooked as another, with the same wind to twist it!" (222). Hareton is made "the uncivil little thing" (252), and Heathcliff glories in his anti-training: "[H]e'll never be able to emerge from his bathos of coarseness, and ignorance. I've got him faster than his scoundrel of a father secured me, and lower; for he takes a pride in his brutishness. I've taught him to scorn everything extra-animal as silly and weak" (253). But Hareton *is* trainable, and it is that fact that determines his value.

In the novel's conclusion, of course, it is not Heathcliff but Catherine who tutors Hareton, in a pedagogic relation that must be distinguished from discipline; because unlike the "guardianship" of Nelly, this relationship is born of mutuality. Catherine's civilizing of Hareton means curbing his hungers, and turning the desire to eat into a hungering after literacy. Observing Hareton in the kitchen at the Heights, Catherine tells Nelly, "He's just like a dog, is he not, Ellen? . . . He does his work, eats his food, and sleeps, eternally! What a blank, dreary mind he must have!" (341). Hareton's dogged pursuit of "daily labour and rough animal enjoyments" (333) is replaced under Catherine's tutelage by an intense focus on literacy. As with the Monster in *Frankenstein,* or with Oliver Twist, or with the young paupers of James Kay's manual, the need to eat is translated into the desire to know. That transformation is signaled when Catherine first emerges from her isolation after Linton's death. Invited by Hareton to "come to the settle, and sit close by the fire; he was sure she was starved," Catherine responds scornfully, "I've been starved a month and more" (327), suggesting, as had her mother before her (126), that hunger might encompass more than bodily claims. Catherine, however, does not feed her appetite with the self-annihilating desire that turns her mother from matter into spirit. Instead, Catherine feeds her mind, a shift away from the body but pointedly not toward a disembodied self. In her isolation at the Heights, Catherine's "torment" is the loss of her books, the words of which are imprinted on her body: "I've most of them written on my brain and printed in my heart, and you cannot deprive me of those" (332). By contrast, it is the mark of Heathcliff that is imprinted on her mother's body. Cathy claims that Heathcliff can never be taken from her, however physically distant he might be, and Heathcliff cannot escape Cathy's words: "Do you reflect that all those words will be branded in my memory, and eating deeper eternally, after you have left me?" (196).

The suggestion that hunger surpasses the claims of matter is borne out as Catherine turns Hareton into a reader. It is obviously their shared examination of books, and the success of Catherine's program in literacy education, that signals the beginning of the change between them. As Nelly tells it: "[O]n looking round again, I perceived two such radiant countenances bent over the page of the accepted book, that I did not doubt the treaty had been ratified, on both sides, and the enemies were, thenceforth, sworn allied" (345). In the union of Catherine and Hareton, pedagogy functions in place of devouring desire. Love is still violent, or at least combative ("enemies"), but domesticated. The covert and coercive influence of Nelly Dean is replaced by the sparring of youthful lovers: "'Con-*trary*!' said a voice, as sweet as a silver bell—'That for the third time, you dunce! I'm not going to tell you, again—Recollect, or I pull your hair!' 'Contrary, then,' answered another, in deep, but softened, tones. 'And now, kiss me, for minding so well.' 'No, read it over first correctly, without a single mistake'" (338).

This both replaces the torture to which Catherine had subjected Hareton earlier, when she humiliated him for the lack of training he had suffered under Heathcliff, and domesticates the brutality that has thus far governed the novel.[16] The need for the proper pedagogy is articulated, oddly enough, by Lockwood, who warns Catherine that "we have each had a commencement, and each stumbled and tottered on the threshold, and had our teachers scorned, instead of aiding us, we should stumble and totter yet" (332).

It is mediated torture, and a more mutual one, partly made safe by the fact that neither Hareton nor Catherine need ever grow up. It is Nelly who points out how "in their several occupations, of pupil and teacher,"

Catherine and Hareton nevertheless "both appeared, in a measure, my children" (351). The violent flames that burned in the hearth of the Heights in times past are now the domestic illumination that allows the pursuit of learning and which light reveals only a limitless childhood: "The red fire-light glowed on their two bonny heads, and revealed their faces, animated with the eager interest of children; for, though he was twenty-three, and she eighteen, each had so much of novelty to feel, and learn, that neither experienced nor evinced the sentiments of sober disenchanted maturity" (352).

Wuthering Heights resolves the problem of custody in relocating the central novelistic subject in the pedagogical child couple. In *The Tenant of Wildfell Hall* tentative narrative closure is achieved in reinventing the custodial couple. Resolution, in *Wuthering Heights,* relies in part on its evacuation of all mothers, and in the disappearing of the act of mothering. Unlike most discourses, fictional and not, that we have examined throughout this book, Brontë fictions deny the idea of sentimentalized motherhood as a potential haven from imprisoning or tortuous antifamilial or institutional structures. While marriage might be seen elsewhere as a prison, the maternal is still a liberating space that can produce a viable subject.

In *Wuthering Heights* Catherine and Hareton are selves produced on the margins of, or in the space between, savagery and civilization, of liberty and imprisonment, and of discipline and torture. The individual members of the couple do not become disciplinary subjects, in part because they do not become adults. Unlike Dickens, where the carceral frights and Gothic horrors of the family are pushed off onto another class or an amoral male, the Brontës expose the violence of the family and conceive of that violence as productive of selfhood. These novels capitalize upon the restrictions family life increasingly poses. Mothering in *Wuthering Heights* is always an absence, or about to become one. It is Nelly who functions in the maternal role, but the peculiar nature of her "mothering" calls the role itself into question. If homes imprison, mothers do not, in this novel, liberate, as they appear to do in Dickens.

Nor can mothers offer freedom in *Wildfell Hall,* where mothering, in contrast to Emily Brontë's novel, is constantly before the reader rather than absent, and its dangerous properties anatomized in excruciating detail. *Wuthering Heights* removes its mothers, and *The Tenant of Wildfell Hall* vigorously disapproves of them. This is true even of Helen Huntingdon, who for all of her efforts on behalf of her beleaguered son, and in spite of her central role in the novel, does not become the exalted beacon of maternal plenitude one might expect.

The novel almost universally portrays motherhood as dangerous, never sanctified. Sanctimonious, yes, in Helen Huntingdon's religious policing of her little son; but this zeal is by no means approved. The problem with Helen's behavior, as the community sees it, is that "you will treat him like a girl—you'll spoil his spirit, and make a mere Miss Nancy of him" (55). Helen's response is an impassioned speech on the gendered nature of the family's teaching:

> You would have us encourage our sons to prove all things by their own experience, while our daughters must not even profit by the experience of others. Now I would have both so to benefit by the experiences of others. . . . I would not send a poor girl into the world unarmed against her foes. . . . [N]or would I watch and guard her, till, deprived of self-respect and self-reliance, she lost the power, or the will, to watch and guard herself;—as for my son—if I thought he would grow up to be what you call a man of the world—one that has "seen life," and glories in his experience. . . . I would rather that he died to-morrow!—rather a thousand times! (57)

The family is the place where gender difference is created. Through "protection" and "influence" a mother forms a daughter; but "making a man" of a boy is achieved by giving him a liberal hand.

Wildfell Hall, like *Wuthering Heights*, is preoccupied with the training of the child-in-custody. Like *Wuthering Heights*, it removes the child from the presumed safety of a "natural" family. Once remanded to a contrived "custody," the way is open for a microscopic investigation of the procedures of child rearing and pedagogy. This is evident in *Wildfell Hall* in the way that Helen's departure from her husband and her isolated retreat as a mother-in-hiding make possible the kind of critical scrutiny to which the community subjects her in the passage we have already examined.

But that scrutiny of child rearing is evident as an obsession at the moment of Arthur's birth, and even before it. Chapter 28, "Parental Feelings," is an extended pedagogical diatribe. Says Helen, "[T]hank

Heaven, I am a mother too. God has sent me a soul to educate for heaven" (252). Her work, as Helen conceives it, will be "to be his shield, instructor, friend—to guide him along the perilous path of youth, and train him to be God's servant" (252). Helen's "constant terror is, lest he should be ruined by that father's thoughtless indulgence" (256). Of course, Arthur senior is not without his views on the practices of child rearing. He tells his wife she is "not fit to teach children, or to be with them"; she has already "reduced the boy to little better than an automaton" (387). Mothering and fathering, and in fact all family life, is a matter of training and teaching, forming and reforming.

Wildfell Hall eventually obscures the difference between inflicting pain and teaching. To a great extent Helen's "torturing" of Arthur Senior resembles her "tutoring" of Arthur Junior. The differences between Helen and Heathcliff, Helen and Arthur Huntingdon, or Helen and Nelly Dean, in their caretaking roles, are perilously unstable. This is because *Wildfell Hall,* like *Wuthering Heights,* understands pedagogy in large part as the control of a literal appetite, a physical hunger that is also always the sign of a potential need—if left unchecked, it threatens to become a self-consuming and annihilating desire.

For Helen's most assiduous efforts to train little Arthur precisely concern his appetite. The Markhams are shocked to see little Arthur refuse wine "as if in terror and disgust . . . ready to cry when urged to take it" (53). Helen explains that he "detests the very sight of wine . . . and the smell of it almost makes him sick. I have been accustomed to make him swallow a little wine or weak spirits-and-water, by way of medicine when he was sick, and, in fact, I have done what I could to make him hate them" (53). We learn more of this interesting method later:

> *I exerted all my powers to eradicate the weeds that had been fostered in his infant mind, and sow again the good seed they had rendered unproductive. . . . I have succeeded in giving him an absolute disgust for all intoxicating liquors. . . . He was inordinately fond of them for so young a creature, and . . . I dreaded the consequences of such a taste. . . . Into every glass I surreptitiously introduced a small quantity of tartar-emetic—just enough to produce inevitable nausea and depression without positive sickness. Finding such disagreeable consequences invariably to result from this indulgence, he soon grew weary of it, but*

> *the more he shrank from the daily treat the more I pressed it upon him,*
> *till his reluctance was strengthened to absolute abhorrence. (375–76)*

This passage goes on at considerable length to describe in detail the bizarre course of training Helen undertakes to "secure him from this one vice" (376).

The tentative and peculiar solution the novel forges is to remove little Arthur from his father's custody, and to both give and refuse the mother's custodial care. In the end this novel, which is more directly concerned with the legislative acts of child custody than any other written in the first half of the century, circumvents politics to offer custody to a stepfather. Mistrusting motherhood as much as family, *Wildfell Hall* suggests that a child might need a mediating presence to protect him from his mother. That need is reflected in the novel's closure, which is achieved not by way of marriage, although there is one of those, but rather when masculinity is redefined as a resistance to desires that threaten self; when stepfatherhood becomes the approved mode, and one concerning literacy; and when custody, not only of the child but of narrative itself, is given over to that stepfather.

It is, in the end, Gilbert Markham who gets custody not only of little Arthur, but of the story of both Arthurs, of Helen, indeed of all the narrative. First, however, he must prove himself able to resist the temptations that confront him. Gilbert reforms during the period of his separation from Helen, especially when he manages to renounce his desire to hear news of Helen after she returns to nurse her husband. He does not beg Lawrence for news of her, "and departed with a cordial pressure of the hand. I posted the letter on my way home, most manfully resisting the temptation of dropping in a word from myself at the same time" (416). Gilbert's reform makes "manliness" a matter of resistance, and it enables him, in the end, to get the girl. More important, he gets the boy—custody of little Arthur.

While the couple at the end of *Wuthering Heights* are children, it is the child at the end of *Tenant of Wildfell Hall* that makes coupling possible, and that child remains central to the narrative. Arthur is present as an enabling force in the growing romance between Helen and Gilbert from the first, as when Helen allows Gilbert to penetrate her isolation "in spite of her prejudice" because, according to Markham, "between myself and my dog, her son derived a great deal of pleasure from the acquaintance

. . . [and] she ceased to object, and even welcomed my coming with a smile" (72–73). The child's role is made explicit when Gilbert says, "Dear Arthur! What did I not owe to you for this and every other happy meeting? . . . In love affairs, there is no mediator like a merry, simple-hearted child" (109).

The simple-hearted child serves such a role in ending the novel when he is the agent of closing the emotional and social gaps between the lovers ("'Why should I stay any longer?' 'Wait till Arthur comes, at least'" [484]). At last, Arthur and Gilbert engage in a scene of reading; Gilbert's domestication and fitness for fatherhood are signaled in his ability to contribute to Arthur's literacy: "'Look, Mr. Markham, a natural history with all kinds of birds and beasts in it, and the reading as nice as the pictures!' In great good humour, I sat down to examine the book and drew the little fellow between my knees. . . . I affectionately stroked his curling locks, and even kissed his ivory forehead: he was my own Helen's son, and therefore mine; and as such I have ever since regarded him" (487). Gilbert oversees little Arthur in his reading, and he reads Helen's diary and all the events of the story into the novel, thus controlling narrative altogether.

Gilbert and Helen *do* produce children of their own, ready and willing to be trained. The language Gilbert uses in ending *his* narrative will return us in closing to *Wuthering Heights:* "As for myself, I need not tell you how happily my Helen and I have lived and loved together, and how blessed we still are in each other's society, and in the promising young scions that are growing up about us" (490). The notion of a family as a productive garden recalls the words of Helen's diary, earlier, in which the contamination of the garden is threatened internally by "the weeds that had been fostered in [Arthur's] infant mind" (375). But it directs us also to the image that closes *Wuthering Heights,* of Hareton and Catherine domesticating the Heights in planting the garden, displacing Joseph's wild profusions, and formally marking the end of Heathcliff's reign. Hareton and Catherine in possession of one another, like little Arthur in the custody of Gilbert Markham, and like the unnamed offshoots of Helen's second marriage, are all, indeed, "scions," twigs grafted onto an older branch, new growth yet still inheritors of the past. And like the scion, the offspring here represent the possibility of a trained and trainable planting that nevertheless contains the seeds of its less controlled beginnings. The image, like *Wuthering Heights,* refigures the problem of heredity as a physiologic one. That is, it is important that Heathcliff's genetic material does not survive; there is a sense in *Wuthering Heights* and in *The Tenant of Wildfell Hall* that neither moral heredity nor economic inheritance is as significant as biology. It is to this notion of "grafting" that we now turn. For in George Eliot, the civilization of selves is accomplished not through moral will alone, but in relationship to physical "scions"—specifically, the bodies of Adam Bede and Dinah Morris.

IV

Civilization and Confession in
Midcentury Representations of
Infanticide and in *Adam Bede*

When the animals entered the Ark in pairs, one may
imagine that allied species made much private remark
on each other, and were tempted to think that so many
forms feeding on the same store of fodder were emi-
nently superfluous, as tending to diminish the rations.
(I fear the part played by the vultures on that occasion
would be too painful for art to represent, those birds
being disadvantageously naked about the gullet, and
apparently without rites and ceremonies.)

George Eliot,
Middlemarch

UNDER THE INFAMOUS tutelage of Monsieur Heger, Emily Brontë
composed a series of essays in 1842 as exercises in mastering a foreign
language. These French compositions, written while twenty-four-year-
old Emily and her sister Charlotte studied at Heger's Belgian *pensionnat,*
hint at concerns that Brontë amplified five years later when she came to
write *Wuthering Heights.* But the essays also contain the germ of ideas that
dominate George Eliot's early fiction as well as other midcentury discourse. Brontë's early essays, like *Adam Bede* and like other writing about
infanticide of the time, puzzle over their revelation of the base and potentially animalistic nature of human selves. Emily Brontë's lessons in
French, concerned as they are with violent natures and the violence of
nature itself, provide a bridge between *Wuthering Heights,* in which family
savagery is tamed pedagogically, and the related problems of "civilized"
and "instinctive" behavior, in relationship to the victimized child-subject
that determines the discourse of infanticide explored in this chapter.[1]

In the short schoolgirl narratives "L'Amour Filial" and "Le Papillon," Brontë portrays people as instinctual beasts, and offers up a natural world that is violent or at best indifferent. In "Le Papillon" the speaker enumerates the horrors of nature in relentless detail. Here, "Nature is an inexplicable problem; it exists on a principle of destruction." It is not only animals who must be prey or predator: "Every being must be the tireless instrument of death to others, or itself must cease to live," and men are no exception. The nightingale's song, for example, serves only to "guide the bullet to your breast or the child to your brood" (176).

In "L'Amour Filial" Brontë first asserts that parental affection is "a principle of nature" (156), something she demonstrates by comparing mothers to animals: "The doe does not fear the dogs when her little one is in danger; the bird dies on its nest." But this "instinct"—a word she uses repeatedly in the brief essay—is absent in ungrateful offspring when "the spark of heavenly fire dies out in their breast, leaving them a moral chaos without light and without order" (156). Both essays end ineffectually with swift recourse to a theology that does nothing to quell the doubts that suffuse the compositions. "Filial Love" urges the necessity of a menacing God who must threaten, for "it is through fear that the maniac must be forced to sanctify himself" (156). Even more bizarrely, "The Butterfly" seeks to quiet a destructive nature with the gentle ministrations of the gleaming insect who suddenly appears "like a censoring angel" (178). In both essays, not surprisingly, the heavenly "god of justice and mercy" (178) begins to resemble an apocalyptic nature a bit too red in tooth and claw: "[E]very grief that he inflicts on his creatures, be they human or animal, rational or irrational, every suffering of our unhappy nature is only a seed of that divine harvest which will be gathered when, Sin having spent its last drop of venom, Death having launched its final shaft, both will perish on the pyre of a universe in flames and leave their ancient victims to an eternal empire of happiness and glory" (178). These two essays form a pair insofar as both emphasize a fierce natural world whose properties are far more powerful, and whose destruction is far more random, than the spiritual forces meant to control it.

Apart from their considerable interest as underread elements of the slim Emily Brontë oeuvre, these essays are fascinating because, in her impotent assertion of faith in the face of an inevitable physical decay, Brontë sounds more like the Tennyson of "In Memoriam" than she does

Romantic precursors with whom she is often associated. But she differs from Tennyson in important ways. It is not mortality that troubles Emily Brontë; she seems ready enough, if not actually eager, to acknowledge the relentless operations of death. Rather, it is earthly relations between mortal creatures, human and animal, that are most troubling. Fish swallow flies, Brontë reminds us in "Le Papillon," and "These will become, in their turn, the prey of some tyrant of the air or water; and man for his amusement or his needs will kill their murderers" (176). Prominent in "L'Amour Filial" is "the baseness of our race" (156). Worst of all is the ungrateful child; "the virtuous soul does well to shun with horror" such "monsters" (156).

Reading the Belgian essays, one begins to suspect a secret admiration on Brontë's part for such "baseness," which—as Dorothy Van Ghent recognized when she called the characters in *Wuthering Heights* "elemental figures almost naked of the web of civilized habits" (154)—is finally more "natural" than the artificial and cloying flutterings of the "lustrous gold and purple" butterfly. In a third essay (chronologically the earliest of the surviving manuscripts), "Le Chat," Brontë comes closest to revealing the "base" concerns underlying her work. Employing a playful tone that wickedly compares felines to humans, Brontë can insist unequivocally that people are misanthropic, and that "civilized" behavior and minding one's manners is merely a method of manipulation. Unmediated by theology, Brontë's world is dominated by predators of little feeling. Speaking to an imaginary "delicate lady, who has murdered a half-dozen lapdogs through pure affection" (56–58), Brontë insists that people, like animals, torment their prey: "You yourself avoid a bloody spectacle, because it wounds your weak nerves. But I have seen you embrace your child in transports, when he came to show you a beautiful butterfly crushed between his cruel little fingers; and at that moment, I really wanted to have a cat, with the tail of a half-devoured rat hanging from its mouth, to present as the image, the true copy, of your angel" (58). The butterfly who will later appear as censoring angel is, in this less mannered composition, the victim of savage childhood. The savagery of untrained childhood, as argued in chapter 3, is at the heart of *Wuthering Heights*. Animals and children are alike in their lack of civility, and it is a failure of decorum Brontë comes very close to approving.

But Brontë's essays finally shy away from such approval in seeking

to resolve in theology what *Wuthering Heights* transforms by way of pedagogy: the animalistic nature of human beings. The French compositions
work a great deal like Hareton Earnshaw's labors over book-learning in
Wuthering Heights insofar as they are literacy exercises and lessons in ac-
culturation for the author herself. Emily Brontë is learning not only her
(French) lessons but her manners as well. In the Belgian essays, Brontë
tames her writing over time, moving from a certain celebration of the
animal to a tacit endorsement of more civilized behavior. In May, when
she wrote "The Cat," children are savage; but by August, their savagery
is punished by a menacing god. Half-child herself, Emily Brontë's linguistic advancement is the pedagogical moment that trains her prose,
however inadequately. As Hareton's reading soothes the savage beast in
him, Emily Brontë's writing at least appears to be a softening of her conception of the natural cruelty of children and of the havenless home.

   Just as the Belgian essays eventually erase the savagery of persons that
the essays themselves inscribe, *Wuthering Heights* closes with a scene of
reading that promises more civilized familial relations in the future; with
the death of Heathcliff and the education of Hareton, animalistic and
primitive behaviors promise to recede. As a text concerned with the
"evolution" of human beings, *Wuthering Heights* is perhaps best seen in
the reflected light of Eliot's evolutionary account of self and society in
Adam Bede. In interesting contrast to Brontë, George Eliot's *Adam Bede*
not only admits but actively celebrates the animal. Comparing the two
novels, it is more possible to see the ways in which Emily Brontë, so often
imagined as a weird sister of the moors, and whose work (beginning with
her sister Charlotte's romanticized account of Emily in her 1850 preface
to *Wuthering Heights*) is sometimes said to defy social norms, might be
seen as a normalizing presence when compared to George Eliot. And
Eliot, in her turn, frequently characterized as the sober realist and moral
voice of Victorian fiction, can be understood—at least in her relation to
animalistic and primitive selves—as a champion of the "elemental" and
uncivilized selves who must die in *Wuthering Heights*. The sometime portrayal of these women as nineteenth-century figures of intellectual sobri-
ety (Eliot) and half-mad utterances (Brontë) is undermined.

   In contrast to Emily Brontë's work both in *Wuthering Heights* and in
her Belgian essays, George Eliot claims neither literacy nor theology as
civilizing forms. In fact, Eliot does not quite argue for the "civilizing" of

primitive selves at all, for in *Adam Bede* and in Eliot's own essays of the time (particularly her essay on Riehl), civilizing forces are understood to be the distorting institutional structures of the state. Eliot writes in direct opposition to reformers who participate in the proliferating discourse of infanticide discussed below, and whose efforts to civilize criminal mothers materialize as social reform projects sponsored by the state. Eliot articulates instead an evolutionary narrative that functions both at the level of social organisms and individual selves. But *Adam Bede* and social reform discourse are alike in at least one respect: for each, the narrative of infanticide is organized around the idea of confession—though confession is understood rather differently in Eliot's fiction.[2]

Lessons of Mercy

The mid-Victorian period saw the proliferation of a massive discourse about infanticide. Even in the absence of any persuasive evidence that infanticide was actually on the rise, reformers of all sorts wrote as if child murder were taking place not just daily, but hourly. The notion of civilizing barbaric selves played an important role in the burgeoning discourse of infanticide developing during the same period Brontë and Eliot were writing, for mid-Victorian infanticide discourse insisted upon an implied relationship between child murder and the failure of civilization. Take, for example, the exhortations of Dr. Edwin Lankester: "It undoubtedly suits the purpose of some writers to draw a veil over this crime, and to endeavor to blind the eyes of the public to the foul blot it is in the eyes of the world on our boasted morality and civilisation; but it is for those who are anxious to maintain the honor of our nation to seek by all means to prevent this crime" (221). To be moral and civilized, he suggested, requires attention to the "foul blot"; moreover, it is "morality and civilisation" that are at risk.[3]

 Or, outside the field of medicine, consider the more popular *Saturday Review,* which deplored the "system of infanticide" in baby-farming, claiming that it "must, from the nature of the case, argue a very debased stage of public morality. It is the characteristic at once of the rudest barbarism and of that more terrible epoch of national life when the wheel has gone its full circle, and society falls to pieces by the vices of civilization. A Bushman or a Patagonian may be almost pardoned for killing his infant, where the necessaries of life are scanty; and if Mr. Darwin's theory of the struggle for existence is really a natural law, there may be cases and places where infanticide becomes comparatively venial, because in some sort unavoidable" (5 August 1865, 161). The *Review* thus reinforced the connection between infanticide and a demoralized and uncivilized nation, even as it brought the drama of evolution into relationship with the idea of civilization.

The uncivilized perpetrators of this great crime were women—specifically, women of the servant class. The paradigmatic infanticidal mother was described by A. Herbert Safford in discussion during a meeting of the National Association for the Promotion of Social Sciences (NAPSS): "It may be said that I am reasoning as if the women most liable to be tempted to infanticide were of one class. I believe they are. . . . I believe that with very few exceptions—in fact, scarcely one—the women accused of child-murder are domestic servants" (*Transactions* 1869, 226). But despite the specificity with which nineteenth-century writers identified the criminal as female, mid-Victorian writing about infanticide—in contrast to both the juridical and the sentimental approaches of earlier periods—is only superficially interested in women. Nineteenth-century writing about infanticide is characterized instead by an effort to widen the scope of the crime, and to see it as a social evil shared communally, across class and gender lines. An individual or private guilt is assigned to the servant girl presumed to have done the deed, but the idea of a social confession takes precedence over any private admission of guilt. In this sense, the notion of civilization is given broader meaning. What is more, the resistance toward recognizing affinity seen in earlier writing discussed in this book—the railroad laborer, the child pauper, the wet nurse—has now apparently undergone a shift. The figure of the Malthusian male, at least in discussions of child murder, has begun to fade.[4]

Consider W. B. Ryan's 1862 essay, "Infanticide: Its Law, Prevalence, Prevention, and History," and its lurid and sensational description of English life:

> *The feeble wail of murdered childhood in its agony assails our ears*
> *at every turn, and is borne on every breeze. The sight is horrified as,*
> *day after day, the melancholy catalogue of murders meets the view, and*

we try to turn away the gaze in hope of some momentary relief. But turn where we may, still we are met by the evidence of a wide spread crime. In the quiet of the bedroom we raise the box-lid, and the skeletons are there. In the calm evening walk we see in the distance the suspicious-looking bundle, and the mangled infant is within. By the canal side, or in the water, we find the dead child. In the solitude of the wood we are horrified by the ghastly sight; and if we betake ourselves to the rapid rail in order to escape the pollution, we find at our journey's end that the mouldering remains of a murdered innocent have been our travelling companion; and that the odour from that unsuspected parcel truly indicates what may be found within. (qtd. Behlmer, "Deadly Motherhood" 404)

The mid-Victorian "sensation" over infanticide is literally registered in the senses of the bourgeois bystander, whose refusal to face the truth is belied by his neurotic inability to sidestep it. Not merely a discoverer of evil, the average citizen virtually produces dead babies wherever he goes. He not only finds these bodies, but he must endure a sensory assault, experiencing the horror of child murder as physiological sensation, in his own body. Entirely absent here is the murdering mother, and agency is postponed in the ambiguous way that "we" is gradually implicated in the ubiquity of the "wide spread crime." Guilt is transferred, by the close of this passage, from the absent perpetrator to the obviously, if peculiarly, responsible party who tries hopelessly to escape his fault.

Ryan's essay is exemplary of the impulse toward social guilt and responsibility in relation to infanticide that is more fully developed as social confession in philanthropic discourse, specifically in John Brownlow's *The History and Objects of the Foundling Hospital*. Brownlow tells the story of the seduced young servant girl to emphasize her shame, but even more powerfully he wants to suggest that all society is responsible. He argues that society is liable for the conditions that make her degradation possible, and that society itself, particularly male society, must own its guilt. Brownlow promotes what he calls a "lesson of mercy" emerging out of the horror of child murder. This lesson must be practiced because "misery . . . has its origin in the moral weakness of our nature" (27). In other words, mercy has benefits for the middle-class philanthropist, whatever its merits in helping the outcast woman.[5]

According to Brownlow, mercy begins with the biblical injunction that only those without sin cast the first stone. He insists upon the shared guilt, the generalizable nature of the infanticidal mother's transgression: "It may be asked, then, where is the man, imbued with Christian charity, who is prepared to take up the stone, and fling it at the poor victim of unprincipled seduction and brutal desertion? Is he ready to bear in like manner the consequences of his own guilt, and to go down the stream of life with her in her shattered bark?" (28). The message for Brownlow in the deserted and murdering mother has less to do with infanticide, and in fact less to do with women at all, than it has to do with defining a generalizable social shame and culpability.

As with Ryan's essay, there is a gradual slippage between the guilty perpetrator and all society, signaled here also in the curious use of "we":

Alas! the descent from virtue to vice is so easy, that but one step inter-venes between them: and often, when we think we are secure, our foot slips, and we are involved in all the misery and degradation of sin! This is the fate of us all: 'tis the fate of him who proudly glories in his recti-tude; for what is the moral history of a man's life? 'Tis but a succession from virtue to vice, from vice to repentance. Shall man, then, who is so weak as not to be able to sustain his own virtue, withhold from a wretched woman, who by wily arts has been deceived, that compassion for her error which he requires for himself? (29)

Brownlow's text seeks to locate guilt in "the public mind," rife with its "morbid morality," and thus establishes a genuine, if limited, "mutual affinity" between the criminal mother and the middle-class male.

One of the effects of producing a social confession is to imagine a more or less Darwinian affinity between the individual, understood as the infanticidal mother, and society, understood as the benevolent man. Such is one aim of Brownlow's text. It should not be surprising that such a strong assertion of social guilt came from a source explicitly concerned to promote an institution: the London Foundling Hospital. Once all so-ciety is at fault, social intervention is almost a given. This is to say, then, that the narrative of infanticide as it was told in the nineteenth century forges a link between specific acts of violence and a generalizable social guilt and therefore responsibility. It is this discourse of responsibility and affinity that results in a conviction that social responsibility requires in-tervention. It is affinity, and not the notion of a despised "other," that authorizes intervention; just as it is a shared humanity, articulated in a certain liberal stance not unlike that demonstrated by William Acton in roughly the same period, discussing wet nurses, that serves as justification for social solutions. State intervention is called for not because criminal or debased others outside society must be contained. On the contrary, institutions promise to minister to those who have fallen on the slippery slope between virtue and vice—a slip possible for all.

Among social scientists and reformers, consequently, there was a strong call for legislative regulation and institutionalization. J. Brendan Curgenven, Secretary of the Harveian Society, called for "the registration of all nurses having the care of illegitimate children, and the placing them under the supervision of the Poor Law medical officers of the districts in which they reside" (*Transactions* 1867, 531). He also demanded a stricter accounting of registration of births and accounting for the illegitimate child, and a state system for dealing with foundlings, as well as for maternity hospitals. Finally, he approved of elaborate measures for dealing with abandoned children. In an 1869 Bristol meeting, Herbert Safford called not for greater punishment of the crime, but for "an Act of Parliament . . . authorising charitable societies to receive illegitimate children and to proceed before a magistrate against both the fathers and the mothers for their support" (*Transactions* 1869, 209). Dr. Elizabeth Blackwell saw reform as the solution: "[G]reat advantage arises from the establishment of private charities to meet the cases of these poor women" (*Transactions* 1867, 213).

Societal intervention is soon made an explicit goal. In discussion of "endangered" children, Barwick Baker said in 1869: "I would have it clearly understood that the child should be entirely separated from its father and mother and brought up as a child of the State, with a payment from the father and the mother" (*Transactions* 1869, 211). At the same meeting Mr. Aspland urged, "The medical officer in every suspected case of death should go to the house and make careful inquiries; and were it known by the public that this was to be the course of procedure in such cases, and if in establishing this system a public prosecutor were to be appointed, you would create machinery by which you would be able to deal with these people" (*Transactions* 1869, 213). NAPSS members are "of the opinion that asylums for the reception of pregnant single women would prevent to a certain extent, the crime of infanticide, and that such asylums should be established, and receive authority from the state to proceed against parents for the maintenance of the children" (*Transactions* 1869, 217). Infanticide was thus separated from a discourse of individual guilt and criminality and was invented instead as a widespread *social* problem. As part of this process the social investigators eagerly took up child murder as a cause. Their emphasis and recommendations, in the main, sought a greater direct intervention into private life, particularly the private life of the poor.

Infanticide discourse produced not only or even especially a mother or a female perpetrator but, most importantly, a victimized child subject—one who happens to be a corpse. The dead child ideally represents a subjectivity that is both determined and independent, because the murdered or unborn child, as publicly imagined by reformers, can never fully occupy a position in society; it exists, in death, as a kind of perpetual reminder of the potential for life, a perpetual marker for a selfhood that can never be marred by the dividing social categories of class or gender. Although dead—or perhaps because of it—the murdered child is constantly produced as an important "citizen," even as an indispensable self. Arguably, because it can never display anything but perfect innocence, compliance, and, in its helpless state just prior to abandonment, the need for social intervention, it is the dead child who is the most perfect Victorian subject.

This plasticity, the way in which the victim of infanticide can be both sovereign and socially enmeshed, may account for the tremendous fascination with child murder at midcentury. Like the fetus among twentieth-century opponents of abortion, this dead child is a figure for the potentiality for life itself. In Victorian terms, the murdered child, or the endangered bastard, is simultaneously a unique self and a "citizen"—he or she is preeminently a social self related to all, suggesting mutual affinity across class boundaries even while preserving borders in the emphasis on servant-class perpetrators.

The child victim served to advance state apparatus and social intervention in the name of the British child. The mother is relatively unimportant; her confession is replaced by a society-wide expression not just of guilt but of responsibility. If individual guilt required social confession, this social confession requires a social and institutional intervention. Civilizing means, at least in part, institutionalizing. But in George Eliot, the mediation of individual guilt through social shame and responsibility is insufficient; the intervention of the state is actively despised. Eliot embraces her own version of instinct and civilization in her discussion of infanticide—but she uses it to resist state intervention by suggesting that change happens over time, happens "in the body," and defies both speech and social practice—her theory of a history that is "incarnate." In George Eliot's work there is no true child-subject because, unlike most of her contemporaries discussed thus far, she finds no solution in the social.

Confessional Instincts

The impulse to confession almost always requires the presence of a fresh ear and a fresh heart; and in our moments of spiritual need, the man to whom we have no tie but our common nature, seems nearer to us than mother, brother, or friend.

George Eliot, "Janet's Repentance"

In earlier chapters of this book, to be "beastly" has been associated with threatening others, whose hungers must be recognized and tamed. Recall the primitive Heathcliff, Mary Shelley's monstrous creation, or the "brute-like" laborer in John Francis's *History of the English Railway.* Even more commonly, despised others have been cast as canine: Ruskin urges the poor to claim their rights "as children, not as dogs"; Oliver Twist is seen, before his decontaminating sojourn among the middle classes, "clutching at the dainty viands that the dog had neglected," and is referred to as "you young dog!" (157); Sikes is associated with the dog whose name is mindful of the violence of which his monstrous master is capable; and Emily Brontë's Hareton Earnshaw, before undergoing his literacy lessons, is to the second Catherine "just like a dog, is he not, Ellen?" (341). It is the transformation from animalistic, especially canine, beings into literate and feeling selves that "humanizes" these beasts—or, significantly, fails to do so.[6]

But in *Adam Bede,* there are no hungering bodies, large or small, deserving or otherwise. For a work touted as a harbinger if not an exemplar of English realism, Eliot's first full-length novel is remarkably immaculate of the gritty facts of starvation that inform much earlier writing. Among the gentry of *Adam Bede*'s parish setting, food is an ornament to conversation, confession, and even financial transaction. Hunger has no home in Hayslope. As Arthur imagines when he heads to the Reverend Irwine's to confess his attraction to Hetty, "One can say everything best over a meal" (207). Indeed, the "progress of civilisation has made a breakfast or a dinner an easy and cheerful substitute for more troublesome and disagreeable ceremonies," and in fact, "for gentlemen in an enlightened age . . . mortal sin is not incompatible with an appetite for muffins" (207). Even, or perhaps especially, among the peasantry, at Mrs. Poyser's harvest supper, the celebration of food is pastorally conceived; it speaks of community more loudly than appetite. This is so much the case that Adam, as he travels toward the "sacred song" of the harvest and food, associates appetite with love, not with the victuals that await him: his misfortunes "left me with a greater need, so as I could crave and hunger for a greater and a better comfort" (559)—a comfort that is, of course, Dinah Morris herself. Even the workers join in the celebration of bucolic rites, Tom Tholer holding his knife and fork erect "as if they had been sacred tapers" (560). Not only at the communal table, but in the fields as well, these laborers are nothing like the animalistic workhouse paupers at Andover, described in chapter 1, or the devouring railroad workers whom John Francis deplored (chapter 2). Instead these docile fellows eat under the hedgerows "with relish certainly, but with their mouths towards the zenith, after a fashion more endurable to ducks than to human bipeds" (560).[7]

In *Adam Bede,* hunger bespeaks community, in a manner quite opposite to earlier writing discussed in these pages, where an emphasis on Malthusian tensions meant that a shared repast revealed only the dangers inherent in recognizing common ground. Like the concern for social guilt in the discourses of infanticide, Eliot's repeated comparisons of persons to animals underscore, ironically, a shared humanity rather than the presence of a monstrous Other. Almost no one escapes comparison to beasts, especially to farm animals and to the gentler creatures of the English countryside. A laborer presents "a slow bovine gaze" (63), Sandy Jim calls his son a "gallows young dog," prompting Chad Cranage's offer to "tie 'm up an' shoe 'm as I do th' hosses" (65). Seth Bede is like "a lamb" (66), as is Hetty (78) and even Dinah (156). Dinah is also a "cade lamb" (156) and "like the birds o' th' air," while the people of Stoniton are "like poultry a'scratchin' on a gravel bank" (121–22). Lisbeth Bede is like "a wounded dog" (152). The Stoniton men carry babies "as if they were no heavier than little birds" (187). To Hetty, children are "buzzing insects" (200). The Poyser boys, in a rare mention of exotic beasts, are like elephants (232, 521); at another point they are "a couple of spaniels or terriers" (237). Bartle Massey compares women to "water-grubs" and "stinging gnats" (285). He excoriates his dog Vixen, but compares himself to her (463). Meanwhile, Wiry Ben is a "dancing monkey" and a "mad grasshopper" (324). As for "gentlefolks's servants—they're mostly like the fine ladies' fat dogs, nayther good for barking nor butcher's meat, but on'y for show" (338). Adam is like "a patient trembling dog" (399). One might go on for pages: Bessy Cranage is a dog (519); Methodists are bats (522); a child is like "a little dog" (548); and Mrs. Poyser is "as uneasy as a new-sheared sheep" (524).[8]

Not surprisingly, animals themselves are frequently represented. As James Eli Adams has argued, in *Adam Bede* animals—especially dogs, and most especially Adam's dog Gyp—are the models for behavior, with the elaborate exception of Bartle Massey's much-maligned Vixen. These two dogs take a star turn; but in addition there are Irwine's canine brood, Arthur's whelps, and Mr. Poyser's "booming bark[ing] . . . dogs" (115). Everywhere one turns, an animal of some sort yips or leaps or lumbers. Mr. Irwine rises on his "grey cob, with his dogs running beside him" (113); at the Hall Farm the "yellow-billed ducks" compete in a concert with "the unwary approach of a cock," and the calves and the "sow with her brood" join in (116–17). No visit to the Bede household can be accomplished, of course, without some canine commentary by Gyp. The physical locations of the novel are generally defined by their animal populations—and the more creatures, the better. Thus, the Hall Farm is the most prized because most bucolic, and animal-friendly, setting of all.

But although people are positively compared to animals, and although the presence of animal life in the novel signals a certain (artificial) "naturalness" in the world, it will not escape the reader's notice that the gentrified world of the Donnithornes and Irwines is far less infused with the animalistic than are the lesser homes and work places of Hayslope. Perhaps this is appropriate in a novel with pastoral impulses; after all, the pastoral classically deals with the lower ranks, from the shepherds of Theocritus perhaps even to the Solitary Reaper and the weaver of Raveloe. But Eliot's first novel is hardly classic pastoral. Although it at times borrows from a Wordsworthian view of nature, as critics have noted, *Adam Bede* is always simultaneously concerned with an evolutionary perspective on nature. And, too, the very ubiquity of so much brute creation might suggest the fecundity and teeming life of Darwin, not to mention the interdependent nature of life as it exists upon the "tangled bank." *Adam Bede* is set at almost the precise moment at which the *Lyrical Ballads* appeared; but it was written in the year that *On the Origin of Species* was first published.⁹

In Eliot, pastoralism is always set in relationship to a less civilized nature, and the pastoral community is frequently in competition with an indifferent and destructive nature—just as, in Emily Brontë's Belgian essays, "natural" filial affection is belied by a predacious instinct. Almost as if to assert a Tennysonian Nature "careful of the type" yet so "careless of the single life," Eliot's narrator underscores the indifference of nature: "For if it be true that Nature at certain moments seems charged with a presentiment of one individual lot, must it not also be true that she seems unmindful, unconscious of another? . . . There are so many of us, and our lots are so different: what wonder that Nature's mood is often in harsh contrast with the great crisis of our lives? We are children of a large family, and must learn, as such children do, not to expect that our little hurts will be made much of—to be content with little nurture and caressing, and help each other more" (338). The ungrateful offspring who embodies brutishness in Emily Brontë's youthful essay has no role here; in this novel, Nature herself is represented as an uninterested parent, less cruel than perpetually neglectful.¹⁰

At another point, the narrator mocks the notion of a kindly and benevolent Nature, showing how it is always *people* who insist upon the idea of a natural world that is in concert with our desires. The young man in love foolishly "considers himself an adept in [Nature's] language," but we soon know that this is an error: "Nature has her language, and she is not unveracious; but we don't know all the intricacies of her syntax just yet, and in a hasty reading we may happen to extract the very opposite of her real meaning" (198–99). In fact, the narrator tells us, the physical qualities for which Nature is responsible must be read as purely biological elements:

> *Long dark eyelashes, now: what can be more exquisite? I find it impossible not to expect some depth of soul behind a deep grey eye with a long dark eyelash, in spite of an experience which has shown me that they may go along with deceit, peculation, and stupidity. But if, in the reac-*

tion of disgust, I have betaken myself to a fishy eye, there has been a surprising similarity of result. One begins to suspect at length that there is no direct correlation between eyelashes and morals; or else, that the eyelashes express the disposition of the fair one's grandmother, which is on the whole less important to us. (199)

The intricacies of Nature's language are more subtle in their science—one face expressing the biological inheritance of another—than in their poetry. This passage can be compared to the emphasis on faces in *Oliver Twist,* discussed in chapter 1. For Dickens, features are both biologically inheritable and also truthful indicators of inner selves; in other words, in *Oliver Twist* there is a reliable connection between eyelashes and morals.

In *Adam Bede,* both Adam and Arthur are fooled by nature, believing that "Nature has written out his bride's character for him in those exquisite lines of cheek and lip and chin" (198). Both men believe Hetty must be good because . . . well, she looks so good. Eliot repeatedly points out that nature allows appearance to be at odds with an internal state (245). Although there are lengthy passages of Romantically influenced descriptions of the countryside, these are often punctured by a revelation of their falsity. A vision of the "parting crimson glory of the ripening summer sun," "the flower-sprinkled tresses of the meadows," (62) and the peaceful village is laid before the admiring eyes of the stranger on horseback at the beginning of the novel. But the narrator almost immediately critiques the stranger's perspective when that stranger observes of Dinah a few pages later that "nature never meant her for a preacher." Eliot's narrator remarks, "Perhaps he was one of those who think that nature has theatrical properties, and, with the considerate view of facilitating art and psychology, 'makes up' her characters, so that there may be no mistake about them" (67).

In its portrayal of the natural world and especially its relationship to social rank, *Adam Bede* presents an evolutionary view unique to Eliot, and indebted to the insights of her 1856 essay, "The Natural History of German Life," in which she puts forward the idea that the pastoral view of peasantry is deeply flawed precisely because such a view imagines that nature has theatrical properties that will serve an art opposed to realism: "The painter is still under the influence of idyllic literature, which has always expressed the imagination of the cultivated and town-bred, rather than the truth of rustic life. Idyllic ploughmen are jocund when they drive their team afield; idyllic shepherds make bashful love under haw-thorn bushes; idyllic villagers dance in the checquered shade. . . . But no one who has seen much of actual ploughmen thinks them jocund; no one who is well acquainted with the English peasantry can pronounce them merry" (109).[11]

Such falseness is to be despised because it is divisive; art can, and Eliot insists it must, express the mutual affinity between persons. In the "realistic" work of Scott, Kingsley, and others, "[M]ore is done towards linking the higher classes with the lower, towards obliterating the vul-garity of exclusiveness, than by hundreds of sermons and philosophical dissertations. Art is the nearest thing to life; it is a mode of amplifying experience and extending our contact with our fellow-men beyond the bounds of our personal lot" (110). Eliot singles out for special dishonor-able mention Dickens's "frequently false psychology, his preternaturally virtuous poor children" (111).[12]

Attending to the truth of rustic life means, above all, to be able to read Nature's syntax in the physical characteristics of the peasant. For while facial features cannot, for Eliot, reflect individual moral propensi-ties, physical selves are reflective of cultural types. In Germany, for ex-ample, the peasants still evoke "the historical type of the national *phy-sique*" (114). Of course, it is not just in their bodies that rustics retain the past; in their clinging to tradition they are also the unwitting bearers of the historical origins of a given culture. The peasantry of Germany, in Eliot's reading of Riehl, is governed by heredity and not by will. Even their clinging to the past is a matter of instinct rather than passion: in the Wetterau, the peasant preserves the "thick fur cap, because it is an his-torical fur cap—a cap worn by his grandfather" (116). But he is perfectly willing to "[tear] down the gothic carving of the old monastic church . . . to mark off a foot-path through his field" (118).

If the peasant is not sufficiently evolved to understand the culture that he nevertheless so thoroughly represents, or at any rate embodies, the solution is vehemently not the imposition of state power and inter-vention. "Disintegrating forces" are destroying the peasant, and "degen-eration is unhappily going on at a greater pace than development" (121). Among these forces are the advances of a market economy and an in-crease in government intervention. Attempts to sophisticate the peasantry with political theory have a worse effect, for "The coarse nature of the peasant has here been corrupted into bestiality by the disturbance of his instincts" (125). Proper development is accomplished over time, and indeed it is a *physical* process, as Eliot describes it in her interpretation of Riehl:

> [Riehl] sees in European society incarnate history, *and any attempt to disengage it from its historical elements must, he believes, be simply destructive of social vitality. What has grown up historically can only die out historically, by the gradual operation of necessary laws. The external conditions which society has inherited from the past are but the manifestation of inherited internal conditions in the human beings who compose it; the internal conditions and the external are related to each other as the organism and its medium, and development can take place only by the gradual consentaneous development of both.* (127)

Although the notion of "incarnate history" is not made entirely clear, it might usefully be connected to Eliot's discussion of the national "physique" embodied by the European peasant. Eliot is describing—even as she, in her words, "interprets" Riehl—an evolutionary process in which "external conditions" can be altered through "inheritance" and "gradual . . . development." [13]

Adam Bede can be read as an extended meditation on Riehl's ideas, and as an expression of not only Riehl's, but Eliot's, belief that "The nature of European men has its roots intertwined with the past, and can only be developed by allowing those roots to remain undisturbed while the process of development is going on, until that perfect ripeness of the seed which carries with it a life independent of the root" (129). *Adam Bede* returns to the (rural) past, and to the parish, as opposed to larger bureaucratic units that dominated later Victorian society, to retrieve the peasant, and to propose an alternative evolution.[14]

Adam, whose name not only forms the title but announces the importance of a "new man" to this novel, will be the agent whose body carries within it the "perfect ripeness of seed" that can advance the "gradual consentaneous development" of society. Adam's fitness for the job is demonstrated in Eliot's loving attention to the details of her protagonist's corporeal self: "[T]he broad chest belonged to a large-boned muscular man nearly six feet high, with a back so flat and a head so well poised that when he drew himself up to take a more distant survey of his work, he had the air of a soldier standing at ease. The sleeve rolled up above the elbow showed an arm that was likely to win the prize for feats of strength; yet the long supple hand with its broad finger-tips, looked ready for works of skill" (50).

As if the power of his muscles and strength of will were not enough, Adam also manifests an embodied connection to England's deep historical past: "Adam Bede was a Saxon, and justified his name; but the jet-black hair, made the more noticeable by its contrast with the light paper cap, and the keen glance of the dark eyes that shone from under strongly marked, prominent, and mobile eyebrows, indicated a mixture of Celtic blood" (50). This worthy body, once it is united with Dinah's at novel's end, promises to overturn the degeneration evident among the gentry and the clergy. That other members of the lower ranks are not yet suitable candidates for this program of gradual change is suggested in the narrator's description of Bartle Massey's pupils in their attempts to become literate: "It was almost as if three rough animals were making humble efforts to learn how they might become human" (281).[15]

Although Arthur Donnithorne's handsome looks and heartiness suggest good, strong stock—not to mention the kingly and nation-building associations of his first name—he is nevertheless biologically unworthy, as is suggested in this exchange between Irwine and his mother, with Arthur looking on:

> "*Thank God you take after your mother's family, Arthur! If you had been a puny, wiry, yellow baby, I wouldn't have stood godmother to you. . . . But you were such a broad-faced, broad-chested, loud-screaming rascal, I knew you were every inch of you a Tradgett.*"
>
> "*But you might have been a little too hasty there, mother,*" said Mr. Irwine, smiling. "*Don't you remember how it was with Juno's last pups? One of them was the very image of its mother but it had two or three of its father's tricks notwithstanding. Nature is clever enough to cheat even you, mother.*"
>
> "*Nonsense, child! Nature never makes a ferret in the shape of a mastiff.*" (108)

But in fact the Donnithornes are exactly that: ferrets with the aristocratic bearing of that traditionally regal dog, the mastiff.

For the squirearchy is a form of authority that the novel suggests must be replaced. At eighty, Squire Donnithorne will soon, as everyone else is happily aware, be replaced by Arthur—and on the unexamined face of things Arthur represents the possibility of a different method of government. He wants to patronize his tenants: "When I was a little fellow, and Adam was a strapping lad of fifteen . . . I used to think if ever I was a rich sultan, I would make Adam my grand-vizier" (106). Arthur is, of course, slated to become the rich sultan, and he often associates himself with the language of monarchic rule: "I think I shall have a lofty throne for you Godmama, or rather two, one on the lawn and another in the ballroom." The improving squire will indulge in a gentle control: "He was nothing if not good-natured; and all his pictures of the future, when he should come into the estate, were made up of a prosperous, contented tenantry, adoring their landlord, who would be the model of an English gentleman—mansion in first-rate order, all elegance and high taste— jolly housekeeping—finest stud in Loamshire—purse open to all public objects—in short, everything as different as possible from what was now associated with the name of Donnithorne" (170).

However differently Arthur paints himself in his daydreams, his coming into his property will not, we are to understand, mark a radical change in his rule. Both old squire and new rely on what Eliot perceives as outmoded aristocratic means of control. The old squire's authority stems purely from his financial control; he can only threaten and blackmail: "'Well, Poyser,' said the squire, shifting his tactics . . . 'I know you will be glad to have your lease renewed for three years . . . otherwise, I daresay Thurle, who is a man of some capital, would be glad to take both the farms'" (393). Arthur's plan simply reverses the threat to remove monetary assistance, replacing it with an equalling controlling "generosity."

The Reverend Irwine, who takes nominal control over the Donnithorne estate after Arthur's departure, is also unable to offer any enduring form of authority. Irwine is, in fact, a kind of type of Arthur, a less aristocratic version of the benevolent control the novel mistrusts. It is Irwine who ascends to a kind of government over the Donnithorne estate. With the old squire's death, and Arthur's downfall, there remains no one to take over the Donnithorne concerns, but Arthur explains to Adam as he prepares to take his leave: "Mr. Irwine is to have the chief authority on the estate—he has consented to undertake that." The Poysers and Hayslope generally "will really be under no man, but one whom they respect and like" (513).

Of course, Irwine is not so very different from Arthur after all, for it is still "respect" and "like" that underwrite his authority. What will bind Irwine is what would have bound Arthur—a gentlemanly urge to do good. Irwine has nominal charge of the economically controlling interests of Hayslope when the novel ends. This signals the close of the paternal era—at least the kind of rigid paternalism represented by the old squire; and it signals the end of Arthur's plans for an aristocratic patronage based on what he imagines to be fair play. Yet it threatens to substitute for that patronage a clerical one perhaps even more dangerously benevolent and well meaning. It would seem, and Arthur certainly suggests to Adam, that this new arrangement represents a more equitable situation for the tenants and townfolk—life under "one whom they respect and like." But Irwine's relaxed morals—it is in part his laxity, he confesses, that has led to Hetty's and to Arthur's downfall—make him an unfit inheritor of the mantle of authority. No matter: Irwine is merely a placeholder, a marker in wait for a future when Adam and Dinah's offspring will themselves reproduce and, just in time for George Eliot's own historical moment, populate the world of Hayslope like Noah's progeny after the flood.

If in this way Eliot suggests an evolutionary solution to social problems, she is at odds with a crucial movement of her time. In "The Natural History of German Life," Eliot fundamentally opposes large-scale social programs, a standard reform method at the time she was writing the novel and the essay on Riehl. During a time of massive legislative activity and bureaucracy building in English society, Eliot returns to the parish and to the past, in order to suggest a dismantling of a state not yet fully formed, urging instead a careful observation and "understanding" of the lower classes. Her opposition to the modern state is informed, as well, by her anthropological imagination, which she reveals in the essay on Riehl, asserting that "a wise social policy must be based not simply on abstract social science, but on the Natural History of social bodies" (131). She insists that "pure instinct is noble, but instinct that has been semi-civilized is corrupt." In *Adam Bede,* pure instinct is to be preserved in the peasant stock of Adam, and refined in the body of Dinah Morris.

When Eliot turns to infanticide, she rejects the social science of her day, and turns to a concern for instinct. For better or for worse, people frequently operate by instinct in *Adam Bede,* in ways that would be unthinkable in many earlier novels because the idea of "will," which so informs the moral vision of a writer like Dickens or Elizabeth Gaskell, is compromised. Dinah's voice, for example, is a fine instrument "touched with the unconscious skill of musical instinct" (71). As she explains to Irwine, "[S]ometimes it seemed as if speech came to me without any will of my own, and words were given to me that came out as the tears come" (135). Arthur's attraction to Hetty is outside his control as well. Arthur tells Irwine a man might be "ruled by moods that one can't calculate on beforehand." But Irwine points out that "the moods lie in his nature. . . . A man can never do anything at variance with his own nature. He carries within him the germ of his own exceptional action" (217). Arthur is helpless when gazing upon Hetty's face, which "had a language that transcended her feelings"; Hetty's facial language is beyond her own control "just as a national language may be instinct with poetry unfelt by the lips that use it" (330). Those same forces bring Arthur and Adam to blows, for "[i]n our instinctive rebellion against pain, we are children again, and demand an active will to wreak our vengeance on" (345). In combat the two men are no longer domestic but wild creatures: they "fought with the instinctive fierceness of panthers in the deepening twilight darkened by the trees" (347). And later, Adam shrinks from Hetty "by an ungovernable instinct" (471).

But instinct is not to be excessively prized, however natural it might be, any more than the German peasant's clinging to his fur cap is lauded. Adam points out, "We can't be like the birds, as fly from their nest as soon as they've got their wings, and never know their kin when they see 'em, and get a fresh lot every year" (211). The analogy is an apt one, for it refers to the way in which animal instinct may be at odds with the nurturing necessities of parenthood. And it is by way of parent-child relations, specifically through an examination of Hetty Sorrel and her act of infanticide, that Eliot spells out both the problem of instinct and the civilizing solution to it. In her portrayal of the infanticidal mother, Eliot moves firmly away from the sentimental to the uncivilized. From the start of the novel, Hetty's instinct has been semicivilized—which is to say corrupted—in her attraction to the gentrified world of the Donnithornes. Eliot uses her narrative of motherhood, instinct, and rustic life to offer a different perspective on social development.[16]

Hetty, as has often been noted, is more frequently compared to animals than any other character in the novel. She is not only a lamb but a downy duck (127), a "young frisking thing" and a "kitten-like maiden" (128), a butterfly (146), "a tropic bird" (175) with a "butterfly soul" (180), a deer (181), "a bright-eyed spaniel," a "frightened bird" and a "silly pet" (182), and a "little perching bird" (187). She more than once displays a "pidgeon-like stateliness" as she parades alone in her room (197). She is ubiquitously a kitten, in Arthur's and in Adam's eyes (255, 308), and even in the view of the narrator (417). She is also, peculiarly enough, an "ant" (267). Although Hetty is often credited with "the luxurious nature of a round, soft-coated pet animal" (425), and compared to other pampered pets, she becomes less domesticated as her pregnancy progresses. Until then she is likely to be compared to kittens and birds. But impending motherhood brings out something more savage in her; eventually she is clinging to life like a brute (435). She becomes a "frightened animal" (463). Hetty's progress during the long "journey in despair" (chapter 37) is a record of her further degeneration, one might even say her further devolution. In her search for the remembered/imagined pool in which she intends to drown herself, Hetty proceeds as if by instinct, guided by a knowledge not clear to her, "going on and on without distinct purpose, yet strangely, by some fascination, taking the way she had come" (429). She has an unexamined desire to preserve her life, "for without knowing what she should do with her life, she craved the means of living as long as possible" (426); and this explains how it is that, planning vaguely to drown herself when she at last finds the pool she had been "dreaming of," she nevertheless appeases her hunger with animal pleasure, taking out the buns she has saved and eating them "eagerly" (431).

And indeed the infanticide itself is strikingly devoid of sentiment of any kind, presented (when we finally hear of it in Hetty's prison cell) as a narrative of instinctual behavior only half-consciously performed. What is more, in the course of her long journey Hetty has become a corpse, reduced from a purely ornamental body to a purely elemental and primitive one. If she lacked depth from the start, she at last becomes nothing but an empty animal shell "clinging to life only as the hunted wounded brute clings to it" (435). Even when our attention is focused on Hetty, it is not at a pitiable victim that we look, but to an animal driven by instinct.[17]

Eliot's infanticidal mother is neither victim nor criminal. She is finally a creature of an indifferent nature, and her description of the mur-

der itself is a battle between the desire to survive and the instinct to preserve one's young: "I longed so to be safe at home. I don't know how
I felt about the baby. I seemed to hate it—it was like a heavy weight
hanging around my neck; and yet its crying went through me" (499).
Hetty's return to the spot where she has left the child to die is not a con-
scious act of conscience; it is more an instinctive act barely within her
control: "I turned back the way I'd come. I couldn't help it, Dinah; it was
the baby's crying made me go: and yet I was frightened to death" (500).
The battle between personal survival and the survival of her offspring
finally paralyzes Hetty, and she waits immobile until she is found. In Eliot
we encounter at least one Victorian mother (indifferently) red in tooth
and claw.[18]

As Adam suggests in his reference to birds, the biological fact of
mothering is insufficient, and instinct alone can hardly produce an evolved
society. Much recent criticism has rightly focused on mothers in this
novel, and especially on Dinah's motherhood at the novel's end. It is argued either that Dinah is subsumed by motherhood, or that her acceptance of mothering is prized as a nurturing rather than biological motherhood. But neither reading is sufficient, for neither view can account
for the fact that *Adam Bede* remains, as evidently Eliot herself remained,
deeply unresolved about mothering.

To explore that ambivalence toward mothers, one might look first
to Eliot's discussion of "those delightful women of France" (9) in her
essay on Madame de Sable, "Woman in France" (1854). There we learn
that although "science has no sex," literature decidedly has, and that "under every imaginable social condition, [woman] will necessarily have
a class of sensations and emotions—the maternal ones—which must
remain unknown to man; and the fact of her comparative physical weakness, which, however it may have been exaggerated by a vicious civilization, can never be cancelled, introduces a distinctively feminine condition into the wondrous chemistry of the affections and sentiments, which
inevitably gives rise to distinctive forms and combinations" (8). It seems
that the feminine condition is defined not just by biology but by "maternal" sensations; and, furthermore, it seems that those very sensations account for both the best and the worst in women writers.

A second example of ambivalence: in a letter to Sara Hennell written the day after her twenty-ninth birthday, Eliot figured her own birth

and relationship to a mother—to "Mother Nature" in fact—as a near-infanticide. In her fanciful yet profoundly disturbing tale, an inexperienced "sprite" creates for Mother Nature "a rough though unmistakable sketch of a human baby"—the infant Mary Anne Evans. Appalled at the "pretty piece of work I should have to patch up this thing into a human body and soul that would hang together," Mother Nature demands that her "Vishnu-sprites 'smother it at once to save further harm.' " Ultimately, this "poor sketch of a soul" is spared, only to be "pitied and helped" as the young George Eliot (*Letters* 1: 272–73). In this imagining of her own birth, Eliot portrays herself as something only *resembling* a human baby, and her mother—indeed all Mothers—as indifferent murderers.[19]

Finally, it is seldom noted that in *Adam Bede,* mothers are hardly prized. For example, both Lisbeth and Hetty are guilty of smothering their children, even if only one of them does so literally. The worthy Mrs. Poyser does not escape criticism: her treatment of the intolerable Totty—more a spoiled puppy than a child—makes her mothering seem worse than inadequate, particularly in comparison with her skilled handling of other household matters.[20] In her treatment of motherhood, Eliot in many ways comes to resemble Anne and Emily Brontë, who (as seen in chapter 3) portray the family as a violent enclosure, and mothers as especially venomous.[21]

Behind all of Eliot's portrayals of motherhood looms the figure of Hetty. It is a picture of a creature torn between self-preservation and a biological—not sentimental, not expressed in language—imperative to preserve one's offspring. Hetty is therefore hardly a Victorian model for maternal behavior. *Instinctual* motherhood is not entirely rejected, however. Hetty's failure to care properly for her own offspring is perhaps prompted by the disruption of the "natural" order of things, her corruption at the hands of the Donnithorne family, and her displacement from familial relations. Under better circumstances, when "peasants" are not interfered with, instinct works well enough. This is seen, peculiarly enough, in the novel's portrayal of motherly canine devotion. The best mother in the novel is probably Vixen, herself nearly a victim of boys' pranks, boys who would have drowned her had Bartle Massey not come to her rescue. Vixen is torn between duty to her pups and devotion to her human master and lord, and existing "in a state of divided affection, had twice run back to the house to bestow a parenthetic lick on her puppies" (292). Ultimately, though, Vixen is subsumed by her motherly duties. As Bartle puts it, in his habitually misogynist way, "But where's the use of talking to a woman with babbies? . . . she's got no conscience— no conscience—it's all run to milk" (292).

Half-savage child-women and half-human dogs: so goes the novel's portrayal of instinctive mothering. In this Eliot reaches a dilemma not unlike that in *Wuthering Heights:* how do we mediate the corrupting effects of civilization, but avoid the uncivilized savagery of animal behavior? Eliot rejects pedagogy, the solution forged by Anne and Emily Brontë. The book-learning offered in Bartle Massey's schoolroom is radically insufficient, if not absurd.[22] Instead she relies upon a highly elaborated form of confession, which trains the body rather than the mind.

George Eliot initiated her novelistic career with the moment of confession clearly in mind, as she noted in a journal entry of 30 November 1858: "When I began to write [*Adam Bede*], the only elements I had determined on besides the character of Dinah were the character of Adam, his relation to Arthur Donnithorne and their mutual relation to Hetty, i.e. to the girl who commits child-murder: the scene in the prison being *of course* the climax towards which I worked" (Haight 198). That "of course," carrying with it an implicit connotation of common sense, is interesting because the confession itself is so queer a climax. The criminal's confession here (that "scene in the prison") can have no legal meaning; Hetty Sorrel has already been condemned to death. And it fails to alter events in the narrative, where it goes largely unremarked. What should "of course" be the moment of supreme self-revelation reveals only the shallow depths Hetty has feebly commanded throughout the novel. Even for Eliot, Hetty is reduced to an act, to "the girl who commits child-murder," or, at another point in the same journal entry, "a very ignorant girl who had murdered her child and refused to confess" (197). If this is the climactic moment of *Adam Bede,* why is it so thoroughly unsatisfying? How is it that the long-postponed confession of guilt should seem, at last, beside the point? Or, to put it another way, in what ways does the insufficiency of confessional content direct our attention to the form of confession in the closing pages of Eliot's novel?

Art performs a social good, Eliot insists as she finishes *Adam Bede,* writing to John Blackwood that she is happy to think that her novel will "tell on peoples' hearts and . . . be a real instrument of culture" (Haight

209). But for Eliot a socially meaningful "picture of human life"—truth—cannot rely upon the precise language of science, as she explains in the essay on Riehl: "Suppose, then, that the effort which has been again and again made to construct a universal language on a rational basis has at length succeeded, and that you have . . . —a patent deodorized and nonresonant language, which effects the purpose of communication as perfectly and rapidly as algebraic signs. Your language may be a perfect medium of expression to science, but will never express *life,* which is a great deal more than science" (128).

In spite of her dismissal of scientific language, Eliot soon declares an analogic relation between the body and writing: "The sensory and motor nerves that run in the same sheath, are scarcely bound together by a more necessary and delicate union than that which binds men's affections, imagination, wit, and humour, with the subtle ramifications of historical language" (128). The writer's task is to achieve the "delicate union" between sensory and motor nerves, between "historical language" and "imagination." It is "the subtle shades of meaning, and still subtler echoes of association, [that] make language an instrument which scarcely anything short of genius can wield with definiteness and certainty" (128). If not absolutely confident of her "genius," Eliot nevertheless nominates herself the authoritative speaker who can unite, in the body of her fiction, both sensory and motor nerves, combining the precision of science with artistic imagination.

But even as Eliot is "aspir[ing] to give no more than a faithful account of men and things as they have mirrored themselves in my mind," she is famously aware, as she states in the oft-quoted passage from chapter 17, that "[t]he mirror is doubtless defective; the outlines will sometimes be disturbed; the reflection faint or confused; but I feel as much bound to tell you, as precisely as I can, what that reflection is, as if I were in the witness-box narrating my experience on oath" (221).

It is to confession that Eliot turns as a way of establishing the truth of language and, perhaps more important, as a way of solving the dilemma of "civilization." Modern culture inscribes confession, to use Foucault's formulation in the first volume of his *History of Sexuality,* "at the heart of the procedures of individualization by power" (59). Secular confession, operating under the sign of liberation, is said to speak truth, especially one that proceeds from or generates a self-examination yielding "the basic certainties of consciousness" (*History of Sexuality* 60). It is a transformative gesture that ritualizes social redemption and constructs liberal subjectivity. Eliot works through the problem of language that she identifies in the "confused reflection" of writing by forming two distinct modes of confession. The first, like infanticide discourse discussed earlier, including Brownlow's *History,* creates confession as a social and moral act spoken *for* the community rather than *by* the individual. But in a second mode of confession, in Hetty Sorrel's private revelations, Eliot brings confession into the body in speech that is neither socially redemptive nor personally revelatory. In fact, in Hetty's apparently empty language is a quite perversely asocial rendering of the speech of confession. In the privacy of the cell, confession transcends language by becoming the authentic language of the body itself, removed from social practice and grounded in private, intense experience.

In Eliot's public mode of confession, guilt is a communal affair, and as such the confession of it is shared; it is mindful of Brownlow's formulation of the tragedy of infanticide and the social failures it represents. Hetty's secret is made a tragic one partly because of Arthur Donnithorne's inability to confess, and his failure to recognize the universal social consequences of his individual desires. In failing to speak, Arthur succumbs to the body, and Hetty's secret soon grows to a hidden dread. Guilt and the repercussions of sin quickly metastasize. For the Poyser family and for Hetty, sin results in an almost archaic shame, for "the home at the Hall Farm was a house of mourning for a misfortune felt to be worse than death. . . . That was the all-conquering feeling in the mind of both father and son—the scorching sense of disgrace, which neutralised all other sensibility" (459). For Adam and Arthur, guilt predominates over shame.[23]

But shamed or guilty, it is certain that in the world of Hayslope there is no solitary position possible, as the Reverend Irwine instructs Adam: "The evil consequences that may lie folded in a single act of selfish indulgence, is a thought so awful that it ought surely to awaken some feeling less presumptuous than a rash desire to punish. . . . There is no sort of wrong deed of which a man can bear the punishment alone: you can't isolate yourself, and say that the evil which is in you shall not spread. Men's lives are as thoroughly blended with each other as the air they breathe: evil spreads as necessarily as a disease" (468–69). Thus, while Hetty herself remains largely unredeemed, neither conscience nor consciousness aroused, those around her are brought to self-examination and social responsibility. Arthur ultimately confesses, and his consequent self-examination issues in a fatal blow to the world he represents. He pleads with Adam: "I only wish to ask you if you will help me to lessen the evil consequences of the past, which is unchangeable. I don't mean consequences to myself, but to others" (510–11).

The shame culture that the Poysers inhabit, and over which Arthur presides, gives way to a new society in Adam, who has also failed to attend to the intricate and interconnected nature of men's lives. Adam's telling Hetty's secret to Irwine represents the beginning of a new order in the novel. "I must do it," Adam says, speaking of his impulse to confess Hetty's secret, for "it's the right thing. I can't stand alone in this way any longer" (449). Adam resolves to "do my work well, and make the world a bit better place for them as can enjoy it" (516). Adam's actions define him as the contemplative, self-examining subject, redeemed by his conscience, brought to consciousness by it, and aiming his moral sights on a common good.

With all of this guilt and redemption under way in the novel, it is perhaps no wonder that we arrive at the scene of Hetty's prison encounter with Dinah somewhat overstuffed with the speech of confession. Hetty is convicted without uttering a word. Nevertheless, in Hetty, Eliot repairs the rupture between the materiality of the body and the insufficiency of the language that would represent it. She seeks to evade the normative, disciplinary economy of (an emerging) modern confession. If, in Foucault's view, we confess the desires of the body in order to bring the body into discourse and to locate points of intersection between the body and the soul, in Hetty's speech that meeting line is dissolved in a discourse remarkable not as language but as experience. Confession, in one important sense, brings the experience of the body into language and "puts it in order." Phrased as liberation, confessional speech disciplines bodily acts and desires. In Hetty, confession neither transforms, redeems, nor even constitutes her as subject. Instead it is the product of Dinah Morris's instruction in what we might think of as the erotics of involuntary confession.[24]

Hetty's speech is made possible not by law, not by coercion, not even by a desire to "speak the truth." In fact the speech really does not proceed from an acknowledgement of or interest in truth itself. Instead, it erupts out of the intense encounter between Dinah and Hetty, in which Dinah's mastery of the art of confession aids Hetty in her efforts to overcome the resistance of her body to the private pleasures of that art. Hetty's confession does not emerge out of her self; it erupts in response to provocation, manipulation, and prodding, one might even say an excitation. And Hetty responds not in language, but in the flesh. Dinah's first words are registered in Hetty's body: "There was a slight movement perceptible in Hetty's frame—a start such as might have been produced by a feeble electrical shock" (493). Far from constituting her status as subject, Hetty loses rather than produces self, loosening the boundaries even of her bodily presence. She begins her progress toward confession by clasping Dinah to her, the two merging, their "faces . . . indistinct" (493).

Hetty's confessional act, unlike Arthur's or Adam's, is defined by its intensity as experience. Hetty's body progresses toward climactic speech. Dinah's intense conjurings over Hetty's slowly responsive body are meant to instruct Hetty in the bliss of release in confession. But that speech must be reabsorbed into the experience of confession itself. It will not be made into *public* speech, or into a subject-producing discourse; it does not function as a site for the production of truth or knowledge. The knowledge Hetty gains, in fact, is secret. It is understood as private practice—in Foucault's words, "not considered in relation to an absolute law of the permitted and forbidden . . . but . . . experienced as pleasure, evaluated in terms of its . . . reverberations in the body and the soul" (*History of Sexuality* 57).[25]

Dinah's success with her disciple is assured and climax achieved when at last Hetty is explosively relieved of the hard despair that makes it impossible for her to feel. "'Dinah,' Hetty sobbed out, throwing her arms round Dinah's neck, 'I will speak . . . I will tell . . . I won't hide it anymore'" (497). Hetty "convulses," and her tears and sobs are at first too violent. Content is subordinated to form, in that what Hetty says, though lengthy, is mostly unremarkable. The interest here lies in the eruption of speech, the "reverberations," and Dinah's careful manipulation of that process. Experience itself must master a content that cannot be interpreted because it is empty of meaning. The prison scene is about the bodily experience of confession itself, one that remains private; it cannot be told because even though it is experienced partly through speech it cannot be spoken of or described, only endured or enacted: "Hetty was silent, but she shuddered again, as if there were still something behind; and Dinah waited, for her heart was so full, that tears must come before words. At last Hetty burst, out with a sob" (500). Confession and the body, in Hetty, are united.[26]

Such a confession can never be heard, and indeed it is barely registered in the narrative. Only Dinah—and the reader—hear the sound of Hetty's climactic moment, or feel the vibrations of her body. The silence that is the speech of the body does, however, reemerge later in the novel, as Dinah's own unspoken desires gradually make themselves felt in, and are advertised by, a body that cannot be still. The secret she cannot tell is expressed in the twitchings of her duster—"how it went again and again round every bar of the chairs, and every leg, and under and over everything that lay on the table, till it came to Adam's papers and rulers" (535)—and demonstrated in the response of her body to Adam's presence: "It was as if Dinah had put her hands unawares on a vibrating chord; she was shaken with an intense thrill, and for the instant felt nothing else" (535). Adam's "very awkward and sudden" confession of love brings out in her a violent and quite physical reaction; Dinah's "lips became pale, like her cheeks, and she trembled violently under the shock of painful joy" (551). While critics in recent years have balefully noted the silencing of Dinah's voice—the prohibition against her preaching—one might argue that Dinah's silence does not represent the disappearance of female speech in the novel, but rather the rise of a powerful, if unspeakable, female sexual desire. That is, Dinah stops talking about God when her body starts confessing her more earthbound desires.[27]

Adam Bede creates George Eliot even as it was soon to become the vehicle for confessing to the truth about George Eliot—that is, exposing Marian Evans. Within the novel itself, however, *Adam Bede* imagines confession as an erotic interchange shared not only between Hetty and Dinah, but even more intimately in the confidential embrace of Eliot and her reader-interlocutor. In the decades that followed the publication of *Adam Bede,* social reformers worked zealously to promote institutional responses to social ills. George Eliot's early work, and especially *Adam Bede,* are fit texts with which to end this book because they demonstrate the ways in which novels symbolically represent social dilemmas; and also the way in which certain novels resist resolution in predictable ways. Eliot has been seen at times as soberly promoting the ends of the middle-class family and midcentury bourgeois life. But in *Adam Bede* the family—and this might be said of Anne and Emily Brontë as well—is distinct from the Dickensian model explored in chapters 1 and 2. In the case of the Brontës and Eliot, middle-class family life is not to be subject to state intervention. In this regard Eliot is anything but a conservative force, at least insofar as she seeks to preserve aspects of the primitive in Hetty and to defy the "civilizing" forces of social apparatus and institutions. By contrast, the discourse of infanticide examined in the first half of this chapter was engaged precisely in civilizing, a "civilization" that served to support the advance of institutional intervention. Even as George Eliot was writing and publishing *Adam Bede,* the institutionalization of social welfare was beginning in earnest. With the advent of social welfare casework, and the invention of the case history, the narrative of the child victim formally became the province of the state. Child welfare had arrived.

Conclusion: From Pulpy Infants to a Nation of Good Animals

It is in the case of children, that misapplied notions of liberty are a real obstacle to the fulfillment by the State of its duties. One would almost think that a man's children were supposed to be literally, and not meta- phorically, a part of himself.

John Stuart Mill, *On Liberty*

IN THE LATE 1850s, Herbert Spencer wrote a series of essays first pub- lished in the *Westminster* and *North British Reviews,* and in the *British Quar- terly.* These were eventually collected under the title *Education: Intellectual, Moral and Physical.* Among Spencer's strongest and most vigorously re- peated arguments is the argument for the primacy of science and scientific method in the deliberation of social issues. In the essay "What Knowl- edge is of Most Worth?" (1859) Spencer answers "the question with which we set out" unequivocally; the most valuable thing to know can easily be defined because "the uniform reply is—Science. This is the verdict on all counts. . . . Equally at present, and in the remotest future, must it be of incalculable importance for the regulation of their conduct, that men should understand the science of life, physical, mental, and so- cial; and that they should understand all other science as a key to the science of life" (84–86).

What Spencer means by "Science," however, is not so easily deter- mined. Certainly he is striving to infuse contemporary debates about education with a "scientific" pedagogy; in addition to philosophizing, Spencer offers precise schedules and detailed recommendations for train- ing children that rival those James Kay produced in the 1830s. And Spen- cer also means to encourage rational discussion and refuse appeals to sentiment; like many of the social reformers of the day, he claims to bring scientific method to the social sphere.

But Spencer's idea of science and his interest in it, at least as it is articulated in these essays, is finally closer to a kind of radical materiality, an insistence on physical matter, the most important of which is the human, especially childish, body. Abstract ideas are to be eschewed in education because "learning the meanings of things, is better than learning the meanings of words" (84). Fully a quarter of the book—an entire essay, "Physical Education"—is given over to a discussion of the proper training of a child's body, taking in matters of exercise, sleep, diet, and numerous other minutiae ("A soft, flabby flesh makes as good a show as a firm one; but though to the careless eye, a child of full, flaccid tissue may appear the equal of one whose fibres are well toned, a trial of strength will prove the difference" [247]). Casting aside what he views as the ornament and fashion of a classical nineteenth-century education, Spencer argues for a training that begins and ends with the body itself. From infancy onward, what matters is matter: "Instead of respecting the body and ignoring the mind, we now respect the mind and ignore the body" (300).

An interest in the corporeal self characterizes much Victorian social-reform writing concerning children, a point made forcefully by Harry Hedrick in his book on child welfare. The discourse of childhood, generally, has focused on childish bodies, as James Kincaid shows. But Spencer's attitude toward the body, particularly the child's body, can be usefully compared to George Eliot's, and to earlier writers. In Shelley's *Frankenstein,* certainly in Malthus, in Dickens, and in the debates over the railroad, the wet nurses, and pauper inmates of the workhouse—in all of these nineteenth-century writings, the body is a central concern. Those concerns, however, tend to be organized around the appetites of the body, and the energy it can or refuses to expend in labor or simply in physical strength. By contrast, Spencer views the body, even the poor body, not as a potential threat but as a source of regeneration. In writings discussed earlier in this book, the fictional model of the Malthusian male was Shelley's monster, a beastly malcontent encountered, albeit in mutated form, in later writings as diverse as the 1834 *Report* of the poor law commissioners and Emily Brontë's *Wuthering Heights.*

This willingness to represent the body in a positive light is, of course, also characteristic of George Eliot. By the time Eliot and Spencer were writing in 1859, it was evidently possible to view the body, even the adult male body, not as monstrously hungry but as merely animal. For Eliot, to be animal is to be part of the tangled web of the world; as seen in discussion of *Adam Bede,* there are times when for Eliot the worthiest human beings *are* the animals, who can be mutely and immutably true to the best instincts of their species and remain uncorrupted by society's civilizing forces. Meanwhile, for Spencer, to be animal is to participate in forming—I am tempted to say bodybuilding—the state: "As remarks a suggestive writer," Spencer approvingly tells us, "the first requisite to success in life is 'to be a good animal'; and to be a nation of good animals is the first condition to national prosperity" (232).

If Carlyle saw children as moldable creatures—"pulpy infants," in his disturbing phrase—Spencer views children as "unfolding" selves. For Spencer the hardened individuals of Carlyle, beings who in their adult state are a potential threat to the social order, can never be "fixed." "For shoe-making or house-building," Spencer points out, "for the management of a ship or a locomotive-engine, a long apprenticeship is needful. Is it, then, that the unfolding of a human being in body and mind, is so comparatively simple a process, that anyone may superintend and regulate it with no preparation whatever?" (49).

There is an implicit but unmistakable connection here between shoemakers and house builders, that is to say laborers, and the "unfolding" individuals who are children only for a time. It is entirely possible for Spencer to imagine his children as adults, where they will necessarily take their place as citizens and workers, their productive and reproductive capacities welcomed as worthy contributions to England's unfolding future. Carlyle's notion of development ends in adulthood, when persons "are fixed and hardened"; Spencer resembles Eliot in his formulation of the human self as progressing. This is to show, then, that by midcentury the reformulation of the body had changed the way social relations could be understood. The mid-Victorian body, as imagined in Spencer and in Eliot, is potentially a progressing evolutionary body, as opposed to a dangerous Malthusian one.

It is probably science that makes this shift in attitude toward the body possible for Eliot and Spencer at this historical juncture. Perhaps it is not only coincidental that both *Adam Bede* and Spencer's essay appeared in 1859, the year Darwin first published *Origin of Species*. Of course it is not only evolutionary theory that makes such thinking possible, but Darwin certainly serves as an important marker on the way to what Robin Gilmour calls the "authority which the idea of science enjoyed by the end of the century" (111). But science is working in the service of the state in Spencer's formulation; it is not supporting the impassioned search for objective inquiry and knowledge unsullied by partisan concerns, if in fact any science can be said to do or have done such a thing. The "good animals," who owe their categorization, and their affinity to other creatures, to the advances of scientific knowledge, are immediately absorbed by Spencer into a prescriptive account of nation making.

The difference between Spencer and Eliot, then, is in their implicit attitudes toward social intervention and institutions. Both place the embodied self at the forefront and imagine bodies as agents of progress; but while Spencer would institute a program of pedagogy that would publicly and uniformly train children as "citizens," and very specifically train them physiologically, Eliot seeks to imagine a body, in Hetty Sorrel and in Hetty's confession, that might oppose the institutionalization of the self. In the muscular and laboring Adam Bede, Eliot's novel might be said to regenerate Victor Frankenstein's monstrous creation, and to nullify the filthy relations of English society as social life grows more interdependent. *Adam Bede* offers a new narrative of origins in which an able-bodied adult male can reproduce without anxiety—in fact, whose reproductive capacity is crucial, and whose "hunger" can be defined as a desire to enter and enrich the labor force. In this novel the male body can be prized for any superior genetic material it might possess, not feared for its brute power or devouring force. If one were to seek a parallel between Shelley's Monster and the world of Hayslope, it could only be found in Hetty Sorrel, who is both a murdering monster and a pitiable victim.

Adam Bede is placed at the end of this book because Eliot's early novel is poised on the threshold of a new era, in which the relationships among the child, subjectivity, and social reform projects are formally, even inflexibly, linked to the institutions of the state. The malleable selves imagined by Carlyle in *Past and Present* are now to be fixed and hardened within the institutional confines of social welfare, where they are to become, in the phrase that serves as title to the 1868 book by Florence Hill (later Hill-Davenport) on training juvenile paupers, the *Children of the*

State. Spencer's essays suggest a welcoming of state intervention, and while his work underscores the importance of institutions, Eliot resists legislative intervention. Her foray into England's past, it turns out, fails to predict the future. It is Spencer's view that will dominate the rest of the century, and which arguably persists into the present, for Spencer makes the absolute connection between pedagogy and citizenship.[1]

Eliot's attempts to forge independent solutions to the dilemma of nineteenth-century social life are almost unique in the period. For most nineteenth-century writers, the child offered an occasion for investigation, regulation, and legislation. This scrutiny of the child in relation to the state is evident in Herbert Spencer when he deplores a lack of training in what is, for him, that most important of citizenship activities—the education of children. Spencer imagines a reader from "the remote future" reviewing the pedagogical materials of the mid-nineteenth century. He mock-marvels at

> *how puzzled an antiquary of the period would be on finding in [our schoolbooks and college examination papers] no indication that the learners were ever likely to be parents. "This must have been the curriculum for their celibates," we may fancy them concluding. "I perceive here an elaborate preparation for many things: especially for reading the books of extinct nations and of co-existing nations (from which indeed it seems clear that these people had very little worth reading in their own tongue); but I find no reference whatever to the bringing up of children. They could not have been so absurd as to omit all training for this gravest of responsibilities. Evidently, then, this was the school course for their monastic orders." (40)*

That parent training, then or now, has never become an important aspect of any curriculum hardly seems to matter, since the force of Spencer's polemic has more to do with authorizing the interventions of the state into the lives of children and families than it does with preparing adults for their familial responsibilities.

This intervention was literalized and legislated eleven years after Spencer wrote these words, in the passage of the Elementary Education Act of 1870, which mandated an education for every school-age child. The purpose of the legislation was to reduce "ignorance," which according to W. E. Forster, the M.P. who introduced the legislation, should be of concern to every citizen, since ignorance is "pregnant with crime and misery, with misfortune to individuals and danger to the community" (qtd. Horn 80). All children were to be taught, a policy that is said in Parliament to be in the best interests of the state: "It is of no use trying to give technical teaching to our artisans without elementary education . . . and if we are to hold our place among . . . the nations of the world we must make up the smallness of our numbers by increasing the intellectual force of the individual" (qtd. Horn 81). Public and political opinion in 1870 had traveled a long way from the anxious discussion in Parliament in the 1830s over James Kay's plan to educate workhouse children.

The Elementary Education Act placed the institution of the school at the center of the experience of all children. For poor children, however, there were to be more and greater institutions. The movement from the mid-Victorian period on was not only toward greater legislation but toward the creation of institutions and social practices that would intervene in the lives of families of all classes, but especially those of the poor, and especially in the growth of child welfare. A series of books and pamphlets, including Hill's *Children of the State*, directly linked the successful operation of the state with the rescue and reform, through social institutions, of children.

Hill takes for granted what had been problematic thirty years before; she quotes Kay and Tufnell as authorities for her argument that children must and should be treated as a separate class within the workhouse, and educated well outside it. Industry and self-reliance are the themes upon which she touches again and again. Her goal is to erect social institutions that mirror the benevolent influence of the domestic family, institutions that will train children to enter society productively. And she is especially interested in calculating the various costs to the state of plans to educate or warehouse paupers: "[T]he future tax upon rate-payers by the return of pupils upon their hands as permanent paupers, or upon the country at large by their sinking into the criminal class, or even the loss of their worth to the community as producers, is to be estimated, not by a few pence more or less a-week, but by many hundreds of pounds" (225). Hill concludes her book with an urgent call to fellow reformers not to allow other nations to surpass the efforts of British subjects: "Shall we be satisfied to achieve less for pauper children in England than is accomplished for criminal children in France? Mettray has converted to useful citizens

94.47 per cent of the youths she has restored to liberty. Let us strive to show no less fair a return for all we expend in money, time, and care on our CHILDREN OF THE STATE!" (274).

As Hill's work suggests, the story of child welfare after the mid-Victorian period is at least in part a narrative of nation and state. Such an attitude was fully and explicitly in place by the turn of the twentieth century, evident in John Gorst's 1906 *Children of the Nation,* the object of which, according to the author, was "to bring home to the people of Great Britain a sense of the danger of neglecting the physical condition of the nation's children" (qtd. Hedrick 9). According to both George Behlmer (*Child Abuse and Moral Reform*) and Hedrick, toward the end of the century "parental authority was substantially reduced as it found itself in conflict with that of the State" (Hedrick 49). The narrative of child victimization had entered into a new arena of discourse; rather than promoting a complex and sometimes contradictory account of self and society, it might be said that, at about the time of the passage of the Elementary Education Act, the story of the child in danger was deployed in a more narrow sphere and toward more narrow and explicitly ideological (and state-sanctioned) ends.

At about the time that state intervention became the norm, and the connection between the state and the state of the child emerged into explicit discussion—that is to say, at about the time that child welfare and social work began to emerge as categories with recognizable and defining limits—the narratives of childhood distress that so dominated nineteenth-century fictional writing began to disappear or, if you will, to evolve. The untroubled connection between child victim narratives in fiction and in social reform discourses, which had held sway for much of the century, began to change. Kingsley's *Water-Babies,* Eliot's *Silas Marner* and *The Mill on the Floss,* and Lewis Carroll's *Alice in Wonderland* are all novels of the 1860s. The major novelists of the 1870s, 1880s, and 1890s seem less interested in the theme of childhood victimization and endangerment. Children do not disappear altogether, of course, but the child victim is not nearly as central in the later period, and almost disappears in modernist writing. Even George Moore's *Esther Waters* is less interested in endangered childhood than it is in the trials of Esther herself. The late Victorian period would seem less enmeshed in the sort of fascination with victimized childhood that can be seen in Shelley, Dickens, the Brontës, early Eliot, Kingsley, Barrett Browning ("The Cry of the Children," as well as "Aurora Leigh"), and which presses at the margins of many industrial novels.

The relative disappearance of the child victim in literary writing took place at about the time that early versions of social welfare invented the idea of the "case history." During the first three-quarters of the nineteenth century the narrative of the child victim could be found in writings of diverse kinds: in novels, in poetry, in open debate in Parliament, in pediatric manuals, in reform pamphlets on a wide variety of subjects, in the daily newspaper, in monthly *Reviews*—in short, the often sensational story of children at risk was endlessly repeated. Though probably too simple an answer, it is hard to dismiss the conclusion that, with the appearance of the formal apparatus of child welfare, the creative and complex use of the figure of the child victim was no longer so readily available. Or perhaps the story of the endangered child split into two different kinds of narratives: the sterile and sociologically inclined accounts of social workers, on the one hand, and the elaborate, literary, and highly suggestive accounts of Freud, on the other. What seems clear is that the particular kind of narrative of child victimization that dominated the first half of the nineteenth century, one characterized by its flexibility and the diverse writings in which it appears, was no longer in force toward the end of the century. But this was by no means the end of the story of what are called, nowadays, "children at risk."

In *Threatened Children,* Joel Best argues that the figure of the child victim in the late twentieth century has increasingly come to play a role in debates over a range of social problems, from drunk driving to AIDS. But we hardly need a sociologist to tell us this. The syndicated Sunday supplement of a local newspaper recently ran a cover story called "Our Endangered Species." The writer, Andrew Vachss, echoes Herbert Spencer's concerns in curious ways: "Although we all believe our human species to be the highest point on the evolutionary scale, there is one critical area in which we have failed to evolve, one area in which we do not represent an improvement upon our predecessors. And this is a failure so fundamental, so critical, that our longterm survival is at stake. . . . That fundamental stake is this: We are not protecting and preserving our own. Our notion of the human 'family' as the safeguard of our species has not evolved. Instead, it has gone in the opposite direction—it has devolved"

(4). Like so much writing about child victims from Spencer onward, the passage works to offer a biological basis for the family. It purports to be a righteous plea for the rights of children, even as it exploits the tear-stained victim reproduced on the cover in the service of a narrative about domesticity.

This kind of polemic existed in the nineteenth century, as I have tried to show. Common sense, not to mention a generation of critics and historians, tells us to read the nineteenth century as the creator and bastion of the bourgeois home, domicile of the Angel in the House, and innovator of the concept of separate spheres. It no longer seems to me so straightforward. Victorians liked to read about, reflect upon, and exclaim over child victims. They wept over Little Nell and identified with Jane Eyre, who at one point calls herself a "pariah of the nursery." Victorians were self-righteously indignant about child labor and outraged at infanticide, and reproduced the story of the child victim as a kind of originating welfare story that promoted state intervention. But they were also capable of using the child victim to explore the possibility that the home and the state are themselves prisons.

I am not certain whether the narrative of the child at risk is told with the same complexity in the twentieth century; most of the time I think not. One of the unexpected effects of writing this book has been my increased sensitivity to what appear to be the public pleasures of present-day stories of childhood distress, and particularly to the political expediency of discursive gestures toward the protection of children. On Father's Day 1997, appropriately enough, the *New York Times* acknowledged the political power inherent in the representation of children, noting, "These days much of the nation's political debate focuses on children—or on the needs and interests of children as defined by politicians and advocacy groups" (15 June 1997). A caption within the article notes that children are "useful to politicians, in ways that adults aren't." This usefulness first emerged as a complex ideological formation in the nineteenth century. And although the representation of childhood and children has evolved considerably during the last two hundred years, the fact of that representation has been more or less a constant, so much so that we seldom recognize the political nature, or question the accuracy, of narratives of childhood distress.

The story of victimized childhood has a specific history; tracing the history of that storytelling is one way of tracing the history of modernity. Almost as soon as "childhood" became a distinct category, stories of children in danger were circulated as part of larger debates about self, nation, class, and family. The story of suffering children proved so enticing that we have never stopped telling it. This book has traced just some of the origins of that telling.

Notes

Introduction

1. On industrial and social problem novels, see Brantlinger (*Spirit of Reform*), Gallagher (*Industrial Reformation*), Kestner, Schor, and Sheila Smith.

2. On the ways in which modern practices of social work have incorporated aspects of other professional practices such as law and medicine, see Donzelot, especially on the juvenile court (106–17) and "The Priest and the Doctor" (171–88). For another very useful discussion of the rise of the social as a domain, see Poovey, *Making* 7. For the "disciplinary subject" of Foucault, see his *Discipline and Punish.*

3. On the Malthusian reformulation of the body, see Gallagher, "The Body." On Malthus and Victorian society, see Himmelfarb (100–132) and Boner (chs. 3 and 4).

4. The notion that legislation concerning itself with private life was steadily on the increase in this period, or was widely thought to be, is articulated as early as A. V. Dicey's *Lectures on the Relation between Law and Public Opinion in England during the Nineteenth Century,* first published in 1905. Historians throughout the twentieth century have persuasively disputed Dicey's account of the period before 1870 as one unmarked by state intervention. Among the more well-known discussions of this issue are those by Polanyi and by Corrigan and Sayer. For a discussion of the issue of public opinion and state intervention, see Lubenow.

5. A founding text for this view of the reciprocally constitutive roles of gender, class, and race, and particularly how these categories are crucially connected to the construction of subjectivity, is Cora Kaplan's. In speaking here and elsewhere of "class," I am thinking in terms of Gareth Stedman Jones's discussion of the word, as Kaplan discusses it in her essay. In *Languages of Class,* Jones dismisses the idea that class is a term that has a necessary and unchanging "reference point in anterior social reality" (7–8). Jones also emphasizes the "linguistic context," for "'class' is a word embedded in language" (7). For a recent discussion of the use of the terms *class* and *rank* and *status* in early Victorian culture, see Ingham (esp. 9–12).

6. In "Work and the Body in Hardy and Other Nineteenth-Century Novelists," and an essay included in her book *Resisting Representations,* Elaine Scarry discusses the intensity of our preoccupation as twentieth-century readers with courtship and desire (61). In Scarry's account, what is under erasure in our reading of the nineteenth-century novel, and what is so difficult to talk about (despite the ubiquity of its representation in fiction), is the idea of work.

7. The idea is stated most baldly by Joseph Boone, who sees the love plot as a "stranglehold of literary convention" (2). There are a number of books that take this connection between marriage and novel writing for granted. Some of the more recent and

most useful are Calder, Cockshut, Green, Kennard, and Tony Tanner. On the resistance of some female authors to this plot, see Foster.

8. For a more recent "take" on the Victorian child and sexuality, see Carol Mavor's fascinating study, especially her discussion of Lewis Carroll (7–42).

9. Coveney and Steedman are not the only critics who have traced the predominance of the child in literature. A surprisingly large number of literary critics have examined childhood—surprising because they have for the most part done so without linking the appearance of the child in literature to the fascination with childhood outside it. Among those I have consulted are Brown, Grylls, Kane, Kuhn, Pattison, and Spilka.

10. Needless to say, this view has not gone uncontested. Exemplary of the resistance to a social-constructionist view is the work of Linda Pollock, who argues that parent-child relations have remained relatively constant over time because they are natural and universal; and that history may alter context, but it can have very little effect on the enduring and formative love between parents and children (see both of her books). Other sources for this discussion, in addition to Aries, Plumb, and Stone, are Gathorne-Hardy and Shorter. See also Andrews, ch. 1, entitled "The Idea of Childhood: A Genealogy," in *Dickens* (9–26).

11. On these matters, see Barry Qualls's helpful discussion, in which he expands on the idea that the Romantics "elevate the child to natural godhead" (4). He points out how the child figure of religious discourse (he speaks especially of Bunyan) is enclosed in the "prison-house"—the Wordsworthian term, from the Immortality Ode, for loss of childhood grace and innocence. For Qualls, the child of religious discourse and the Wordsworthian child come together in that ubiquitous Victorian figure, the orphan.

12. This is especially true of progress narratives that deplore the "cruelties of the past" at the same time they champion the road to modern welfare "enlightenment," the source for which some critics and historians have found in specific historical events of the nineteenth century. See Bruce, Poynter, and Michael E. Rose. For an insightful account of the historiography of welfare, see Thomson.

13. Throughout this chapter I am quoting from the Penguin edition of the novel, which consists of Shelley's 1831 version of *Frankenstein*. For the 1818 version, see Rieger.

14. *Frankenstein* has, of course, been connected to any number of social and psychological issues in the period; perhaps the novel has received more widely varying interpretations than any other early-nineteenth-century work. See Michie and Morretti on the Creature and issues of class and social rank. Tim Marshall seeks an explicit connection between Victor's labors and the 1832 Anatomy Act. Gilbert and Gubar read the novel as a feminist revision of Milton, in which Eve is crucial: "[F]or Mary Shelley, the part of Eve *is* all the parts" (230). Gilbert and Gubar are by no means the only feminist critics to take *Frankenstein* to heart; for a survey of such work, see Catherine Gallagher and Elizabeth Young, "Feminism and *Frankenstein*."

On the use of *Frankenstein* in relation to "political" issues in the 1830s and well afterward, and their translation into "psychological" concerns, see Sterrenburg (166–71). In a now famous essay, Spivak uses Shelley's novel to consider imperialism, as Barbara Johnson has taken up Shelley's novel to deal with deconstruction. Botting has written insightfully on the many ways in which Frankenstein has been taken up by critics and by culture. See also O'Flinn.

15. On the issue of body snatching and the Anatomy Act, see Laqueur ("Pauper Funer-

als"), Marshall, and Richardson. For a novel approach to the "problem" of Victor's creation of the Creature, see Sutherland, who argues (half-seriously?) that the Monster is literally Victor's child (33).

16. The only discussion of the Monster's vegetarianism of which I am aware is that of Carol J. Adams, who devotes an entire chapter of *The Sexual Politics of Meat* to Shelley's novel.

17. There is a large and excellent body of work on reproduction, sexuality, mothers, and women in *Frankenstein,* far too large a body to summarize here. See the survey written by Gallagher and Young, cited above. The essays I have found especially helpful include those of Kate Ellis, Gilbert and Gubar (213–47), Knoepflmacher ("Aggression of Daughters"), Mellor (*Mary Shelley*), Moers ("Female Gothic"), Poovey (ch. 4 of *Proper Lady*), Rubenstein, and Veeder.

18. James O'Rourke provides a thorough discussion of Mary Shelley's relation to Rousseau, particularly concerning the issue of child abandonment.

19. On the 1831 revisions, see Butler ("The First *Frankenstein*"), Mellor ("Choosing a Text"), and Poovey (*Proper Lady,* 133–42). Suggesting *Frankenstein* as a beginning framework for understanding realism, George Levine has provided a model for this study, in one sense at least. While I am not specifically concerned with realism here, I find, like Levine, that "Frankenstein and his monster will turn up frequently in the chapters that follow" (*Realistic* 24). Although our projects are quite different, I share Levine's opinion that "the monster is also kin to the oppressed women and children of Victorian fiction" (30). See also Levine, "*Frankenstein* and the Traditions."

I. Hideous Progeny Made Clean

1. This is from the London *Times,* Monday, 4 May 1846. The *Times* printed further Andover testimony on 7, 16, 20, and 25 May. Another source is the debate in the House of Commons that took place on 5 March 1846, and which has been reprinted in the Irish University Press edition of the *British Parliamentary Papers.*

2. For background on the Andover scandal, see Crowther, who uses the scandal as a kind of touchstone throughout her book on the workhouse, as well as Anstruther, Driver, Henriques (55), Longmate (ch. 10), and Wood (81).

3. Evidence given before the House of Commons, Thursday, 5 March 1846, *British Parliamentary Papers* 633. As a rule, the bones crushed by workhouse inmates were not human bones. But as reported in Parliament, skeletal remains from the burial grounds were included in the heap on at least one occasion, a fact that was rapidly made part of the discussion.

4. On the issue of social control or an incipient liberalism in Kay's writing, see Richard Johnson and Tholfsen. Crowther comments on the collision of these two perspectives on Kay's educational contribution in relation to class conflict in this way: "[Kay] was a Benthamite who believed in the type of social mobility later popularized by Samuel Smiles" (202).

5. This is not to suggest that education, especially the education of the poor, was not an important or widely debated topic in this period. In fact, as Richard Johnson rightly points out, "the education of the poor was, indeed, one of the strongest of early Victorian obsessions" (96).

6. References to the 1834 *Report for Inquiring into the Administration and Practical Operation*

of the Poor Laws are to the modern edition published in Lubove, *Social Welfare in Transition.*

7. This redefinition has been noted before. See, for one such source, Laqueur ("Pauper Funerals"), who says that in the nineteenth century the poor law articulated legally a notion that had been evolving unevenly since the seventeenth century: "The poor, instead of being those who would always be amongst us and who indeed occupied a spiritually-privileged category, became those who could not or would not sell their labor and who consequently had to be supported, more to assure political stability than by reason of benevolence, at some minimal levels above starvation" (120–21). Hadley makes the same point (80).

8. Comparing the Victorian reforms to earlier practices of relief and definitions of the poor, Himmelfarb says that the "Elizabethan laws were, in fact, genuinely and un-ambiguously 'poor' laws precisely because they did not make any sharp distinction between poor and pauper" (160).

9. On the conflict between the "less eligibility" theory and children, see Pinchbeck, who notes, "The principle that 'children should follow their parents' was adopted in the 1834 Poor Law Amendment Act, with the result that, in practice, there was wide variation of treatment largely depending on whether or not they lived in Unions governed by the Outdoor Labour Test Order" (500). On the effort to depauperize children, see her chapter "The Release of Children from Pauperism." Pinchbeck believes that Kay's effort to reform educational practices in the workhouse was approved and philosophically sanctioned by the poor law commissioners who "became aware that containing and reducing pauperism was fundamentally connected with a more positive approach to the relief of children than the principle of less eligibility . . . readily allowed" (501). But see Crowther, whose view is closer to my own, when she asserts that "Tufnell and Kay-Shuttleworth had to persuade the Commissioners that to educate workhouse children would not encourage their parents to become paupers" (202).

10. Throughout this chapter I am quoting from a reprint of *The Training of Pauper Children,* published by J. Morten in 1970.

11. *Sixteenth Report,* "Minutes of Evidence" (3). The "Minutes of Evidence" Kay gave before Parliament in March 1838 (abbreviated here as the *Sixteenth Report* and *Fourteenth Report*) largely cover the matter of his proposal to reform pauper education.

12. On what he calls "parental substitution," see Richard Johnson, who argues that "Kay and his colleague and friend, E. C. Tufnell, added a new dimension to Poor Law policy. They argued that the Poor Law should not only sweep away incentive to idleness, but should also provide a positive machinery for rehabilitating the children of paupers" (111).

13. On these points, see Driver (95–99). Driver reads Kay's educational reforms as a fairly straightforward Foucauldian imposition of discipline. He thus makes much of the "fixed timetables, regimented drills," and the like that made up parts of Kay's proposal.

14. Although school districts were established under the Poor Law Amendment Act of 1844, "the new powers were so circumscribed as to be inoperable" (Duke 71). Some changes were effected with the District Schools Act of 1848, but by 1849 it was clear that there was not to be any uniform or systematic plan for district schools. On this history, and on the practical problems encountered in attempting to implement vari-

ous aspects of Kay's plan, see Duke. Driver also touches on this issue in important ways. In spite of the legislation I have named, he says, "Outside London . . . the official campaign for the establishment of district schools was frustrated by the reluctance of individual Boards of Guardians to adopt the provisions of these Acts" (97). He goes on to assert that outside official circles "the district schools policy proved to be deeply unpopular" (97).

Digby has an entirely different view in her chapter entitled "Pauper Education," claiming, "That the education of poor children was essential in order to achieve social stability was widely believed in the 1830s" (180). She goes on to say that there was widespread support for a system of pauper education. Two things make Digby's assertion plausible: that hers is a close study of a single union, Norfolk (and therefore her work can locate one of the many variations in workhouse policies and practices), and also that the particular union about which Digby is writing happens to be the one in which James Kay mainly worked. I suspect Digby's claims are true for her local study but not generalizable.

15. Duke analyzes the rejection of the apprentice this way: "One major objective after 1834 was to destroy the parish apprenticeship system, by moulding children into valuable employees who could hold their own in a genuinely free labour market" (68).

16. Although Ruskin wrote the series of essays that were eventually published as *Unto This Last* in 1860, his sentiments and his tone sound more like Carlyle of the 1830s and 1840s, as Brantlinger has pointed out. *Unto This Last* was perceived as "socialistic," and the essays seen as "out of step with the times. If he had written *Unto This Last* in 1843, it would have appeared as a reinforcement of *Past and Present*" (*Spirit* 3–4).

17. On the relationship between fiction and blue books, see Sheila Smith (135–71).

18. The reprint of an early section of *Oliver Twist* was taken from *Bentley's Miscellany* and appeared on 31 January 1837. The novel's explicit relationship to the new poor law has been vigorously debated. Although *Oliver Twist* was almost immediately taken up by opponents of the law, critics have complained from the start that the novel quickly leaves poor relief behind. More recent, and fruitless, debate has centered on whether the novel takes place before or after the new law. On this issue see House and Fairclough. It is not actually possible to determine when the novel is meant to take place, and Dickens's portrayal combines elements of the old and new systems.

There is, however, ample reason to associate *Oliver Twist* with protest against the new poor law. One critic who has made this connection is Steven Marcus in *From Pickwick to Dombey*. His powerful essay on *Oliver* also connects Dickens to Malthus (65), and in many other ways has influenced my thinking here. On the direct relations between *Oliver Twist* and the poor laws, see House and Schlicke.

Still one of the best discussions of the relationship between reform efforts and fiction in this period is Brantlinger's *Spirit*. Brantlinger makes a point that in some ways supports my own readings throughout the book: "Stated most broadly, the history of the Victorian novel parallels the history of the social sciences, and the images of human nature and society characteristically projected by Dickens, Mrs. Gaskell, George Eliot, and even Trollope and Thackeray are in many respects those also projected by blue books" (28).

19. On the *Times*'s reporting of workhouse conditions and the accuracy of those reports, see Roberts, "How Cruel."

20. Quoted in Collins, *Critical Heritage* (46). It was apparently possible to possess and consume Oliver in the usual overstuffed three volumes, or in a reduced recipe, accessible to the less wealthy: "Some editions of the text came in three expensive volumes; other publishers pirated the novel and reprinted it in cramped double columns, selling the whole narrative for only a penny" (Paroissien xiii).

21. On food and consumption in this novel, and in all of Dickens, see Houston and Watt.

22. Bodenheimer has a different way of reading the inheritance plot, informed by her interest in the "pastoral rhetoric" she finds in the novel. Inheritance is suspect because it is part of the social and legal worlds, which in *Oliver Twist* stand for injustice and evil. The pastoral language of the novel "acts as a cleansing agent, erasing the social stigma of Oliver's illegitimacy and his mother's sexual fall by referring them to an asocial realm of judgment" (120).

23. J. Hillis Miller approaches the problem this way: "There is no acceptance of the doctrine of original sin in Dickens' anthropology. Each human creature comes pure and good from the hands of God and only *becomes* evil through the effects of an evil environment. Some are, however, like Oliver, paradoxically more naturally good than others . . . and are thus able to withstand the pressure of evil surroundings" (67).

24. As Anny Sadrin points out, "Baseness is Monks's true inheritance" (42). See Sadrin generally on issues of inheritance.

25. The reading of *Oliver Twist* I have in mind here is D. A. Miller's, especially in *The Novel and the Police,* although he also discusses *Oliver* in "Discipline in Different Voices." Miller's ideas about Dickens, and about Victorian fiction generally, have influenced much of my own thinking in this chapter and elsewhere; this is as good a spot as any to acknowledge his (disciplinary) presence in the very early stages of this book.

   Hadley comments usefully on Miller's reading. Considering Dickens's use of melodrama and the famous scene of Oliver's (criminal) reading in Fagin's den, Hadley argues that Dickens "does not invoke melodrama in chapter 17 in order to facilitate the project of novel reading and thus to imprison Oliver in the darkened domain of private subjectivity. Rather, with melodramatic techniques, Dickens hopes to continue the long defense of his popular subject matter and style that he had launched in his preface; in so doing, he also stages Oliver's escape from Fagin's 'bastile,' the site of private reading" (122). She points out that "Oliver, in contrast to Monks, resists what most modern critics identify as the 'realistic' portrayal of private subjectivity that becomes the fate of Sikes and Fagin" (126).

   Hadley's reading of the novel touches on several of the issues that concern me here: inheritance, classification, and subjectivity. Although Hadley takes a very different view of the novel—most notably, she reads *Oliver Twist* as eschewing the classificatory impulse that motivates the new poor law—her essay has been both useful and influential here. I am grateful to her for sending me a copy of the essay before the appearance of her book.

26. Talking about what she calls "physiognomical reading," Jaffe comments on the way narrators and characters "read" faces, in Dickens and in other nineteenth-century novels, as an act of empowerment-through-knowledge that also reveals "their own concerns and desires" (19). See also Hollington, who focuses on the importance of appearance in the novel. His essay especially takes up Cruikshank's drawings for *Oliver Twist.* He argues that characters in the novel are represented as failed physiognomers,

and the reader is invited to do as the narrator and the illustrator do—to transcend the limits of textual interpreters of appearance. I am not interested here to discuss the complexities of nineteenth-century theories of phrenology, since I am concerned with Dickens's attention to the face itself, and merely as a surface; but for potential connections, see Cooter.

27. J. Hillis Miller talks about this passage as among those in *Oliver Twist* that "abound . . . in intimations of immortality" (78). As he points out, however, the point is not to accentuate the contours of a "prenatal paradise," but rather to emphasize the shortcomings of postnatal sociality; in other words, here is yet another register of Dickens's—and Victorian society's—distance from Wordsworth and Romanticism generally.

28. Brantlinger has defined another compelling reason for the failure of bourgeois education in his essay "How Oliver Twist Learned to Read." He demonstrates convincingly that literacy is equally—if not more thoroughly—associated with criminality than right living. *Oliver Twist* is itself, Brantlinger argues, as much one of Brownlow's volumes as it is to be counted among Fagin's red-with-gore books: "Clearly a single novel can lead a double life by playing both roles in a cultural game of cops and robbers, crime and punishment" (78). Brantlinger's essay bears on my argument in other ways as well, since he provides a discussion of pauper education and the dilemma of pedagogy and the poor.

II. In the Bosom of the Family

1. This is the third (American) edition of Routh's text. I believe the first London edition was published, in substantially the same form as quoted here, in 1860. The book-length text is largely a compilation of articles Routh wrote for *The Lancet* and the *British Medical Journal* during the late 1850s, and in many cases the text of *Infant Feeding* is a verbatim reprint of articles written in 1858 and 1859.

2. Readers of the novels will quickly come up with exemplary breast-feeding and dry-nursing mothers of their own, but some obvious choices include Mrs. Mann in *Oliver Twist;* the lone woman on the prairie in *American Notes; David Copperfield*'s Mrs. Micawber; Mrs. Plornish in *Little Dorrit;* the French women in *A Tale of Two Cities;* and Pip's Mrs. Joe.

3. On the politics of the breast, see Perry and Schiebinger. Or the history of wet-nursing and breast-feeding, see both of Fildes's books.

4. By coincidence, Dr. Charles West not only was an acquaintance of but also worked in a sort of collaboration with Dickens. West was a prime force behind the establishment of the Great Ormond Street Children's Hospital, a project that Dickens supported in various ways. The story of this relationship is recounted by Jules Kosky in his book *Mutual Friends,* an unquestioning account of both Dickens's and West's pure and total devotion to the cause of children; both men are said by Kosky to be prone to "brooding on the suffering and the waste, the inevitable concomitants of death in the young" (31). West himself would make a compelling study, particularly his relationship to the formation and official sanction of pediatrics as a discrete science. His habit of performing postmortems on slum children on important days of state is especially fascinating; he deliberately spent both the day of Wellington's funeral and that of the queen's coronation examining the corpses of children in poor London.

5. Jill Matus also deals briefly with the exchange between Acton and Routh, but she sees Acton's reformative narrative as a minor one wielding little influence. As do I, Matus finds that by midcentury the focus is on "delinquent middle-class mothers" (158).

6. The importance of "simultaneity of production" derives from Marx's discussion of spatial relations and capitalism: "This locational movement—the bringing of the product to the market, which is a necessary condition of its circulation, except when the point of production is itself a market—could be more precisely regarded as the transformation of the product *into a commodity*" (qtd. Schivelbusch 46). Spatial movement, Marx claims, creates in part the strictly economic value a product has at market.

7. Schivelbusch comments that typically the "nineteenth-century English bourgeoisie gains no authentic experience of the reality of the great industries of Manchester and Sheffield. It becomes aware of them only indirectly, by means of the displays of world exhibitions and humanitarian fiction. Yet the railroad, the industrial process in transportation, does become an actual industrial experience for the bourgeois, who sees and feels his own body being transformed into an object of production" (123).

8. Francis's concern, it should be pointed out, is specific to the navvy, a distinct and isolated role in Victorian economic terms, and in relation to Victorian life. Mr. Toodle is not, of course, a navvy. I would suggest that Francis's "brute" lurks, albeit at some distance, behind Mr. Toodle. The fears concerning the railroad represented in this essay—the social proximity, enabled as well as emblematized by increased mobility, and contamination anxieties—are structurally similar to those of Francis, as portrayed in his *History*.

9. See Jones on the street clearances (*Outcast* 180).

10. The remarkable passage in which Dickens describes Dombey's trip, and in fact the representation of the railroad in the entire novel, is extensively discussed by Murray Baumgarten. For Baumgarten, as for me, the railroad functions somewhat ambivalently, although ultimately the negative aspects of advancing technology are contained, in Baumgarten's view, since they appear in Dombey's "stunted imagination." Baumgarten argues that "Dickens evokes not only the positive force of the railroad world but the new possibilities provided by the expanding cities of Victorian England. His novels provide us with examples of the achievements of industry and commerce as well as the self-alienation of the underground man" (84). Other important accounts of the railroad in *Dombey* include those of Arac (105–10), Nelson, and Marcus, in his originating argument in *From Pickwick to Dombey*.

11. Of particular interest here is Moynahan's essay on "firmness" and "wetness" in this novel.

12. Other critics have noted the smothering or near-malevolent nature of Florence's care. See, for example, Nina Auerbach in *Romantic Imprisonment* (115). Using *Dombey and Son* to address issues of feminist theory and scholarship, Helene Moglen has pointed out how the "solution" Dickens engineers to the problem of separate spheres mirrors one strand of feminist criticism. Moglen would have us focus on the subversive elements in Charles Dickens's fiction—to take up Edith's melodramatic (and therefore, Moglen argues, subversive) performance, rather than Florence's sentimental one. In adapting *Dombey* to this use, Moglen acknowledges critics like Auerbach, Dianne Sadoff, Louise Yelin, and Lynda Zwinger, recognizing the ways in which these feminist readings of the family in Dickens enable later discussion.

13. An important and very useful discussion of the early Victorian idea of influence, and

of *Dombey and Son* (one that intersects at some points with my own), is that by Judith Newton; see especially 127–34.

III. Tender Tyranny

1. Throughout this chapter I will be referring to the first Catherine (Earnshaw) Linton as "Cathy," and to her daughter as "Catherine," simply for reasons of clarity and simplicity.

2. The changing nature of the family, and particularly the growth of domestic ideology and its relation to industrial society, has been well documented. See Stone, Trumbach, Gillis, and Davidoff and Hall, to name only selected examples.

3. On the history of the law, see Glendon, Graveson and Crane, Holcombe, Shanley, and Stetson.

4. This is Brougham during the second reading in Lords (*Hansard's* 44:780). The bill was introduced in 1837 to the House of Commons by Sergeant Talfourd, debated on the second reading, and passed by the House rapidly. It was defeated in the Lords by a majority of two after Brougham's speech. In the following year Talfourd again introduced a very similar bill into the House of Commons. It passed and was introduced into the Lords, as it had been the year before, by Lord Lyndhurst. This time Brougham was not present at the second reading, and the only opposition came from Lord Wynford, who called the measure inadequate. It was passed and received the Royal Assent. See *Hansard's* volumes 38, 40, 42, 44, 47, 48, 49, and 50 (1837–39). Further citations are to these volumes.

5. Published commentary on child labor reform may be found, to name just one standard source, in Thompson (331–49). The literature on this topic has, of course, been extensively discussed by both historians and literary critics.

6. While perhaps not expressed in just this way, this is the general ground covered by Donzelot.

7. For an excellent discussion of this, which focuses on the United States, see Zelizer.

8. The work of these two Brontë sisters in relation to one another has been usefully discussed by several critics. See Gordon and Jacobs. An interesting essay that reads Anne Brontë's novel in relation to George Eliot, especially her story "Janet's Repentance," is Kunert's.

9. Levy makes this point when she says, "By imaginatively elaborating the realm of the individual, the family, and the household, *Wuthering Heights* naturalized the notion of an 'inside' drained of the materials of the 'outside'—social, political, and historical content" (76).

10. One need go no farther than the back cover of the Penguin edition of the novel, which announces fearlessly, "In all their judgements on the subject of sex, the Brontës—and Anne most stoutly of all—were eloquent in proclaiming the equality of men and women. . . . *The Tenant of Wildfell Hall* might be described as the first sustained feminist novel."

11. Although all of the essays I cite here are quite different from each other, they are minimally united in recognizing marriage and male/female relations as primary in this novel: Gilbert and Gubar, Langland ("Feminine Desire"), and McMaster.

12. For an interesting reading of male masochistic pleasure in *Wuthering Heights* (and a provocative account of the dominance of psychoanalytic theory in discussions of masochism), see Siegel.

13. Eagleton believes that the marriage between Helen and Gilbert does not represent any significant intermixing of class, insisting that Markham is more gentleman than farmer, and that Helen's social standing is ambiguous (128–29).

14. The presence of the institution—Lowood, "governessing," the church, the school, even the factory (*Shirley*)—in Charlotte Brontë's work sets her apart from her sisters, and puts her outside the paradigm for subjectivity that I am developing in this chapter. Nevertheless, Jane Eyre (who calls herself a "pariah of the nursery" at one point) is a central figure among Victorian child victims.

15. On the complex and interesting topic of *Wuthering Heights* and "evolution," see Goff.

16. On this scene, see Armstrong, *Desire* 185.

IV. Civilization and Confession in Midcentury Representations of Infanticide and in Adam Bede

1. For Gaskell's account of the pedagogical methods that produced Charlotte and Emily's essays, see *The Life of Charlotte Brontë,* ch. 11.

   For the original and English translations of Emily Brontë's essays, I am using Sue Lonoff's excellent edition, *The Belgian Essays.*

2. In speaking of Eliot in this way, I am obviously gesturing toward the relationship between Eliot's fictional narratives and notions of evolution (Darwinian, Spencerian, and otherwise) current at the time. Many writers have considered the complex relationship between "evolution" (in all of the various ways the term was understood in the mid-Victorian period) and fiction, and therefore Eliot and evolution is not my explicit subject in this chapter. See especially Beer, Irvine, Levine (*Darwin*), and Ritvo.

   My argument is also related to the literary-critical consensus that George Eliot, as Graver has put it, "participated in a tradition of social thought that was preoccupied with the rediscovery of community" (3). In other words, there is a connection (as others have noted) between a certain evolutionary narrative critics have detected in Eliot, and the Darwinian concept of "the mutual affinities of organic beings" (*Origin of Species* 36). See also Shuttleworth, whose introductory chapter in *George Eliot and Nineteenth-Century Science* is quite useful here, and who asserts that Eliot's notion of organic order was a "dynamic one" which could account for "reciprocal interaction between the individual and the social whole" (2).

3. While Victorians themselves insisted, especially in the popular press and in the medical world, that infanticide had reached epidemic proportions, it is not at all clear to what extent there was any change at all in the number of cases of child murder— a number that would at any rate be impossible to guarantee. Central sources for the debate on infanticide are Jackson and Laquer ("Bodies, Details"). See Hoffer and Hull, Behlmer ("Deadly Motherhood") and Lionel Rose (*Massacre*). Additional sources for the history of infanticide include Langer and Malcolmson. Higginbotham leans toward a belief in an increase in child murder in the Victorian period. I am skipping over here some of the interesting ways in which infanticide figured in nineteenth-century culture. The growth of professional authority, particularly the office of the coroner, and the idea of professionalism in *Adam Bede,* is a subject I have explored in a forthcoming essay. Behlmer ("Deadly Motherhood") gives an excellent account of infanticide in Victorian society.

The specific link between civilization and infanticide had actually been made earlier in the century, when missionaries and writers urged their fellow English citizens to take responsibility for the acts of colonial subjects in India. English readers had for some time been treated to stories of child murdering abroad, especially in the "less civilized" reaches of India. Official and unofficial travelers to India returned with accounts of "this unnatural custom," which echoed throughout England in various pamphlets and government reports as, in the title of one such report, "India's Cries to British Humanity." Over a period of some forty or more years, numerous booklets were published describing, in the clinical tones employed to belie fascination, this "shocking custom."

4. Mid-Victorian writing about infanticide represents a distinct and historically specific discourse, demonstrated in its difference from earlier attitudes toward, and writing about, child murder. The early modern period, for example, was unambiguously punitive in its approach. Infanticide was defined juridically and seen as the likely, even the exclusive, recourse of fallen women. Child murder was a capital crime, and legislation was enacted the better to ensure conviction. Guilt was assumed, and confession, to a certain extent, was unnecessary. Criminality and femininity, and the relationship between them, informed the judicial approach to combatting infanticide in Elizabethan and Jacobean England. For more on this, see Hoffer and Hull.

In the course of the eighteenth century, public sentiment swayed, and the judicial response to infanticide shifted from certain and severe punishment to greater leniency, even to a sentimental tenderness for the perpetrator. Courts were increasingly uneasy and then unwilling to convict, and acquittal became possible on the thinnest of defenses. Producing some childbed linen or infant clothing was sufficient to show that a mother had intended to care for the child, and merely displaying these items often resulted in her release. Judges instructed juries that the child must be proven to have been alive at birth in order for conviction to take place. This was obviously a difficult fact to establish with certainty, given the state of eighteenth-century forensic medicine, not to mention the dangers of childbirth itself. These legal changes suggest that the infanticidal mother was no longer narrowly viewed by the judiciary as a lewd woman, or as a murderess subject to the highest penalty, but that she was at least partly imagined as a victim. This new perspective was even more evident in medicine, as demonstrated in the widely read medicolegal treatise by William Hunter, *On the Uncertainty of the Signs of Murder in the Case of Bastard Children* (1783).

5. On the history of the hospital and its roots in the eighteenth century, see McClure. Brownlow was himself a foundling at the hospital, who rose from secretary's assistant to treasurer's clerk and, eventually, in 1849 was unanimously appointed as the general secretary. For an excellent discussion of the role of the Foundling Hospital in early Victorian culture, which relates to the changing nature of the concept of motherhood as it concerns illegitimacy and infanticide, see Weisbrod.

6. On Queen Victoria's association with the canine world, and especially on the relationship between domesticity and dogs, see Munich (127–55).

7. On the pastoral mode generally, see Alpers; on the relationship of pastoral conventions to social ideology, see Patterson. The relationship between food and pastoral can be traced at least as far back as the *Idylls* of Theocritus. And see Raymond Williams (*The Country and the City*).

8. Harvey comments at length on the animal imagery in the novel, and on the relationships among science, "nature," ideology, and fiction.

9. The categories of "Romantic Nature" and "evolutionary perspective" are not necessarily mutually exclusive, especially at this time. As has sometimes been pointed out, for example, Darwin himself tends to read nature as essentially Romantic. Thus, Eliot's blending of the Romantic and the evolutionary is less an opposition than a demonstration of the extent to which ideas of nature and creation were in deep flux at the time. However, as I argue, Eliot ultimately abandons the pastoral modes of the novel to embrace an anthropologized/evolutionary perspective, one which she is inventing as she writes the novel.

    There are many useful sources that consider *Adam Bede* as a pastoral novel. Carroll deals with what he calls the novel's "pastoral theodicies" (73–105); Gregor with the novel's "two worlds." Marotta considers, as do I, the contradictions of Eliot's version of pastoral, if indeed it is a version of pastoral. Other critics who have taken up this notion include Hussey and Creeger. And for a book-length treatment of the pastoral in fiction, which includes a chapter on *Adam Bede,* see Squires. See also Raymond Williams (*The Country and the City*).

    The phrase "tangled bank," of course, is Darwin's. As Goode puts it, "The animal imagery which is so prevalent in the novel is not merely serving an aesthetic function; it also establishes an evolutionary scale. And it is on this scale that human change bases itself" (22).

10. On the idea of nature in *Adam Bede,* see Herbert. Herbert discusses the influence of Wordsworth on *Adam Bede,* and identifies an essentially Wordsworthian perspective on nature in the novel, which he locates in the Reverend Irwine (419). He also emphasizes a Tennysonian view of nature in the novel; the two views function dialectically. This territory is covered differently by Sadoff in "Nature's Language"; she demonstrates how the complexities and contradictions of Eliot's view of nature unravel the novel's attempts at "coherence, stability, and symbolic unity" (411).

11. A number of critics have discussed the relationship between Eliot's essay and the novel *Adam Bede,* among them Goode and Shuttleworth.

12. For an interesting discussion of the related idea of sympathy, affinity, social order, cultural inheritance, and nationalism, see Semmel, who argues that (among other things) for "Eliot the idea of sympathy became increasingly identified with a sharing of the inheritance of the past, and more specifically with the sharing of one's national past with others belonging to the national community" (13).

13. On Eliot's knowledge of Darwinian theories of evolution, and on her relationship to Spencer's related theories, see Paxton, especially her ch. 2, in which she notes that, first, Eliot was very much aware of evolutionary ideas as she began *Adam Bede;* and, second, that Eliot's first encounter with "developmental theory" came through her acquaintance with Spencer (Paxton 15–16).

14. Many critics have discussed the relationship between the broad category of "evolution" and George Eliot's novels, most especially Beer and Paxton. Among those who concern themselves particularly with *Adam Bede* is Dalal, who understands the gradual development of certain characters as an intellectual and emotional process, rather than as a biological one (16–18).

15. For a discussion of the failure of this novel to incarnate history, see Qualls, who argues that only private and individual solutions can be forged within the limits of *Adam*

Bede (143). He says that the union of Dinah and Adam, at novel's end, is "a fine pastoral scene," but that it never "makes the human case of the novel as do the stories of Arthur and Hetty" (145). Interestingly, though, he sees Arthur and Hetty as unformed children.

16. In this Eliot is, I think, less sentimental about motherhood than most writers of the mid-nineteenth century. She is, as a matter of fact, less sentimental than Darwin, who in *Origin of Species,* as Beer has pointed out, fills the space God once occupied in creation theory with a maternalized Nature who "orders" creation (Beer 70).

17. Knoepflmacher asserts that Hetty "is so narcissistic that she denies the most basic instincts of motherhood; she kisses her own limbs before giving birth to her child and then promptly looks for a spot to drown the unwanted 'babby'" (*Early Novels* 120). Knoepflmacher says that *Adam Bede* reveals "the novelist's fear of the indifference of the natural order" (122). Alternatively, feminist readings view Hetty as a scapegoat: see Langbauer (*Consolation*) and Manheimer.

18. The relationship between instinct and motherhood is at the center of Paxton's reading of this novel. In her interpretation, a central aim of *Adam Bede* is to demonstrate the difference between sex and gender (see Paxton's ch. 3).

19. For a different reading of the birthday letter, see Paxton (21–23).

20. See Paxton and especially Matus (167–79) for discussions of Dinah as mother.

21. For a psychological account of Eliot's ambivalence toward mothering, see Redinger (43).

22. James Eli Adams explores the necessarily ironic nature of literacy and eloquence, and particularly the limits of human expression, in an essay that also accounts cleverly for Gyp's place in the novel. On the "problem" of education in Eliot, see Cottom (33–57).

23. Welsh remarks that in *Adam Bede,* as in "Amos Barton," "there is again a remarkable attention to these external relations of social life and the management of shame rather than guilt" (137). He views the scene in the cell as one of "enormous condescension" (*Blackmail* 138), and views the confession itself as an evolution from shame to the responsibility of guilt.

24. Matus believes Hetty's confession "focuses issues of subjectivity and relationship and has an important bearing on the question of what makes a mother" (168).

Although I came upon it after formulating the argument in this essay, I find an interesting relationship between my reading of *Adam Bede* and Katherine Bond Stockton's suggestive discussion of *Middlemarch.* To name just one provocative point, Stockton reads the narrator's relation to text and character in ways that are related to my reading of Hetty and Dinah: "[*Middlemarch*] comes to climax, after all, in a scene between women. Their erotic dynamics—an orgasmic encounter between saint and supplicant—conveys the possibility that a woman might (unconsciously) desire another woman for the purpose of maintaining access to her 'own' opacity in marriage, which is to say her 'own' desire. In this way the narrator's gaze upon women might represent a woman yearning after herself. The narrative could be read as *functioning autoerotically for a narrator* who, within the text and through the telling, takes the place of a desiring woman" (169–70).

25. For a virtually opposite reading of the prison scene and its relation to Foucauldian theories of knowledge production, see Paxton (62).

26. The reading of the novel that I have found most useful, not least because I find myself

most in contention with it, is that of Langbauer. Langbauer reads Hetty as a scapegoat: "[S]he becomes the little piece of trash discarded to save the rest" (*Consolation* 208). But Langbauer's richly suggestive account of the novel goes further than to simply note Eliot's "conservative" scapegoating of Hetty; she points out the identification between Eliot/Eliot's narrator and Hetty in order to demonstrate the persistent and powerful struggle between realism and romance in the novel. Eliot "remains a culprit and a victim even as she tries to exercise power" (212).

27. The sharp criticism of feminist commentators has joined that of feminist critics concerned with the intersection of class and gender issues in the novel. For one example of such a reading, see Homans, for whom *Adam Bede* is straightforwardly a novel that helps consolidate "middle-class hegemony." She reads Dinah's emergence into sexuality as part of the novel's conservative project of annihilating class boundaries and universalizing and naturalizing the British middle class: "When she marries Adam and gets plump, Dinah is simultaneously a bourgeois sexual self and a selfless angel" (168).

On the matter of Dinah's desires, and on the featherduster passage, see Sedgwick, who reads Dinah's (interestingly canine) passion here as "a new, silent, doglike eros whose only expressive faculty is through the eyes, and whose main erogenous zone is the featherduster" (142).

Conclusion

1. Wallace, noting recently how "'childhood,' like 'femininity,' stands in for and mediates larger social anxieties" (288), deplores "the continuing absence of children in theories of subjectivity, particularly in emerging theories of citizenship." Some work on the ideological work performed in the name of children has been done, although for the most part, as Wallace goes on to say, "the child remains an unacknowledged and therefore unexamined organizing principle—not only of the modern nation-state . . . but also . . . of 'oppositional' theory" (286).

I have found the recent work of Hacking and Best of greatest interest in relation to the social use of the child in the twentieth century.

Eliot does make at least one more attempt to resolve the problems of self and society in her 1861 novel, *Silas Marner,* also worth discussion because it is so clearly an example of Eliot's interest in the victimized child. Many of the same issues are raised here as are taken up in *Adam Bede:* work, confession, and the corruption of the gentry. Adam is a carpenter whose work, to make and to build, is mirrored in his role as builder of a new and better society. Silas Marner's labor, as weaver, is to knit society together, a task he is singularly incapable of completing at the start of the novel, when his existence is defined by its isolation. It is through the child, through Eppie-as-savior, that Silas is able to bring things together in the novel's society. Eliot abandons the dilemma of mothers, choosing instead the paternal embrace of a foster father. Rejecting the institution of the church, the corrupt rich (Godfrey and family), and the corrupted poor (Molly, Eppie's opium-addicted mother), Eliot turns to confession as a form of redemption—a confession enabled by the child savior.

Works Cited

Acton, William. "Child-Murder and Wet-Nursing." *British Medical Journal* 16 February 1861: 183–84.

———. "Unmarried Wet-nurses." *The Lancet* 1 (1859): 175–76.

Adams, Carol J. *The Sexual Politics of Meat: A Feminist-Vegetarian Critical Theory.* New York: Continuum, 1990.

Adams, James Eli. "Gyp's Tale: On Sympathy, Silence and Realism in *Adam Bede.*" *Dickens Studies Annual* 20 (1991): 227–42.

Alpers, Paul. *What Is Pastoral?* Chicago: Univ. of Chicago Press, 1996.

Andrews, Malcolm. *Dickens and the Grown-up Child.* London: Macmillan, 1994.

Anstruther, Ian. *The Scandal of the Andover Workhouse.* Gloucester: Alan Sutton, 1984.

Arac, Jonathan. *Commissioned Spirits: The Shaping of Social Motion in Dickens, Carlyle, Melville and Hawthorne.* New Brunswick, NJ: Rutgers Univ. Press, 1979.

Ariès, Philippe. *Centuries of Childhood: A Social History of Family Life.* New York: Knopf, 1962.

Armstrong, Nancy. *Desire and Domestic Fiction: A Political History of the Novel.* New York: Oxford Univ. Press, 1987.

———. "Emily Brontë In and Out of Her Time." *Genre* 15 (1982): 243–64.

Auerbach, Nina. "Dickens and Dombey: A Daughter After All." *Romantic Imprisonment.* New York: Columbia Univ. Press, 1986.

Barrett Browning, Elizabeth. "The Cry of the Children." In *Victorian Women Poets,* ed. Angela Leighton and Margaret Reynolds. Cambridge, MA: Blackwell, 1995. 75–80.

Baumgarten, Murray. "Railway/Reading/Time: *Dombey and Son* and the Industrial World." *Dickens Studies Annual* 19 (1990): 65–89.

Beer, Gillian. *Darwin's Plots: Evolutionary Narrative in Darwin, George Eliot and Nineteenth-Century Fiction.* London: Routledge, 1983.

Behlmer, George K. *Child Abuse and Moral Reform in England, 1870–1908.* Stanford: Stanford Univ. Press, 1982.

———. "Deadly Motherhood: Infanticide and Medical Opinion in Mid-Victorian England." *Journal of the History of Medicine and Allied Sciences* 34.4 (1979): 403–27.

Best, Joel. *Threatened Children: Rhetoric and Concern about Child-Victims.* Chicago: Univ. of Chicago Press, 1990.

Bicknell, B. A. *The Law and Practice in Relation to Infants.* London: The Solicitor's Law Stationery Society, Ltd., 1928.

Blackstone, William. *Commentaries on the Laws of England.* Vol. 1. Chicago: Univ. of Chicago Press, 1979.

Bodenheimer, Rosemarie. *The Politics of Story in Victorian Social Fiction.* Ithaca, NY: Cornell Univ. Press, 1988.

Boner, Harold A. *Hungry Generations: The Nineteenth-century Case against Malthusianism.* New York: Russell & Russell, 1955.

Boone, Joseph Allen. *Tradition Counter Tradition: Love and the Form of Fiction.* Chicago: Univ. of Chicago Press, 1987.

Botting, Fred. *Making Monstrous: Frankenstein, Criticism, Theory.* Manchester: Manchester Univ. Press, 1991.

Brantlinger, Patrick. *The Spirit of Reform: British Literature and Politics, 1832–1867.* Cambridge: Harvard Univ. Press, 1977.

————. "How Oliver Twist Learned to Read, and What He Read." In *Culture and Education in Victorian England,* ed. Patrick Scott and Pauline Fletcher. Lewisburg, PA: Bucknell Univ. Press, 1990. 59–81.

Brontë, Anne. *The Tenant of Wildfell Hall.* Harmondsworth, Middlesex: Penguin, 1979.

Brontë, Emily. *Wuthering Heights.* London: Penguin, 1965.

Brontë, Emily, and Charlotte Brontë. *The Belgian Essays.* Ed. and trans. Sue Lonoff. New Haven: Yale Univ. Press, 1996.

Brown, Penny. *The Captured World: The Child and Childhood in Nineteenth-Century Women's Writing in England.* New York: Harvester-Wheatsheaf, 1993.

Brownlow, John. *History and Objects of the Foundling Hospital, with a Memoir of the Founder.* 3d ed. London, 1865.

Bruce, Maurice. *The Coming of the Welfare State.* London: B. T. Batsford, 1961.

Bull, Thomas. *The Maternal Management of Children in Health and Disease.* 2d ed. Philadelphia: Lindsay & Blakiston, 1853.

Butler, Marilyn. "The First *Frankenstein* and Radical Science." *Times Literary Supplement,* 9 April 1993: 12–14.

Cadogan, William. "Essay Upon Nursing and the Management of Children." 1748. In *The Father of Child Care: Life of William Cadogan (1711–1797),* ed. Morwenna and John Rendle-Short. Bristol: Wright, 1966.

Calder, Jenni. *Women and Marriage in Victorian Fiction.* New York: Oxford Univ. Press, 1976.

Carlyle, Thomas. *The French Revolution: A History, Vol. 1.* New York: AMS Press, 1969.

————. *Past and Present.* Ed. Richard Altick. New York: Gotham/New York Univ. Press, 1965.

Carroll, David. *George Eliot and the Conflict of Interpretations: A Reading of the Novels.* Cambridge: Cambridge Univ. Press, 1992.

Chadwick, Edwin. "The New Poor Law." *Edinburgh Review* 63 (1836): 487–537.

Clark, G. S. R. Kitson. *An Expanding Society: Britain, 1830–1900.* New York: Cambridge Univ. Press, 1967.

Cockshut, A. O. J. *Man and Woman: A Study of Love and the Novel, 1740–1940.* London: Collins, 1977.

Collins, Philip. *Dickens: The Critical Heritage.* New York: Barnes & Noble, 1971.

Combe, Andrew. *Treatise on the Physiological and Moral Management of Infancy.* 4th ed. Boston: Saxton & Kelt, 1846.

Cooter, Roger. *The Cultural Meaning of Popular Science: Phrenology and the Organization of Consent in Nineteenth-Century Britain.* Cambridge: Cambridge Univ. Press, 1984.

Corrigan, Philip, and Derek Sayer. *The Great Arch: English State Formation as Cultural Revolution.* New York: Basil Blackwell, 1985.

Cottom, Daniel. *Social Figures: George Eliot, Social History and Literary Representation.* Minneapolis: Univ. of Minnesota Press, 1987.

Coveney, Peter. *Poor Monkey: The Child in Literature.* London: Rockliff, 1957.

Crowther, M. A. *The Workhouse System 1834–1929.* London: Batsford Academic, 1981.

Cunningham, Hugh. *The Children of the Poor: Representations of Childhood since the Seventeenth Century.* Oxford: Blackwell, 1991.

Dalal, D. S. *George Eliot: Self and Society in Her Novels.* New Delhi: Reliance, 1989.

Darwin, Charles. *Darwin: A Norton Critical Edition.* 2d ed. Ed. Philip Appleman. New York: Norton, 1979.

Davenport, Florence Hill. *Children of the State.* New York: Macmillan, 1889.

Davidoff, Leonore, and Catherine Hall. *Family Fortunes: Men and Women of the English Middle Class, 1780–1850.* London: Hutchinson, 1987.

Dicey, A. V. *Lectures on the Relation between Law and Public Opinion in England during the Nineteenth Century.* London: Macmillan, 1930.

Dickens, Charles. *American Notes for General Circulation.* New York: Penguin, 1985.

———. *Dombey and Son.* New York: Penguin, 1988.

———. "Dullborough Town." In *Selected Journalism 1850–70,* ed. David Pascoe. New York: Penguin, 1997.

———. *Oliver Twist.* New York: Penguin, 1970.

Digby, Anne. *Pauper Palaces.* London: Routledge, 1978.

Donzelot, Jacques. *The Policing of Families.* Trans. Robert Hurley. New York: Pantheon, 1979.

Driver, Felix. *Power and Pauperism: The Workhouse System, 1834–1884.* Cambridge: Cambridge Univ. Press, 1993.

Duke, Francis. "Pauper Education." In *The New Poor Law in the Nineteenth Century,* ed. Derek Fraser. New York: St. Martin's, 1976.

Dyos, H. J. "Railways and Housing in Victorian London." *Journal of Transport History* 2.1 (1955): 11–21.

Eagleton, Terry. *Myths of Power: A Marxist Study of the Brontës.* New York: Harper & Row, 1975.

Eliot, George. *Adam Bede.* New York: Penguin, 1980.

———. *The George Eliot Letters.* New Haven: Yale Univ. Press, 1954–55.

———. *Middlemarch.* New York: Penguin, 1965.

———. *Selected Essays, Poems and Other Writings.* Ed. A. S. Byatt and Nicholas Warren. New York: Penguin, 1990.

———. *Silas Marner.* New York: Penguin, 1985.

Ellis, Kate. "Monsters in the Garden: Mary Shelley and the Bourgeois Family." In *The Endurance of Frankenstein: Essays on Mary Shelley's Novel,* ed. George Levine and U. C. Knoepflmacher. Berkeley: Univ. of California Press, 1979. 123–42.

Ellis, Sarah Stickney. *The Wives of England.* London: Fisher, Son, & Co., 1843.

Fairclough, Peter. Appendix A. *Oliver Twist,* by Charles Dickens. New York: Penguin, 1966. 481–85.

Ferguson, Frances. "Malthus, Godwin, Wordsworth, and the Spirit of Solitude." In *Literature and the Body: Essays on Populations and Persons. Selected Papers from the English Institute, 1986,* ed. Elaine Scarry. Baltimore: Johns Hopkins Univ. Press, 1986.

Fildes, Valerie A. *Breasts, Bottles and Babies, A History of Infant Feeding.* Edinburgh: Edinburgh Univ. Press, 1986.

———. *Wet Nursing: A History from Antiquity to the Present*. New York: Basil Blackwell, 1988.

Finlayson, Geoffrey. *Citizen, State, and Social Welfare in Britain 1830–1990*. Oxford: Clarendon Press, 1994.

Forsyth, William. *A Treatise on the Law Relating to the Custody of Infants, in Cases of Difference between Parents or Guardians*. Philadelphia: T. & J. W. Johnson, 1850.

Foster, Shirley. *Victorian Women's Fiction: Marriage, Freedom and the Individual*. London: Croom Helm, 1985.

Foucault, Michel. *Discipline and Punish: The Birth of the Prison*. New York: Vintage, 1979.

———. *The History of Sexuality*. Vol. 1: *An Introduction*. New York: Vintage, 1980.

Fourteenth Report from the Select Committee on the Poor Law Amendment Act, with Minutes of Evidence and Appendix, 14 March 1838.

Francis, John. *A History of the English Railway, Its Social Relations and Revelations 1820–1845*. Vol. 2. London: Longman, Brown, Green & Longmans, 1851.

Fraser, Derek. *Evolution of the British Welfare State: A History of Social Policy since the Industrial Revolution*. New York: Barnes & Noble, 1973.

Gallagher, Catherine. "The Bio-Economics of *Our Mutual Friend*." In *Subject to History*, ed. David Simpson. Ithaca, NY: Cornell Univ. Press, 1991.

———. "The Body versus the Social Body in the Works of Thomas Malthus and Henry Mayhew." *Representations* 14 (1986): 83–106.

———. *The Industrial Reformation of English Fiction: Social Discourse and Narrative Form, 1832–1867*. Chicago: Univ. of Chicago Press, 1985.

Gallagher, Catherine, and Elizabeth Young. "Feminism and *Frankenstein:* A Short History of American Feminist Criticism." *The Journal of Contemporary Thought* 1 (January 1991): 77–87.

Gaskell, Elizabeth. *The Life of Charlotte Brontë*. New York: Penguin, 1985.

Gathorne-Hardy, Jonathan. *The Rise and Fall of the British Nanny*. New York: Dial, 1972.

Gilbert, Sandra M., and Susan Gubar. *Madwoman in the Attic: The Woman Writer and the Nineteenth-Century Literary Imagination*. New Haven: Yale Univ. Press, 1979.

Gillis, John R. *For Better, for Worse: British Marriages, 1600 to the Present*. New York: Oxford Univ. Press, 1985.

Gilmour, Robin. *The Victorian Period: The Intellectual and Cultural Context of English Literature 1830–1890*. New York: Longman, 1993.

Glendon, Mary Ann. *The Transformation of Family Law: State, Law, and Family in the United States and Western Europe*. Chicago: Chicago Univ. Press, 1989.

Goff, Barbara Munson. "Between Natural Theology and Natural Selection: Breeding the Human Animal in *Wuthering Heights*." *Victorian Studies* 27 (1984): 477–508.

Goode, John. "Adam Bede." In *Critical Essays on George Eliot*, ed. Barbara Hardy. New York: Barnes & Noble, 1970.

Gordon, Jan B. "Gossip, Diary, Letter, Text: Anne Brontë's Narrative *Tenant* and the Problematic of the Gothic Sequel." *ELH* 51 (1984): 719–45.

Graver, Suzanne. *George Eliot and Community: A Study in Social Theory and Fictional Form*. Berkeley: Univ. of California Press, 1984.

Graveson, R. H., and F. R. Crane. *A Century of Family Law 1857–1957*. London: Sweet & Maxwell, 1957.

Green, Katherine Sobba. *The Courtship Novel 1740–1820: A Feminized Genre*. Lexington: Univ. Press of Kentucky, 1991.

Gregor, Ian. "The Two Worlds of *Adam Bede*." In *The Moral and the Story*, ed. Ian Gregor and Brian Nicholas. London: Faber & Faber, 1962. 13–32.

Grylls, David. *Guardians and Angels: Parents and Children in Nineteenth-Century Literature*. Boston: Faber & Faber, 1978.

Hacking, Ian. "The Making and Molding of Child Abuse." *Critical Inquiry* 17 (1991): 253–89.

Hadley, Elaine. *Melodramatic Tactics: Theatricalized Dissent in the English Marketplace, 1800–1885*. Stanford: Stanford Univ. Press, 1995.

Haight, Gordon, ed. *Selections from George Eliot's Letters*. New Haven: Yale Univ. Press, 1985.

Hansard's Parliamentary Debates: Third Series. Vols. 38, 40–42, 44, 47–50. London: Thomas Curson Hansard, 1837–39.

Harvey, W. J. "Idea and Image in the Novels of George Eliot." In *Critical Essays on George Eliot*, ed. Barbara Hardy. New York: Barnes & Noble, 1970.

Henriques, Ursula. *Before the Welfare State: Social Administration in Early Industrial Britain*. London: Longman, 1979.

Hedrick, Harry. *Child Welfare: England 1872–1989*. New York: Routledge, 1994.

Herbert, Christopher. "Preachers and the Schemes of Nature in *Adam Bede*." *Nineteenth-Century Fiction* 29 (March 1975): 412–27.

Higginbotham, Ann R. "Sins of the Age: Infanticide and Illegitimacy in Victorian London." *Victorian Studies* 32.3 (spring 1989): 319–38.

Himmelfarb, Gertrude. *The Idea of Poverty: England in the Early Industrial Age*. New York: Knopf, 1984.

Hoffer, Peter C., and N. E. H. Hull. *Murdering Mothers: Infanticide in England and New England 1558–1803*. New York: New York Univ. Press, 1981.

Holcombe, Lee. *Wives and Property: Reform of the Married Women's Property Law in Nineteenth-Century England*. Toronto: Univ. of Toronto Press, 1983.

Hollington, Michael. "Dickens and Cruikshank as Physiognomers in *Oliver Twist*." *Dickens Quarterly* 7.2 (June 1990): 243–54.

Homans, Margaret. "Dinah's Blush, Maggie's Arm: Class, Gender and Sexuality in George Eliot's Early Novels." *Victorian Studies* 36.2: 155–78.

Horn, Pamela. *Children's Work and Welfare 1780–1880s*. London: Macmillan, 1994.

House, Humphrey. *The Dickens World*. 2d ed. Oxford: Oxford Univ. Press, 1960.

Houston, Gail Turley. *Consuming Fictions: Gender, Class and Hunger in Dickens's Novels*. Carbondale: Southern Illinois Univ. Press, 1994.

Hunter, William. *On the Uncertainty of the Signs of Murder in the Case of Bastard Children*. London: J. Callow, 1818.

Hussey, Maurice. "Structure and Imagery in *Adam Bede*." *Nineteenth-Century Fiction* 10 (1955): 115–29.

Ingham, Patricia. *The Language of Gender and Class: Transformation in the Victorian Novel*. New York: Routledge, 1996.

Irvine, William. *Apes, Angels and Victorians: The Story of Darwin, Huxley and Evolution*. New York: McGraw Hill, 1955.

Jackman, W. T. *The Development of Transportation in Modern England*. Cambridge: Cambridge Univ. Press, 1917.

Jackson, Mark. *New-born Child Murder: Women, Illegitimacy, and the Courts in Eighteenth-Century England*. Manchester: Manchester Univ. Press, 1996.

Jacobs, N. M. "Gender and Layered Narrative in *Wuthering Heights* and *The Tenant of Wildfell Hall.*" *Journal of Narrative Technique* 16 (1986): 204–19.

Jaffe, Audrey. *Vanishing Points: Dickens, Narrative, and the Subject of Omniscience.* Berkeley: Univ. of California Press, 1991.

Johnson, Barbara. "My Monster/Myself." *Diacritics* 12.2 (1982): 2–10.

Johnson, Edgar. *Charles Dickens: His Tragedy and Triumph.* New York: Simon and Schuster, 1952.

Johnson, Richard. "Educational Policy and Social Control in Early Victorian England." *Past and Present* 49 (1970): 96–119.

Jones, Gareth Stedman. *Languages of Class: Studies in Working Class History 1832–1982.* Cambridge: Cambridge Univ. Press, 1983.

———. *Outcast London.* New York: Pantheon, 1984.

Kane, Penny. *Victorian Families in Fact and Fiction.* London: Macmillan, 1995.

Kaplan, Cora. "Pandora's Box: Subjectivity, Class and Sexuality in Socialist Feminist Criticism." In *Making a Difference: Feminist Literary Criticism,* ed. Gayle Green and Coppelia Kahn. New York: Methuen, 1985.

Kay, James Phillips. *The Training of Pauper Children.* 1839. Didsbury, Manchester: E. J. Morten, 1970.

Kennard, Jean. *Victims of Convention.* Hamden, CT: Archon Books, 1978.

Kestner, Joseph A. *Protest and Reform: The British Social Narrative by Women, 1827–1867.* Madison: Univ. of Wisconsin Press, 1985.

Kincaid, James. *Child-Loving: The Erotic Child and Victorian Culture.* New York: Routledge, 1992.

Knoepflmacher, U. C. *George Eliot's Early Novels: The Limits of Realism.* Berkeley: Univ. of California Press, 1968.

———. "Thoughts on the Aggression of Daughters." In *The Endurance of Frankenstein,* ed. U. C. Knoepflmacher and George Levine. Berkeley: Univ. of California Press, 1974.

Kosky, Jules. *Mutual Friends: Charles Dickens and the Great Ormond Street Children's Hospital.* London: Weidenfeld and Nicolson, 1989.

Kucich, John. *Repression and Victorian Fiction: Charlotte Brontë, George Eliot and Charles Dickens.* Berkeley: Univ. of California Press, 1987.

Kuhn, Reinhard. *Corruption in Paradise: The Child in Western Literature.* Hanover, NH: Univ. Press of New England, 1982.

Kunert, Janet. "Borrowed Beauty and Bathos: Anne Brontë, George Eliot, and Mortification." *Research Studies* 46 (1978): 237–47.

Langbauer, Laurie. "Swayed by Contraries: Mary Shelley and the Everyday." In *The Other Mary Shelley: Beyond Frankenstein,* ed. Anne Mellor, Audrey Fisch, and Esther Schor. New York: Oxford Univ. Press, 1993.

———. *Women and Romance: The Consolation of Gender in the English Novel.* Ithaca, NY: Cornell Univ. Press, 1990.

Langer, William L. "Infanticide: A Historical Survey." *History of Childhood Quarterly* 1 (1974): 353–65.

Langland, Elizabeth. *Anne Brontë: The Other One.* London: Macmillan, 1989.

———. *Nobody's Angels: Middle-Class Women and Domestic Ideology in Victorian Culture.* Ithaca, NY: Cornell Univ. Press, 1995.

————. "The Voicing of Feminine Desire in Anne Brontë's *Tenant of Wildfell Hall*." In *Gender and Discourse in Victorian Literature and Art*, ed. Anthony A. Harrison and Beverly Taylor. Dekalb: Northern Illinois Univ. Press, 1992. 111–23.

Lankester, Edward. "Can Infanticide Be Diminished by Legislative Enactment?" *Transactions of the National Association for the Promotion of the Social Sciences* (Bristol Meeting, 1869 ed.). London: Edwin Pears, 1870.

Laqueur, Thomas. "Bodies, Death, and Pauper Funerals." *Representations* 1 (1983): 109–31.

————. "Bodies, Details, and the Humanitarian Narrative." In *The New Cultural History*, ed. Lynn Hunt. Berkeley: Univ. of California Press, 1989.

————. *Making Sex: Body and Gender from the Greeks to Freud*. Cambridge: Harvard Univ. Press, 1990.

Laslett, Peter. *The World We Have Lost*. New York: Scribner, 1965.

Levine, George. *Darwin and the Novelists: Patterns of Science in Victorian Fiction*. Cambridge: Harvard Univ. Press, 1988.

————. "*Frankenstein* and the Traditions of Realism." *Novel* (fall 1973): 14–30.

————. *The Realistic Imagination: English Fiction from Frankenstein to Lady Chatterley*. Chicago: Univ. of Chicago Press, 1981.

Levy, Anita. *Other Women: The Writing of Class, Race and Gender 1832–1898*. Princeton: Princeton Univ. Press, 1991.

Longmate, Norman. *The Workhouse*. New York: St. Martin's Press, 1974.

Lubenow, William C. *The Politics of Government Growth: Early Victorian Attitudes toward State Intervention*. Hamden, CT: Archon Books, 1971.

Lubove, Roy, ed. *Social Welfare in Transition: Selected English Documents, 1834–1909*. Pittsburgh: Univ. of Pittsburgh Press, 1966.

Malcolmson, R. W. "Infanticide in the Eighteenth Century." In *Crime in England, 1550–1800*, ed. J. S. Cockburn. Princeton: Princeton Univ. Press, 1977.

Malthus, Thomas Robert. *An Essay on the Principle of Population*. Ed. Philip Appleman. New York: Norton, 1976.

Manheimer, Joan. "Murderous Mothers: The Problem of Parenting in the Victorian Novel." *Feminist Studies* 5.3 (1979): 530–46.

Marcus, Steven. *Dickens: From Pickwick to Dombey*. New York: Basic Books, 1965.

Marotta, Kenny. "*Adam Bede* as Pastoral." *Genre* 9 (1976): 59–72.

Marshall, Tim. "Frankenstein and the 1832 Anatomy Act." In *Gothick Origins and Innovations*, ed. Allan Lloyd Smith and Victor Sage. Atlanta: Rodolpi, 1994. 57–64.

Martineau, Harriet. *History of the Peace: Pictorial History of England during the Thirty Years' Peace, 1816–1846*. London: W. & R. Chambers, 1858.

Matus, Jill L. *Unstable Bodies: Victorian Representations of Sexuality and Maternity*. New York: Manchester Univ. Press, 1995.

Mavor, Carol. *Pleasures Taken: Performances of Sexuality and Loss in Victorian Photographs*. Durham, NC: Duke Univ. Press, 1995.

McClure, Ruth K. *Coram's Children: The London Foundling Hospital in the Eighteenth Century*. New Haven: Yale Univ. Press, 1981.

McMaster, Juliet. "'Imbecile Laughter' and 'Desperate Earnest' in *The Tenant of Wildfell Hall*." *Modern Language Quarterly* 43 (1982): 352–68.

"Medical Annotations: Wet-nurses from the Fallen." *The Lancet* 1 (1859): 113–14.

Mellor, Anne. "Choosing a Text of *Frankenstein* to Teach." In *Approaches to Teaching Shelley's* Frankenstein, ed. Stephen C. Behrendt. New York: Modern Language Association [hereafter MLA], 1990. 31–38.

———. *Romanticism and Gender.* New York: Routledge, 1983.

———. *Mary Shelley: Her Life, Her Fiction, Her Monsters.* Berkeley: Univ. of California Press, 1988.

Michie, Elsie B. "*Frankenstein* and Marx's Theories of Alienated Labor." In *Approaches to Teaching Shelley's* Frankenstein, ed. Stephen C. Behrendt. New York: MLA, 1990. 93–98.

Miller, D. A. "Discipline in Different Voices: Bureaucracy, Police, Family and *Bleak House.*" *Representations* 1 (1983): 59–129.

———. *Narrative and Its Discontents: Problems of Closure in the Traditional Novel.* Princeton: Princeton Univ. Press, 1981.

———. *The Novel and the Police.* Berkeley: Univ. of California Press, 1988.

Miller, J. Hillis. *Charles Dickens: The World of His Novels.* Cambridge: Harvard Univ. Press, 1958.

Moers, Ellen. "Female Gothic." In *The Endurance of Frankenstein,* ed. George Levine and U. C. Knoepflmacher. Berkeley: Univ. of California Press, 1979. 77–87.

———. *Literary Women.* Garden City, NY: Doubleday, 1976.

Moglen, Helene. "Theorizing Fiction/Fictionalizing Theory: The Case of *Dombey and Son.*" *Victorian Studies* 35 (1992): 159–84.

Mommsen, Wolfgang, ed. *The Emergence of the Welfare State in Britain and Germany, 1850–1950.* London: Croom Helm, 1981.

Montgomery, James, ed. *The Chimney-Sweeper's Friend, and Climbing-Boy's Album.* London: Longman, Hurst, Rees, Orme, Brown & Green, 1824.

Morretti, Franco. *Signs Taken for Wonders: Essays in the Sociology of Literary Forms.* London: Verso, 1983.

Moynahan, Julian. "Dealings with the Firm of Dombey and Son: Firmness v. Wetness." In *Dickens and the Twentieth Century,* ed. John Gross and G. Pearson. London: Routledge, 1962.

Munich, Adrienne. *Queen Victoria's Secrets.* New York: Columbia Univ. Press, 1996.

Nelson, Harland S. "Staggs's Gardens: The Railway Through Dickens." *Dickens Studies Annual* 3 (1974): 41–53.

Newton, Judith Lowder. "Making—and Remaking—History: Another Look at 'Patriarchy.'" In *Feminist Issues in Literary Scholarship,* ed. Shari Benstock. Bloomington: Indiana Univ. Press, 1987.

Oliphant, Margaret. "The Laws Concerning Women." *Blackwood's Edinburgh Magazine* 79 (April 1856): 379–86.

O'Flinn, Paul. "Production and Reproduction: the Case of *Frankenstein.*" *Literature and History* 9 (1983): 194–213.

O'Rourke, James. "'Nothing More Unnatural': Mary Shelley's Revision of Rousseau." *ELH* 56 (1989): 543–69.

Paroissien, David. *Oliver Twist: An Annotated Bibliography.* New York: Garland, 1986.

Patterson, Annabel M. *Pastoral and Ideology: Virgil to Valéry.* Berkeley: Univ. of California Press, 1987.

Pattison, Robert. *The Child Figure in English Literature.* Athens: Univ. of Georgia Press, 1978.

Paxton, Nancy. *George Eliot and Herbert Spencer: Feminism, Evolutionism, and the Reconstruction of Gender.* Princeton: Princeton Univ. Press, 1991.

Paz, D. G. "Sir James Kay-Shuttleworth: The Man Behind the Myth." *History of Education* 14.3 (1985): 185–98.

Perkin, Harold. *The Origins of Modern English Society 1780–1880.* London: Routledge, 1969.

Perry, Ruth. "Colonizing the Breast: Sexuality and Maternity in Eighteenth-Century England." *Eighteenth Century Life* 16 (1992): 185–213.

Pinchbeck, Ivy, and Margaret Hewitt. *Children in English Society.* London: Routledge, 1969–73.

Plumb, J. H. "The New World of Children in Eighteenth-Century England." *Past and Present* 67 (1975): 64–95.

Polanyi, Karl. *The Great Transformation.* Boston: Beacon, 1985.

Pollock, Linda A. *Forgotten Children: Parent/Child Relations from 1500–1900.* New York: Cambridge Univ. Press, 1983.

———. *A Lasting Relationship: Parents and Children over Three Centuries.* London: Fourth Estate, 1987.

Poovey, Mary. *The Proper Lady and the Woman Writer: Ideology as Style in the Works of Mary Wollstonecraft, Mary Shelley, and Jane Austen.* Chicago: Univ. of Chicago Press, 1984.

———. *Making a Social Body: British Cultural Formation 1830–1864.* Chicago: Univ. of Chicago Press, 1995.

———. *Uneven Developments: The Ideological Work of Gender in Mid-Victorian England.* Chicago: Univ. of Chicago Press, 1988.

Pope, Norris. *Dickens and Charity.* New York: Columbia Univ. Press, 1978.

Poynter, J. R. *Society and Pauperism: English Ideas on Poor Relief, 1795–1834.* London: Routledge, 1969.

Qualls, Barry V. *The Secular Pilgrims of Victorian Fiction: The Novel as Book of Life.* Cambridge: Cambridge Univ. Press, 1982.

Redinger, Ruby. *George Eliot: The Emergent Self.* New York: Knopf, 1975.

Reed, John R. *Victorian Will.* Athens: Ohio Univ. Press, 1989.

Richardson, Ruth. *Death, Dissection and the Destitute.* London: Routledge, 1987.

Ritvo, Harriet. *The Animal Estate: The English and Other Creatures in the Victorian Age.* Cambridge: Harvard Univ. Press, 1987.

Roberts, David. "How Cruel Was the Victorian Poor Law?" *Communications* 6 (1963): 97–107.

———. *Paternalism in Early Victorian England.* London: Croom Helm, 1979.

———. *Victorian Origins of the British Welfare State.* New York: Archon, 1969.

Rousseau, Jean-Jacques. *Emile: Or, On Education.* Trans. Allan Bloom. New York: Basic Books, 1979.

Rose, Lionel. *The Erosion of Childhood: Child Oppression in Britain 1860–1918.* New York: Routledge, 1991.

———. *The Massacre of the Innocents: Infanticide in Britain, 1800–1939.* Boston: Routledge, 1986.

Rose, Michael E. *The Relief of Poverty 1834–1914.* London: Macmillan, 1986.

Routh, C. H. F. *Infant Feeding and Its Influence on Life.* 3d ed. New York: William Wood & Company, 1879.

———. "On the Selection of Wet Nurses from Among Fallen Women." *The Lancet* 1 (1859): 580–82.

Ruskin, John. *Unto This Last and Other Writings.* New York: Viking Penguin, 1985.

Sadoff, Dianne F. *Monsters of Affection: Dickens, Eliot and Brontë on Fatherhood.* Baltimore: Johns Hopkins Univ. Press, 1982.

———. "'Nature's Language': Metaphor in the Text of *Adam Bede.*" *Genre* (11): 411–26.

Sadrin, Anny. *Parentage and Inheritance in the Novels of Charles Dickens.* Cambridge: Cambridge Univ. Press, 1994.

Saturday Review. 5 August 1865: 161.

Scarry, Elaine. *Resisting Representation.* New York: Oxford Univ. Press, 1994. 49–90.

Schiebinger, Londa. "Why Mammals Are Called Mammals: Gender Politics in Eighteenth-Century Natural History." *American Historical Review* 98 (1993): 382–411.

Schivelbusch, Wolfgang. *The Railway Journey: Trains and Travel in the Nineteenth Century.* Trans. Anselm Hollo. New York: Urizen Books, 1979.

Schlicke, Paul. "Bumble and the Poor Law Satire of *Oliver Twist.*" *The Dickensian* 71 (1975): 149–56.

Schor, Hilary. *Scheherezade in the Marketplace: Elizabeth Gaskell and the Victorian Novel.* Oxford: Oxford Univ. Press, 1992.

Sedgwick, Eve Kosofsky. *Between Men: English Literature and Male Homosocial Desire.* New York: Columbia Univ. Press, 1985.

Semmel, Bernard. *George Eliot and the Politics of National Inheritance.* New York: Oxford Univ. Press, 1994.

Shanley, Mary Lyndon. *Feminism, Marriage, and the Law in Victorian England, 1850–1895.* Princeton: Princeton Univ. Press, 1989.

Shelley, Mary. *Frankenstein.* New York: Penguin, 1985.

———. *Frankenstein; or, The Modern Prometheus, the 1818 Text.* Ed. James Rieger. Chicago: Univ. of Chicago Press, 1982.

Shorter, Edward. *The Making of the Modern Family.* New York: Basic Books, 1975.

Shuttleworth, Sally. *George Eliot and Nineteenth-Century Science: The Make-Believe of a Beginning.* New York: Cambridge Univ. Press, 1984.

Siegel, Carol. "Postmodern Women Novelists Review Victorian Male Masochism." *Genders* 11 (1991): 1–16.

Sixteenth Report from the Select Committee on the Poor Law Amendment Act, with the Minutes of Evidence, and Appendix. 16 March 1838.

Smith, Frank. *The Life and Work of James Kay-Shuttleworth.* London: John Murray, 1923.

Smith, Sheila. *The Other Nation: The Poor in English Novels of the 1840s and 1850s.* Oxford: Clarendon Press, 1980.

Spencer, Herbert. *Education: Intellectual, Moral, and Physical.* Akron, OH: The Werner Company, 1860.

Spilka, Mark. "On the Enrichment of Poor Monkeys by Myth and Dream; or, How Dickens Rousseauisticized and Pre-Freudianized Victorian Views of Childhood." *Sexuality and Victorian Literature,* ed. Don Richard Cox. *Tennessee Studies in Literature* 27 (1984): 161–79.

Spivak, Gayatri Chakravorty. "Three Women's Texts and a Critique of Imperialism." In *"Race," Writing and Difference,* ed. Henry Louis Gates Jr. Chicago: Univ. of Chicago Press, 1985.

Squires, Michael. *The Pastoral Novel: Studies in George Eliot, Thomas Hardy, and D. H. Lawrence.* Charlottesville: Univ. Press of Virginia, 1974.

Staves, Susan. "British Seduced Maidens." *Eighteenth-Century Studies* 14 (1980–81): 109–34.

Steedman, Carolyn. *Strange Dislocations: Childhood and the Idea of Human Interiority, 1700–1930.* London: Virago Press, 1995.

Sterrenburg, Lee. "Mary Shelley's Monster: Politics and Psyche in *Frankenstein.*" In *The Endurance of* Frankenstein: *Essays on Mary Shelley's Novel,* ed. George Levine. Berkeley: Univ. of California Press, 1979.

Stetson, Dorothy M. *A Woman's Issue: The Politics of Family Law Reform in England.* Westport, CT: Greenwood Press, 1982.

Stockton, Katherine Bond. *God between Their Lips: Desire between Women in Irigaray, Brontë and Eliot.* Stanford: Stanford Univ. Press, 1994.

Stone, Lawrence. *The Family, Sex and Marriage in England 1500–1800.* New York: Harper, 1977.

Sussman, George D. *Selling Mother's Milk: The Wet-Nursing Business in France 1715–1914.* Urbana: Univ. of Illinois Press, 1982.

Sutherland, John. *Is Heathcliff a Murderer? Puzzles in Nineteenth-Century Fiction.* New York: Oxford Univ. Press, 1996.

Tanner, T. H. *A Practical Treatise on the Diseases of Infancy and Childhood.* Philadelphia: Lindsay & Blakiston, 1861.

Tanner, Tony. *Adultery in the Novel: Contract and Transgression.* Baltimore: Johns Hopkins Univ. Press, 1979.

Tholfsen, Trygyve R. *Sir James Kay-Shuttleworth on Popular Education.* New York: Teacher's College Press, 1974.

Thompson, E. P. *The Making of the English Working Class.* New York: Vintage, 1963.

Thomson, David. "Welfare and the Historians." In *The World We Have Gained: Histories of Population and Social Structure,* ed. Lloyd Bonfield, Richard M. Smith, and Keith Wrightson. New York: Blackwell, 1986.

Trollope, Frances. *Jessie Phillips, A Tale of the Present Day.* London: Henry Colburn, 1844.

Trumbach, Randolph. *The Rise of the Egalitarian Family.* New York: Academic Press, 1978.

Vachss, Andrew. "Our Endangered Species." *Parade,* 29 March 1998, 4–5.

Van Ghent, Dorothy. *The English Novel: Form and Function.* New York: Harper, 1961.

Veeder, William. *Mary Shelley and Frankenstein: The Fate of Androgyny.* Chicago: Univ. of Chicago Press, 1986.

Wallace, Jo-Ann. "Technologies of 'the Child': Toward a Theory of the Child-Subject." *Textual Practice* 9 (1995): 285–302.

Watt, Ian. "Oral Dickens." *Dickens Studies Annual* 3 (1974): 165–81.

Weisbrod, Bernd. "How to Become a Good Foundling in Early Victorian London." *Social History* 10.2 (May 1985): 193–209.

Welsh, Alexander. *From Copyright to Copperfield: The Identity of Dickens.* Cambridge: Harvard Univ. Press, 1987.

———. *George Eliot and Blackmail.* Cambridge: Harvard Univ. Press, 1985.

West, Charles. *Lectures on the Diseases of Infancy and Childhood.* 4th ed. London: Longman, 1859.

Williams, Karel. *From Pauperism to Poverty.* London: Routledge, 1981.

Williams, Raymond. *The Country and the City.* New York: Oxford Univ. Press, 1973.

Wollstonecraft, Mary. *A Vindication of the Rights of Woman. The Works of Mary Wollstone-craft.* Ed. Janet Todd and Marilyn Butler. Vol. 5. New York: New York Univ. Press, 1989.

Wood, Peter. *Poverty and the Workhouse in Victorian Britain.* Wolfeboro Falls, NH: Alan Sutton, 1991.

Yelin, Louise. "Strategies for Survival: Florence and Edith in *Dombey and Son.*" *Victorian Studies* 22 (1979): 279–319.

Zelizer, Viviana. *Pricing the Priceless Child: The Changing Social Value of Children.* New York: Basic Books, 1985.

Zwinger, Lynda. *Daughters, Fathers and the Novel: The Sentimental Romance of Heterosexuality.* Madison: Univ. of Wisconsin Press, 1991.

Index

Victorian Literature and Culture Series

———••◅∞▻••———

ALLAN C. DOOLEY
    Author and Printer in Victorian England

SIMON GATRELL
    Thomas Hardy and the Proper Study of Mankind

JEFFREY SKOBLOW
    Paradise Dislocated: Morris, Politics, Art

MATTHEW ROWLINSON
    Tennyson's Fixations: Psychoanalysis and the Topics of the Early Poetry

BEVERLY SEATON
    The Language of Flowers: A History

BARRY MILLIGAN
    Pleasures and Pains: Opium and the Orient in Nineteenth-Century British Culture

GINGER S. FROST
    Promises Broken: Courtship, Class, and Gender in Victorian England

LINDA DOWLING
    The Vulgarization of Art: The Victorians and Aesthetic Democracy

TRICIA LOOTENS
    Lost Saints: Silence, Gender, and Victorian Literary Canonization

MATTHEW ARNOLD
    The Letters of Matthew Arnold, vols. 1–3
    Edited by Cecil Y. Lang

EDWARD FITZGERALD
    Edward FitzGerald, Rubáiyát of Omar Khayyám: *A Critical Edition*
    Edited by Christopher Decker

CHRISTINA ROSSETTI
    The Letters of Christina Rossetti, vols. 1–2
    Edited by Antony H. Harrison

BARBARA LEAH HARMAN
    The Feminine Political Novel in Victorian England

JOHN RUSKIN
    The Genius of John Ruskin: Selections from His Writings
    Edited by John D. Rosenberg

ANTONY H. HARRISON
    Victorian Poets and the Politics of Culture: Discourse and Ideology

JUDITH STODDART
    Negotiating a Nation: Ruskin's Fors Clavigera *in the Late Victorian Culture Wars*

LINDA K. HUGHES AND MICHAEL LUND
    Victorian Publishing and Mrs. Gaskell's Work